city baby

THE ULTIMATE GUIDE FOR
NEW YORK CITY PARENTS
FROM PREGNANCY TO PRESCHOOL

Second Edition

KELLY ASHTON AND PAMELA WEINBERG

UNIVERSE · NEW YORK

for our city babies:
alexander, angela, rebecca, and benjamin

First Universe Edition published in 2003
by UNIVERSE PUBLISHING
a Division of Rizzoli International Publications, Inc.
300 Park Avenue South
New York, NY 10010

Copyright © 2003, 2001, 1997 by Kelly Ashton and Pamela Weinberg
Previous published by City and Company
Illustrations by Liselotte Watkins
Text Design by Leah Lococo
Cover Design: Paul Kepple and Jude Buffum @ Headcase Design
Cover Illustrations by Mary Lynn Blasutta

2003 2004 2005 2006 2007 / 10 9 8 7 6 5 4 3 2
Second Edition
Printed in the United States

Library of Congress Catalog Control Number: 2002094036
ISBN: 0-7893-0832-0

PUBLISHER'S NOTE: Neither Universe Publishing nor the authors have any interest, financial or personal,

in the locations listed in this book. No fees were paid or services rendered in exchange for inclusion in these pages.

Please also note that while every effort was made to ensure accuracy at the time of publication, it is always best to call ahead

to confirm that the information is still up-to-date. All area codes are 212 unless otherwise noted.

acknowledgments

We would like to thank the following people for their encouragement and support in the writing of this book: Carlo Sant Albano and Matthew Weinberg, Susan and Joel Kastin, Sander and Mechele Flaum, Harris and Angela Ashton, Victoria Ashton, Ronni Soled, Erica-Cheyenne Moore, Daria Masullo, Nicole L. Hirsh, Andrea DiNoto, Kiki Schaffer, Leah Lococo, Kim Hertlein, Nicole Clifford, Jill Dietz, Alexandra Partow, Sharon Watts, Ros and Seth Berger, Emerson Bruns, Kathy Goldman and Sarah Barnett.

With great appreciation to our City Baby Girls, for all of their patience and persistence in updating each and every entry: Cassiah Ward, Marisa Guber and Carolyn Turgeon. With special thanks and gratitude to Helene Silver of City & Company and Andrea Thompson, our editor, whose invaluable help and advice make this book possible.

contents

PART THREE
the city baby brooklyn guide

chapter 14 · brooklyn babies 239

preface to the second edition

Can this be New York with strollers everywhere?

Since the first edition of *City Baby* was published in 1997, we've witnessed something of a baby boom here in New York. Now, more than ever, couples are opting to raise their children in the Big Apple. There are indeed strollers everywhere—uptown, downtown and Brooklyn, too. Amazingly, New York has become a kindler, gentler kid-friendly town, no longer just a stop on the way to the suburbs. Dare we say we told you so?

We knew we were on to something when the first edition of *City Baby* quickly went into second and third printings. The book filled a niche. There was nothing like it, and we were delighted to find parents virtually lining up to buy a copy. We caught the attention of television news shows, newspapers and parenting magazines. The local weekly *Midtown Resident* called *City Baby* "the Fodor's of baby guides," while news anchor Carol Jenkins on Fox News at Noon exclaimed, "Everybody should have a book like this. It's great! What a wonderful idea!" We were hailed as authorities on the awesome experience of childbirth and childcare, as well as on children's shopping and activities in Manhattan. For two years, we wrote a column on kid-friendly restaurants in the city. We spoke at the New York Junior League and at several Jewish centers, and Pamela launched a luncheon series for new mothers. And not incidentally, Kelly gave birth to a second child, bringing our author total to four.

But, being a New Yorker, *City Baby* demanded more: a thoroughly updated second edition, to be exact. Here it is, a new and improved all-purpose parenting guide, with many new sources for you and your child. We have added a wealth of new information on programs for preschoolers; a chapter on Brooklyn; an A to Z yellow pages section that serves as a handy phone reference; and an index that puts every major *City Baby* category at your fingertips. So pack us into your baby bag, gear up the stroller and take us along for the incredible ride called parenthood. Whether you're an experienced mother or new mother, we know that *City Baby* will remain your New York baby "bible."

KELLY ASHTON
PAMELA WEINBERG
2001

introduction

By the time you're about to be a City Mom, you've probably negotiated a few promotions and raises for yourself, planned your wedding, and mastered the Internet. So why should having a City Baby seem daunting?

Maybe it's because in a city full of competent women, here's one neighborhood you haven't visited yet. Fear not. We were once in your shoes; and it was daunting for us too. We became first-time mothers within a few months of each other, and we swapped pregnancy, childbirth, newborn, and baby stories. Still, it wasn't until we began searching for great maternity clothes, adorable baby furniture and trustworthy child care, that we realized how much time, energy, and expertise it can take to prepare for and raise a child in the Big Apple.

Wouldn't it have been easier if someone had written a book/central resource—to help us find everything this city offers? So that's what we did. *City Baby* is that resource, guiding you through mountains of choices that can paralyze even the smartest New York woman.

This new edition offers more choices and information than ever before on subjects like where to take a Lamaze class; how to hire a baby nurse; baby swim and parenting classes; kid-friendly restaurants; the best parks and playgrounds; where to throw a great birthday party; and how to choose an indestructible stroller. We toured hospitals, received pregnancy massages, visited indoor play spaces, and shopped every maternity, children's furniture and clothing store you could think of—and even checked out their rest rooms. (You won't believe how important this will become to you!)

Throughout the book, we've starred * our favorite selections to indicate what we view as the best in each category. Whenever possible, we provide an address, phone number, and a ballpark price for every item or service but please call ahead to confirm. Prices, hours, and services change constantly. We know it's expensive to live in this great city, and if you can save here and there, we will show you how. After all, height-of-fashion clothes and state-of-the-art cribs are not what make for a happy, well-adjusted baby. *You*—the loving parent—are the most important thing.

Congratulations! You're about to embark upon your greatest adventure, one that will take the rest of your life to complete. Let *City Baby* help to make those first few years of parenthood easier.

PART ONE

preparing for a city baby:

everything you need to know

1 · from obstetric care to childbirth

Congratulations! The pregnancy test is positive! Tell the prospective grandparents, aunts, and uncles about the new addition to the clan, then start making the decisions that will keep you busy for the next nine months. First, you will have to consider:

Who will provide you with prenatal care throughout your pregnancy?
Who will deliver your baby?
Where will your baby be born?

Who will look after you and your baby during your pregnancy? Basically, you have two choices: a doctor (who may be the obstetrician/gynecologist you saw in your pre-pregnancy days or another doctor you select at this time) or a midwife. Both of these professionals will essentially perform the same service—meet with you during your pregnancy to monitor your progression and help deliver your baby on the big day.

Where your baby will be born is easy: a hospital, a birthing center, or at home. Yes, the occasional New York City baby has made his or her way into the world via taxi cab in the middle of the Triborough Bridge, but that is a remote possibility. Chances are, you'll make it to the right place at the right time.

You have had the good sense (or blind luck) to be having a baby in a city that seems to have an obstetrician on every other block and some of the best hospitals in the world. Finding excellent care won't be a problem.

This chapter provides everything you need to know about the birthing business in New York—doctors, midwives, hospitals, birthing centers, childbirth preparation classes, labor coaches, lactation consultants, and more.

Looking back on our own birthing experiences with all four of our children, we know that being comfortable with and confident in your doctor is the most important part of a positive birth experience.

All of the hospitals and birthing centers we list have the qualifications to provide an excellent birthing experience, whether you choose to deliver with an obstetrician or midwife.

THE BIRTH ATTENDANT

Whether it's an obstetrician or midwife, you should choose this person as soon as you discover you're pregnant.

Obstetricians

Most women in New York deliver their babies in a hospital under the care of an obstetrician. You probably already have an obstetrician/ gynecologist whom you've been seeing for annual checkups, and you may be perfectly happy to continue together throughout your pregnancy. But you may want to find a new doctor for one of several reasons: your current ob/gyn is fine for the routine checkups, but friends have told you about a wonderful new doctor; your ob/gyn is farther away from your apartment than you'd like; your ob/gyn is affiliated with a hospital that doesn't appeal to you; or you may be over thirty-five years old, considered high risk, and want an ob/gyn who specializes in high-risk pregnancies.

If you're a high maintenance mom, especially a first-timer, you may want an ob/gyn who is very good at hand-holding, one who gets on the phone to comfort you every time you call, or tells you to come to the office. If you are more laid back, you might want an ob/gyn more in keeping with that style. If you're comfortable and happy with your current ob/gyn, stick with her. If you would like to

find someone else, do so. With the large number of good obstetricians in New York, you can afford to pick and choose.

To find an obstetrician:

Ask friends who have had babies or the mother down the hall in your apartment building. A recommendation based on the personal experience of a woman who's already been through what you're just beginning is a good way to go.

✳ **Ask your internist or general practitioner to recommend an obstetrician.**

✳ **Call the hospital where you would like to deliver, and ask for a referral from their obstetrical department. (After you check out the hospital chart starting on page 22, you may find a hospital that is especially suited to your needs.)**

✳ **Go to the library and look up *New York Magazine*'s most recent "The Best Doctors in New York" issue.**

✳ **Call the New York County Medical Society (684-4670) for a listing of obstetricians who practice in the city.**

✳ **Log onto www.newyork.urbanbaby.com for an extensive listing of doctors' names and addresses.**

Once you have a candidate or two, call for a consultation. Any doctor should be willing to sit down with you and discuss what you can expect over the next nine months and during the birth. Come for your appointment armed with a list of questions, a pen and pad, and your husband or partner—two listeners are better than one.

After this initial consultation, you should be able to decide whether this is the doctor for you. He or she should listen to you carefully, answer your questions thoroughly, and inspire your trust. You need to feel confident that this doctor will be there for you any time night or day during your pregnancy. Feeling confident and comfortable with your ob/gyn is the most important thing.

Here are some questions that you should ask:

Are you part of a group practice? If so, will I see the other doctors in the practice? What is the likelihood that you will deliver my baby, rather than one of your colleagues? (Ask when the doctor typically takes vacation. You will be able to figure out what month you are delivering, so inquire early on. Many doctors take off two weeks in March, when the private schools are on break.) Do you have school-age children?

❋ **How often will I need to have an office visit?**

❋ **What tests should I expect to have and when?**

❋ **What is the fee for a vaginal birth? Cesarean birth? What extra charges should I expect? (Many good doctors now charge the same fee for a vaginal or a cesarean delivery, because they do not want to be accused of performing unnecessary cesareans.)**

❋ **What are your thoughts on natural childbirth, anesthesia, episiotomy, Cesarean section, induction of labor? (Ask these and other questions about the doctor's birthing philosophy that are of concern to you.)**

❋ **With which hospital are you affiliated? Does the hospital have birthing rooms; labor, delivery, and recovery rooms; rooming-in for baby and husband; a neonatal intensive care unit?**

❋ **What do you consider "high risk" birth factors?**

❋ **How do I get answers to my questions between visits? If you are busy, is there another doctor in the office who will take my call?**

❋ **Do you have nurses trained to answer basic prenatal questions? (Obstetricians spend half their day doing hospital deliveries or patient check-ins, so it is important to know that if your doctor is not there, someone will be available to answer your questions in a timely manner.)**

While you're at the doctor's office for your consultation, check out the waiting room. If you can, ask one or two of the pregnant women, leafing through the latest *Parents* magazine, how long they usually wait to see the doctor. Routine visits should take about ten minutes, and there is nothing more frustrating than waiting an hour for a ten-minute visit. Also, ask whether the doctor works in a collaborative way with patients, making joint decisions, or whether he likes to call the shots. Again, the doctor's personality must jibe with yours.

The usual schedule for visiting your ob/gyn in a low-risk, normal pregnancy is every three weeks for the first seven months, every two weeks in the eighth month, and every week in the ninth month. Of course, this may vary with different practices, and if your pregnancy is high risk you may see your doctor more often.

Some common tests to expect in the course of your pregnancy are:

Sonogram. Typically, a woman has two or three sonograms (ultrasounds) during her pregnancy. The first will be done in the second month (about nine weeks) to date her pregnancy; the second more extensive sonogram will be done in the fifth month (about twenty weeks), sometimes at the hospital, to check the growth and internal organs of the fetus; a third may be done in the ninth month (about thirty-six weeks) to get an idea of the baby's size and position. During Kelly's second pregnancy, her ob/gyn had acquired an in-office sonogram machine. In fact, many New York ob/gyn's now have a sonogram machine in their office and will do sonograms more often.

✳ *MSAFP (Maternal Serum Alpha-Fetoprotein Screening.)* The MSAFP screening is performed in the fourth month (sixteen to eighteen weeks). This simple blood test determines the levels of alpha-fetoprotein (blood protein) present in the mother's blood. High or low levels may indicate serious problems in the development of the fetus. If the MSAFP level comes back either too high or too low, the doctor will probably recommend a second test to confirm the results of the first.

✳ *Amniocentesis.* Known to moms as an amnio, this procedure is performed in the fourth month (sixteen to eighteen weeks) of pregnancy. The technician, guided by an ultrasound image of the uterus, inserts a long hollow needle through the woman's abdominal wall and withdraws a small amount of amniotic fluid. Amniocentesis is recommended for women over thirty-five (although many women over thirty choose to have it performed as well) and in cases in which genetic disorders or chromosomal abnormalities might be suspected.

These tests and procedures are routine, and the obstetrician you choose will have conducted, ordered, or overseen them on hundreds of pregnant women before you. But remember: this is your pregnancy. You should feel perfectly comfortable asking what you think are "dumb questions" about the need for tests and what the results mean. If you are thirty-five or older, you are considered high risk in New York City. Statistics show that women over thirty-five have a slightly greater risk of problems during pregnancy. Other circumstances can also determine a high-risk pregnancy-a previous period of infertility, multiple miscarriages, high blood pressure, diabetes, obesity, and other serious health problems. Make sure your doctor knows your full medical history.

A number of obstetricians specialize in high-risk pregnancies. *New York* magazine's "The Best Doctors in New York" issue lists many of them, as does www.urbanbaby.com. Your own ob/gyn can also refer you to such a specialist. Or call the obstetrical department of any of the hospitals (starting on page 22), and ask for a referral based upon your specific needs.

Midwives

A growing number of New York women opt for a midwife, rather than an obstetrician, to guide them through pregnancy and delivery. A midwife may be a good fit for you if you're low risk, and if you like the idea of working one-on-one. A midwife will likely be more available than an obstetrician to talk with you about the emotional aspects of what you're experiencing, and will probably be more oriented toward natural childbirth.

If this sounds good to you, you will want to find a Certified Nurse Midwife (CNM), a registered nurse who has undergone extensive formal training through an accredited nurse-midwifery program. The American College of Nurse Midwives, based in Washington, D.C., provides midwife certification nationally and sets the standards for the practice of nurse-midwifery. Only ACNM-certified midwives are able to practice in hospitals. Midwives can prescribe pain medications for women in labor and they can call an anesthesiologist when in a hospital.

Two other categories of midwives are Direct Entry Midwives, often referred to as Lay Midwives, and Physician-Assistant Midwives. The latter may also be certified through the ACNM and therefore can practice in hospitals. Direct Entry Midwives, trained through a combination of coursework and apprenticeship, are not permitted to practice in hospitals but do perform or assist at many home births in the New York City area.

When you choose a CNM, find out about her hospital affiliation. You may prefer to deliver in a birthing center or at home, but in the event of a medical complication, it is critical that your practitioner has access to a hospital nearby. Many CNMs in New York do practice in hospitals and will deliver your baby in the same birthing rooms that the obstetricians use.

With a CNM, you can expect the same schedule you would have with an obstetrician: a visit every three or four weeks at the beginning of your pregnancy, every three weeks in the seventh month, every two weeks in the eighth month, and every week in the ninth month. Like an obstetrician, the midwife will ask how you are feeling and if you have any questions. She will give you an external exam, take your blood pressure and weight, and listen to the baby's heartbeat.

If you would like to check out midwifery, call any of the names listed here, and set up an appointment for a consultation, just as you would for an obstetrician. Use the list of questions we have provided for choosing an obstetrician (see page 15). In addition, you may be especially interested in learning how the midwife will help you through the stages of labor and delivery, the point at which the practices of CNMs and obstetricians usually differ. Many CNMs are skilled at relaxing and preparing the perineum so that anesthesia and episiotomies are rarely necessary.

The following is a list of the hospital-based independent Certified Nurse Midwives practices in New York City:

Beth Israel Midwifery Group
Beth Israel Medical Center
Phillips Ambulatory Care Center
10 Union Square East
bet. 14th and 15th Streets
844-8569

CBS Midwifery, Inc.
Barbara Sellars
(affiliated with St. Luke's Roosevelt)

103 Fifth Avenue at 17th Street
366-4699

Elizabeth Seton Childbearing Center
(affiliated with St. Vincent's Hospital)
222 W. 14th Street
bet. Seventh and Eighth Avenues
367-8500

Midwifery Services, Inc.
(affiliated with St. Luke's-Roosevelt)
135 W. 70th Street bet. Broadway
and Columbus Avenue
877-5556

SOHO Women's Medical Center
(affiliated with St. Vincent's)
135 Spring Street, 2nd floor,
bet. Greene and Wooster Streets
274-0900

Note: You and your doctor or midwife should decide jointly, based on your wishes and her expertise, on a birthing plan for the big day. Sometime after you begin your visits, but well before your due date, decide what will happen regarding anesthesia, IVs, and episiotomies. Your ideal birthing plan (barring any unexpected surprises) should be in writing, in your doctor's file, and on hand at the hospital when you arrive.

THE BIRTH PLACE
Hospitals

All obstetricians are affiliated with a hospital, or maybe two, so once you have selected your obstetrician, you will deliver at her hospital.

If you are still in the process of choosing an obstetrician, you may want to work backward—find the hospital you prefer, and then find an agreeable obstetrician who practices there. Knowing as much as you can about the place your baby will be born is very helpful and comforting.

Here's what's important to know about the hospital: the number of birthing rooms, Cesarean rate, level of care provided in the neonatal unit, policies on husbands in the delivery room, rooming-in (husband and baby staying overnight in your room), and sibling and family visitors. New York has many hospitals, but some are newer and more comfortable than others. Mount Sinai and Roosevelt hospitals have decorated their labor, delivery, and recovery rooms with Laura Ashley-style touches, so they feel more like a bedroom than a hospital room. While it may be tempting to choose a hospital based upon decor, trust us when we tell you that once you are in labor, the color of the wallpaper in the labor room will be the last thing on your mind.

New York Hospital was one of the last to renovate. When Kelly delivered Alexander it looked like a war zone, but the new wing, opened earlier this year, is state of the art and beautiful, and they continue to provide outstanding care.

We toured all the private hospitals in New York City where babies are delivered and found them to be similar in many ways. They provide birthing beds, showers, or squatting bars to help your labor and delivery. And in most, if not all, cases, it is your own doctor or midwife—not the hospital or staff—who makes the important decisions concerning your labor.

Other general points to keep in mind:

All the hospitals allow you to preregister. This is a good idea, because once you are in labor, you won't want to fill out forms—registering in advance can keep the paperwork to a minimum upon your arrival.

❋ **Check your insurance company's policy on length of hospital stay permitted for childbirth.** Most insurance companies cover either a twenty-four or forty-eight-hour stay for a vaginal delivery and three to four days for a Cesarean delivery.

❋ **Contact your insurance company when you become pregnant** so that later there won't be any problems with the forms you submit. Some insurance companies require notification before you check into the hospital.

❋ **Private rooms are available at each of these hospitals.** But keep in mind that the cost of a private room is not covered by insurance—your out-of-pocket expenses will range from $150 to $300 per night. Rooming-in for husbands and newborns is permitted in all hospitals in a private room. (In some hospitals it is also permitted in a semiprivate room so long as your roommate doesn't object.)

❋ **All the hospitals have twenty-four-hour parking lots nearby** and will provide you with a list. Find out which hospital entrance to use in case you arrive in the middle of the night.

❋ **All hospitals offer weekly classes for new mothers:** bathing the baby, breastfeeding, and basic child-care. If you cannot make it to a class, ask

Top Ten Hospital Tips

1. Decide whether you want a private room *before* you go into labor.
2. Bring a pillow with a colored pillowcase from home.
3. Bring your robe and slippers.
4. Bring a bath towel and washcloth. (Hospital towels are tiny!)
5. Bring sanitary napkins.
6. Have a friend or family member present as much as possible to go for drinks, run errands, and get the nurse.
7. Have key phone numbers with you—baby nurse, furniture delivery, hotel, etc.
8. Call your insurance company as soon as possible after the baby is born.
9. Rest as much as possible: you are not going to get much rest for the next ten years.
10. Let the nurse feed the baby at 2 or 3 A.M. if you are not exclusively breast feeding (and even if you are, one feeding won't cause nipple confusion!). You need your sleep!

the nurses, who are trained to help. From our own experience, you must ask to have these lessons. You are in charge, so speak up about your needs.

❋ **Many of the hospitals have extremely generous visiting hours.** The nurse conducting our tour at New York Hospital gave excellent advice in this regard: She said to be selfish and careful about your visitors for your own health and well being and for that of the baby. Use your hospital stay to get some rest, if possible, and to bond with your baby. There will be plenty of time for visitors when you and your baby get home.

❊ Bring two pillows from home for your postpartum room. You will be a lot more comfortable sleeping on your own pillows, as most hospital pillows are flat as a board. Make sure your pillow cases are any color but white so they don't get mixed in with the hospital laundry.

❊ You should also consider bringing towels from home. If you plan to shower at the hospital, the bath towels are the size of face towels, and can barely fit around a postpartum woman's body!

After touring ten hospitals, we became experts at predicting the questions we'd most often hear from fellow expectant parents:

Can we bring music into the delivery room?

❊ **Can the baby be wrapped in a receiving blanket that we bring from home instead of a regulation hospital blanket?**

❊ **Can we dim the lights in the labor room?**

❊ **Can my husband/partner cut the umbilical cord?**

The answer to all these questions is yes, but we can tell you that once labor begins your only concern is delivering that baby any way you can, music or no music.

The following chart provides information to consider while evaluating the hospital in which you will deliver your baby. It includes:

Hospital: The name, address, key phone numbers and visiting hours.

Labor rooms: The number and type of delivery rooms. In a labor, delivery, and recovery room, known as an LDR room, you will do just that before you are transferred to a postpartum room. An operating room is where Cesareans and complicated vaginal births take place. A labor room is for labor only. A delivery room is where you will be taken when you are ten centimeters dilated and ready to deliver. From delivery you go to a recovery room for one to two hours before going to your own room, where you will stay until you leave the hospital.

Midwives: Hospitals with midwives on staff, and those which allow midwives to deliver babies.

Cesarean birthrate: Numbers indicate the percentage of births by Cesarean section each year. The percentages listed are the most recent figures available from each hospital. Generally, hospitals with midwives have the lowest rates; hospitals with a large infertility /high-risk patient base (very New York City) have the highest. The national Cesarean rate for 1999 is 22 percent.

Nursery level: Neonatal intensive care units are classified in Levels I through IV, with Level IV being the most advanced. Choosing a hospital with a Level III or Level IV nursery is recommended, especially for high-risk pregnancies.

Childbirth classes: Prenatal classes for women and their husbands or partners, including Lamaze, breastfeeding, and preparation for Cesarean birth. These classes are given at the hospital (unless otherwise noted), and you must sign up in advance. For second time moms, many hospitals offer sibling classes.

Pamela took Rebecca to one at Mt. Sinai before Benjamin was born, and it was an excellent way to prepare her for having a new baby at home.

Other information: Any unique features about the hospital.

Birthing Centers

If you choose a midwife, she may deliver at one of the hospitals listed above or at a birthing center. Many women find the nonhospital-like atmosphere and amenities of the birthing center enormously appealing.

Not only your husband or coach, but your mother, father, best friend, and your new baby's older brother or sister can be with you throughout your birth experience. During your labor you can usually walk around, sip tea, or relax in a Jacuzzi or tub, all of which many women find more labor-enhancing and less alarming than being in a hospital bed hooked up to a monitor. At a birthing center, you can choose to labor, and even deliver your baby in a special tub of soothing warm water!

One caveat to delivering at a birthing center: You must be committed to a natural childbirth. No pain relief, such as Demerol or an epidural block, can be administered.

Two birthing centers exist in Manhattan:
The Birthing Center
(attached to St. Luke's-Roosevelt Hospital Center)
1000 Tenth Avenue bet. 58th and 59th Streets
523-BABY

Elizabeth Seton Childbearing Center
(Affiliated with St. Vincent's Hospital)
222 W. 14th Street bet. Seventh and Eighth Avenues
367-8500

If the idea of a birthing center appeals to you, call either of these to schedule a tour and an interview with the director. At both, you can ask for a CNM referral. Or, call a midwife who is affiliated with one of the centers (see pages 17-18) and schedule a consultation.

Note: Ask detailed questions about what procedures the center follows should a medical emergency arise at the time of delivery.

CHILDBIRTH METHODS

Once the who and the where of your pregnancy and delivery have been settled, you will start to focus—more and more as you grow and grow—on the how of it all. What are the best, easiest and most pain-free ways to get that baby out?

As you talk with other pregnant women and new mothers, you will hear about the relative merits of one birthing technique over another. Here is a very short course on the three most well-known and popular.

The Lamaze Method. This method, named after its developer, Dr. Fernand Lamaze, head of an obstetrical clinic in Paris in 1950, is popularly, if not entirely accurately, known as childbirth without pain. The method combines learned breathing techniques (the hoo-hoo-hoo, hee-hee-hee) used during contractions, with relaxation exercises designed to help a woman get

HOSPITAL	LABOR RMS/OTHER	CLASSES

Beth Israel Hospital
16th St. & 1st Ave.
420-2000 (General)
420-2999 (Classes)
420-2935 (Patient Care)
www.bethisraelny.org
VISITING HOURS:
  General: 11 A.M.–8 P.M.
  Fathers: 10 A.M.–10 P.M.
  24 hrs. in private rooms
	9 LDR (6 recently renovated with showers)
	1 Recovery Suite (with 5 beds)
	3 Operating Rooms
	MIDWIVES: Yes
	CESAREAN RATE: 20%
	NURSERY LEVEL III
	Has mother/baby nursing (family center-ed—the same nurse takes care of you and your baby). One of the largest mid-wifery programs in the state—over 10% of births are delivered by a midwife. All birthing rooms are private and beautifully decorated, and furnished with an easy chair that can be converted into a bed.
		Pregnancy and Beyond Fitness Program (Prenatal Yoga, Pregnancy Exercise and Yoga Shape Up for New Moms); Promoting a Healthy Pregnancy; Childbirth Pre-paration (Lamaze); Prepara-tion for Parenthood; Lamaze Refresher Course; Sibling Preparation; How to Succeed at Breastfeeding; Baby Saver CPR and Child Safety; New Mother's Support Group

Columbia Presbyterian Hospital/Babies Hospital/ Sloane Hospital for Women
3959 Broadway at 166th St.
www.nyph.org
305-2500 (General)
305-2040 (Parent Ed.)
VISITING HOURS:
  General: 12–8 P.M.
  Fathers: 8 A.M.–10 P.M.
  24 hrs. in private rooms
	8 LDR/2 Delivery
	1 Operating Room
	MIDWIVES: No
	CESAREAN RATE: 20–22%
	NURSERY LEVEL III
	Aesthetically the most impressive. Spacious postpartum rooms are beauti-fully decorated, with bathroom and shower. Moms bring baby to postpartum floor by themselves—provides nice bonding time. On-staff post-natal masseuse available.
		Preparation for Childbirth; Breastfeeding; Cesarean Birth; Sibling Tours

Lenox Hill Hospital 100 E. 77th Street bet. Lexington & Park Aves 434-2000 (General) 434-2273 (Parent Ed.)	11 LDR/3 Operating 1 Recovery suite (holds 7) MIDWIVES: No CESAREAN RATE: 31% NURSERY LEVEL III	Patients are referred to the 92nd Street Y (996-1100). Small group and individual classes are available in Lamaze (434-3512).

HOSPITAL	LABOR RMS/OTHER	CLASSES
434-3152 (Babies' Club) www.lenoxhillhospital.org VISITING HOURS: 　Father: 24 hrs. 　Family: 3–8 P.M. 　General: 12–1:30 P.M.; 　　7–8 P.M.	LDR in one room. Many of our friends have delivered here over the years. Some of the best child/ birth preparation classes are offered here. Also, we hear great praises for the outstanding nurses in the maternity ward.	
The Mount Sinai **Medical Center** One Gustave L. Levy Place Klingenstein Pavilion 1176 Fifth Ave. at 98th St. 241-6500 (General) 241-7491 (Women's 　& Children's Office) 241-6578 (Breastfeeding 　Warm Line) VISITING HOURS: 　General: 9 A.M.–8 P.M. 　Father: 24 hrs.	15 LDR/1 Recovery (holds 5 women) 3 Operating MIDWIVES: Yes CESAREAN RATE: 18.7% NURSERY LEVEL IV LDR rooms are decorated with Laura Ashley in mind and resemble hotel rooms more than hospital rooms. Pam had both her children at Mount Sinai and was thrilled with the care she received. Pam's daughter Rebecca was in intensive care for seven days, and Pam credits Mt. Sinai with saving her life.	**Breastfeeding; Lamaze;** **Weekend Lamaze;** **Labor and Delivery Sibling** **Preparation Classes;** **Sibling Preparation for** **3-7 years; Preparation** **for Cesarean;** **Infant Massage;** **Refresher Lamaze**
NY Presbyterian Hospital **at the NY Weill** **Cornell Center** 525 E. 68th Street bet. 　York Ave. & East River 746-5454 (General) 746-3215 (Parenthood Prep.) www.nyp.org VISITING HOURS: 　General: 9 A.M.–8 P.M. 　Father: 24 hrs.	11 Birthing/2 Operating Rooms/ 2 Delivery/1 Recovery (holds 6) MIDWIVES: Yes CESAREAN RATE: 27% NURSERY LEVEL IV Semi-private rooms sleep two. Private rooms are lovely and roomy. Kelly delivered Angela and Alexander here and although she was very happy the first time, the new renovations have made this first class hospital even better.	Lamaze; Breastfeeding; Baby Care; Adapting to Parenthood; New Mother Support Group; Cesarean Preparation Classes; Breast- feeding Consultation Class; Sibling Classes; Multiples Class

HOSPITAL	LABOR RMS/OTHER	CLASSES
New York University Medical Center 560 First Ave. at 32nd St. 263-7300 (General) 263-7201 (Classes) www.msnyuhealth.org VISITING HOURS: General: 8:30 A.M.–8:30 P.M. Father, Family: 8:30 A.M.–10 P.M.	9 Birthing (LDR) 3 Delivery and Operating Rooms 1 Jacuzzi Room MIDWIVES: Yes CESAREAN RATE: 34% NURSERY LEVEL IV One of the first NYC hospitals to renovate in style. NYU is pristine. Very modern facilities with TV/VCR/CD Player and shower in each room. Spacious Birthing Rooms (LDR) with rockers, wood floors. Request upon arrival in Labor.	Prepared Childbirth; Prepared Childbirth Review, Accelerated Childbirth; Cesarean Birth; Sibling Class Breastfeeding; Breastfeeding Support Group; Father, Family: Infant Care; New Moms Group; Getting a Good Start
Roosevelt Hospital 1000 Tenth Ave. at 59th St. 523-4000 (General) 523-6222 (Classes) www.wehealny.org VISITING HOURS: General: 11 A.M.–8 P.M. Father: 24 hrs.	12 LDR/3 Operating 2 Recovery/3 Birthing MIDWIVES: Yes. Midwives deliver in LDR and Birthing rooms at Birthing Center. CESAREAN RATE: 22.3% NURSERY LEVEL III New and attractive facilities. Only NYC birth center attached to hospital. Center has jacuzzis, kitchen, special meals, fancy decor, allows siblings to observe birth. Private birthing rooms are furnished with a rocking chair and an easy chair which converts to a bed.	Preconception Seminar; Choices in Childbirth; Why Lamaze; Sensuality and Sexuality in Pregnancy; Prenatal Yoga for Expectant Parents; Preparation for Childbirth Classes; Prepared Parenthood; Baby Care/Feeding/ Infant CPR; Breastfeeding; Infant CPR; Child CPR; Combined Infant/Child CPR; First Aid, a Primer for Parents; Sibling Preparation Course; Breastfeeding & New Parent Support Group
St. Luke's Hospital 1111 Amsterdam Ave. at 114th St.	5 LDR/2 Operating/1 Recovery MIDWIVES: Yes CESAREAN RATE: 26%	All classes given at Roosevelt hospital location.

HOSPITAL	LABOR RMS/OTHER	CLASSES

523-4000 (General)
523-6222 (Parent/
  Family Ed.)
www.wehealny.org
VISITING HOURS:
  General: 11 A.M.–8:30 P.M.
  Father: 24 hrs.
	NURSERY LEVEL III
	Huge, comfortable private rooms–
	two-bed rooms used for one woman if
	requested. Least expensive private room
	at $100 extra per night. Rooms have own
	showers, plus a rocking chair and an easy
	chair which converts to a bed. Two guests
	are allowed during labor and birth.	

**St. Vincent's Hospital
and Medical Center**
170 W. 12th St. at 7th Ave.
604-7000 (General)
604-7946 (Maternity Ed.)
www.stvincents.
  healthcentral.com
VISITING HOURS:
  General: 10 A.M.–10 P.M.
  Father: 10 A.M.–10 P.M.;
  24 hrs. in private rooms
	8 LDR/2 OR/1 Recovery
	MIDWIVES: Yes
	CESAREAN RATE: 20%
	NURSERY LEVEL III
	Sunny and spacious private rooms
	with two beds. Family-centered care—
	mom and baby share the same nurse.
	Birth suites allow single-room mater-
	nity care, and feature a love seat
	that folds out for overnight guests.
		**Preparation for Childbirth;
		Childbirth Refresher; Breast-
		feeding; Newborn Care;
		Welcome to Parenthood
		Infant CPR; Sibling
		Preparation Class**

through labor comfortably.

Most hospitals offer Lamaze classes. Call to sign up. (Also, most of the obstetrical nurses listed are trained in Lamaze and can assist your coach in the labor room if needed.) Couples usually begin Lamaze in the seventh month.

Some large obstetrical practices also offer Lamaze or will make referrals to private instructors, so ask your obstetrician or midwife. Kelly took Lamaze with Fritzi Kallop (906-9255) and was very happy with her. Kallop, formerly an R.N. at New York Hospital, has published an excellent book on Lamaze called *Fritzi Kallop's Birth Book.* Fritzi is very funny and down to earth, answers questions day and night, and is there for you long after the birth of your little one.

The Bradley Method Husband-Coached Childbirth. This method was developed by Dr. Robert A. Bradley, a Toronto-based obstetrician. The Bradley Method is based on a calming pattern of relaxation, deep abdominal breathing, and close teamwork between husband (or partner) and wife. Bradley's goal is a completely unmedicated pregnancy (no aspirin or cold remedies) and labor and birth (no epidural block or Pitocin).

With Bradley, the pregnant woman learns various positions for first, second, and third stage labor. She is encouraged to approach her entire pregnancy as training for labor and to prepare her muscles for birth and her breasts for nursing.

Few New York City hospitals offer Bradley instruction for childbirth. To find the name of a certified Bradley instructor in your area, write to The American Academy of Husband-Coached Childbirth, P.O. Box 5224, Sherman Oaks, CA 91413. Or call (800) 4-ABIRTH.

Water Labor and Water Birth. Water birth, popular in Russia since the 1960s, has attracted a small but enthusiastic number of supporters in the United States. Studies have shown that warm water can reduce the hours and stress of labor, offer support to the laboring woman, and help relax blood flow, making the baby's journey into the world easier.

Some women use this method's water-filled tub only as a comfort during labor. Others deliver while still in the tub, and the baby takes his first breaths while most of his body is submerged in water, a gentle and familiar medium from his time in the womb.

The Birthing Center at Roosevelt Hospital makes water labor and water birth available as an option. Our friend Judy delivered her daughter there with Judith Halek attending (see below) and was thrilled with her experience. Should you wish, you can rent a birthing tub and have a water birth at home with the help of a midwife.

CHILDBIRTH EDUCATORS, CLASSES, AND OTHER RESOURCES

If you are having a normal pregnancy, you're happy with your OB or CNM, and you've signed up for childbirth education/Lamaze classes through your doctor's office or hospital—congratulations! You are in good shape for a successful pregnancy and delivery.

If you want to know even more about what's going on with your body and what's to come during pregnancy, labor, delivery, and after, New York has many experts who work on a one-on-one basis or in a small group.

Here is a list of resources. These private practitioners specialize in a variety of birth-related areas: Lamaze, Bradley, water birth, labor support, and childbirth education. Some practitioners offer more than one kind of service; make some phone calls, and you may find just the right match for you.

Class lengths vary, but most childbirth series cost between $200 to $400 per couple. If you use more than one service from a practitioner, you can probably negotiate a package deal.

The following are specialists in pregnancy and childbirth education:

Ellen Chuse, C.C.E.
718-789-1981

Ellen Chuse has been working with birthing women and their families since 1984. She has served as president of the Childbirth Education Association of Metropolitan New York, and remains active on the Board of Directors. Her childbirth preparation series includes information on labor, birth, postpartum, breastfeeding, and newborn care; classes are held in Park Slope and lower Manhattan locations and cost $325 per couple. These classes fill quickly, so call early. Ellen also maintains a private practice as a pregnancy and birth counselor, and leads new mother's groups at the Elizabeth Seton Childbirthing Center. Please call for specifics. Ellen is the mother of two daughters herself.

Choiceful Birth and Parenting
Ellen Krug, CSW, C.C.E.
718-768-0494
www.members.aol.com/choiceful

A certified social worker and childbirth educator, Ellen Krug has been offering childbirth classes and counseling since 1984. Ellen offers an eight-class series on natural childbirth for pregnant women and their partners. Classes cover birth planning, labor support techniques, and relaxation; private classes are available, as well as counseling on any pregnancy, birth, or parenting issues. Ellen also runs a New Mom/Newborn circle, a support group for new moms and their babies that meets weekly. Parenting issues, adjustment to new family roles, sleeping issues, health care, and ways to balance work and parenthood are among the topics discussed. All classes and counseling are offered at a Park Slope, Brooklyn location.

Mary Lynn Fiske, C.C.E., AAHCC
718-855-1650

Mary Lynn Fiske has been teaching the Bradley method for over six years. She offers an eight-class series at a few locations in Cobble Hill, Brooklyn, and also teaches privately in her own and her clients' homes. Classes focus on pain coping techniques, good birth planning, coaching tools for partners, and what to expect during labor and birth. They include labor rehearsals and role-play, discussion of interventions and Cesarean, videos, and relaxation practice. Mary Lynn is an open and generous instructor; she makes her clients feel comfortable with the decisions they reach about their pregnancy and birth.

Judith Halek
309 W. 109th Street
bet. Broadway and Riverside Drive
222-4349
e-mail: watrbaybee@earthlink.net

One of the first labor support doulas in New York City, Judith is a fitness instructor, birth counselor, and specialist in pre- and post-natal massage, as well as the founder of Birth Balance, where she has been the director for over twelve years. She writes and speaks nationally on birth issues. She attended the first

New York City water birth in 1987, currently runs the East Coast Resource Center for Water Birth, and is a water birth consultant. Judith is also the only photographer/videographer in New York who specializes in pregnancy, labor, birth and postpartum documentation. She works with clients in their home, birth center, or hospital. You can watch Judith's weekly cable program on birth topics, particularly the integration of water in labor and birth, on Channel 34, Manhattan Neighborhood Network Cable Station. Check your television listings.

Risa Lynn Klein
1490 Second Avenue bet. 77th
and 78th Streets
249-4203

Risa Lynn Klein is a certified Bradley childbirth educator who has been teaching group and private classes, as well as refresher classes, for over ten years. She is certified in prenatal birth educational counseling, and will serve as a labor assistant at home, hospital or birthing center, for couples who prepare for labor and birth with her. Risa herself took Bradley classes and gave birth to her daughter (now 11) naturally. The experience changed her life; she left a career in television production for one in birth production. She also gives a three-part workshop to help couples prepare for birth, and serves as a breastfeeding consultant.

Diana Simkin
Upper East Side locations
348-0208

A certified personal trainer, Diana has been offering one-to-one fitness for pre- and post-natal women for eighteen years. She gives private or group Lamaze classes and rents Medela breast pumps. Diana has also written three books on pregnancy: *The Complete Pregnancy Exercise Program*, *The Complete Baby Exercise Program*, and *Preparation for Birth*.

Nancy Vega
206 W. 104th Street bet. Broadway
and Amsterdam Avenues
316-6337

Nancy has been involved in natural childbirth since 1990 and is the founder of the New York City chapter of the International Cesarean Awareness Network (ICAN/NYC). She is a childbirth educator through the Childbirth Education Association of Metropolitan New York. Although she now teaches only occasionally, Nancy is a source of support and referral for homebirth and VBAC and never turns away a family in need of support. Nancy is the single mother of two children and had a VBAC birth at home.

Martine Jean-Baptiste, C.N.M., C.C.E.
769-4578

A certified nurse midwife, registered nurse, and certified childbirth educator, Martine has worked in women's health for over 14 years. If you have questions about pregnancy or childbirth options, she would be happy to talk with you.

Gayatri Martin, R.N.
Choices for Childbirth
725-1078

Gayatri has been teaching yoga for over 10 years and Co-operative Childbirth Preparation classes for over eight years. Her classes encourage expectant mothers to be central to the experience of planning and preparing for birth. Gayatri is also a certified Prenatal Holistic Counselors and uses body-centered hypnosis to help women address the emotional and psychological aspects of birth. She conducts private and group classes.

Wellcare Center
161 Madison Avenue
bet. 32nd and 33rd Streets
Long Island College Hospital
349 Henry Street, Brooklyn
696-9256

Wellcare has been providing comprehensive services for expectant and new mothers since 1995. Laura Best-Macia, IBCLC and Ilana Taubman, RN, IBCLC are the core lactation consultant staff (both previously coordinated the Breastfeeding Program at Beth Israel Medical Center). The center offers lactation consulting seven days a week, childbirth education classes that combine the Lamaze and Bradley approaches, breastfeeding, child care, and infant CPR classes. It also provides continuing education courses on lactation management for lactation consultants and other health care providers. Wellcare is also a resource for pump rentals/sales and nursing bras and pillows.

The International Cesarean Awareness Network (ICAN)/NY Chapter
662-2554 (Dierdre McLary);
718-275-3389 (Vanessa Anton-Paultre)
www.icannyc.org

The International Cesarean Awareness Network is an international grass roots organization that was formed to lower the Cesarean rate through education. ICAN/NY is co-led by Dierdre McLary and Vanessa Anton-Paultre. The group provides a support network for women (and their husbands or partners) who have suffered from trauma after having a Cesarean. ICAN also provides a forum for childbirth options, and many midwives, labor coaches, childbirth educators, and water birth experts are members. Free monthly meetings are held at various locations in Manhattan; visit ICAN/ NY's Web site or call for information. ICAN's national Web site is www.ican-online.com.

2 · taking care of yourself

Once you have assembled your support team, from Lamaze instructor to lactation consultant, checked out the hospital room or birthing center in which your baby will first set eyes upon the world, it's time to be good to yourself. Since the first edition of *City Baby*, being pregnant has become truly chic. Like so many supermodels and Hollywood actresses, many New York women have discovered the benefits, physical and emotional, of staying fit during the whole nine months.

Pamela's friend Debby didn't even appear pregnant until her seventh month. She had perfect skin and hair that got thicker and shinier. She looked and acted as if she felt like a million bucks. She may be the luckiest woman we know. If you are like the rest of us, however, the weight gain, the bulging belly and exhaustion might make you feel unattractive on occasion. Now is the time to pamper and indulge yourself. Take advantage of some of the terrific body-strengthening and spirit-lifting services New York has to offer. Treat yourself to a manicure when you're in your ninth month and feel as though you can't stand to be pregnant for one more day.

Most importantly, get involved with a physical fitness program early on. It will help you feel your best throughout your pregnancy and prepare you for labor. Our friend Matty worked until ten days before her delivery, taking the subway from her upper West Side apartment to her downtown East Side office and back again every day. She said climbing up and down all those stairs, carrying what turned out to be her ten-and-a-half pound son, gave her legs of steel. This is good. Strong leg muscles are useful for getting you through the last months of pregnancy, as well as labor and birth.

You can do even more for yourself by checking out one or another of the facilities described in this chapter. You'll find information about health clubs, exercise studios, and private practitioners that offer pre- and postnatal exercise classes, fitness training, yoga, and massage, all fine-tuned and appropriate for pregnant women.

Kelly swears by the Medical Massage Group; the massages she had there relaxed her and the foot reflexology helped her morning sickness. The second time around Kelly tried massage more frequently, worked out regularly, and had a much easier pregnancy.

EXERCISE

Most experts agree that exercising throughout your pregnancy is safe, healthy, and beneficial to your overall well being. If your pregnancy is *low risk* and *normal*, you can participate in a moderate exercise program throughout your nine months. If you're a long-time jock or have exercised regularly prior to pregnancy (at least three times per week), you should be able to safely maintain that level of activity, with some modifications, throughout pregnancy and postpartum. Of course, check with your obstetrician or midwife before starting or continuing any exercise regimen, whether you are low- or high-risk. Also, be aware of the following recommendations adapted from guidelines issued by the American College of Obstetricians and Gynecologists (ACOG):

- **Regular exercise (at least three times per week) is preferable to intermittent activity.**
- **Avoid exercise that involves lying flat on your back after the fourth month. Lying on your back is associated with decreased cardiac output in pregnancy. Also avoid prolonged periods of standing.**
- **During pregnancy, you have less oxygen available for aerobic exercise. Modify the intensity of your exercise. Stop exercising when fatigued, and never exercise to the point of exhaustion.**
- **Weight-bearing exercises, such as jogging, may be continued throughout pregnancy, at lower intensities. Nonweight-bearing exercises, such as cycling and swimming, minimize risk of injury.**
- **During exercise, be sure that your heart rate does not exceed 140 beats per minute.**
- **Avoid exercise that could cause you to lose your balance, especially in the third trimester. Avoid any type of exercise with the potential for even mild abdominal trauma.**
- **Be sure to eat enough prior to your workout. Pregnancy requires an additional 300 calories a day just to maintain your weight.**
- **Drink water and wear comfortable clothing to augment heat dissipation during exercise.**

Many of the body changes of pregnancy persist four to six weeks postpartum. After your baby is born, resume your pre-pregnancy routines gradually, according to how you feel.

Fitness/Health Clubs

If you don't already have an exercise routine and want to get started, walking is a safe way to stay in shape. For those who desire a more structured workout environment, the following health clubs offer special classes and/or training for pregnant women. Many personal trainers in these health clubs are certified to work with pre- and postnatal women, just inquire. (In many clubs, pregnant women work out right next to their non-pregnant counterparts.)

Membership fees in most full-service health clubs (Equinox, New York Sports Club,

Top Ten Tips for Prenatal Exercising

1. Do it!
2. Try as many classes as necessary until you find one you like.
3. Remember to do your Kegels.
4. Don't lie on your back after the fourth month.
5. Drink plenty of water.
6. Don't exercise on an empty stomach; make sure to have a snack first.
7. Exercise with other pregnant women; you won't feel as big.
8. Try yoga for excellent stretching and relaxation.
9. Don't let your heart rate exceed 140 beats per minute.
10. Consult your obstetrician before starting any kind of new exercise.

New York Health & Racquet Club, Reebok Sports Club, and David Barton) range from $900 to $2,000 per year, with a one-time initiation fee between $200 and $500. These fees are often negotiable and may be discounted if you join with a friend or spouse, or pay the entire amount upon joining, or work for an affiliated company. The fee for a personal trainer varies from club to club, but is normally $55 to $100 per hour. With some club memberships, you can use all locations in the chain; others limit workout locations.

Private clubs offer pleasant accoutrements: roomy changing areas, lots of towels, and nice snack bars. Check your local Y classes as well. They are the most economical and offer a wide range of classes and equipment.

Bally Total Fitness
Bfit Baby Club
Various locations in all boroughs
(877) 888-3228; (800) FITNESS
to find the club nearest you.

The Bfit Baby Club was developed to help women experience the benefits of working out during pregnancy. For $29.99 the Bfit Baby Club package includes: recommendations for safe exercise, information on monitoring the heart rate and adapting your workout during pregnancy, a videotape showing 14 core exercises for pregnant and postnatal women, a two week pass to Bally Total Fitness, information on personal training, and a maternity tank top. They also offers personal training for pregnant women.

David Barton
30 E. 85th Street bet. Madison
and Fifth Avenues
517-7577
552 Sixth Avenue at 15th Street
727-0004

David Barton offers personal trainers who are specialists in working with pre- and postnatal women and will design a regimen that is right for your level of fitness. For postpartum women, Barton offers Strollercize classes in which women bring their babies in strollers and perform a series of exercises using the strollers as resistance. These classes are included in the membership fee.

Barton is small and tightly packed with equipment so it is difficult to move around. The design and low lighting give it a nightclub feel; there is a big screen TV where you can watch a movie. There is no baby-sitting available.

Body by Baby
Jane Kornbluh
677-6165
www.bodybybaby.com

Body by Baby offers prenatal and postpartum exercise classes throughout Manhattan and Brooklyn. Prenatal exercises help you stay fit and comfortable during pregnancy, while mommy/baby workouts help you and your baby get strong together. Childbirth preparation classes are also offered, providing couples with the necessary skills to understand and cope effectively with the challenge of labor and delivery.

Equinox
250 E. 54th Street at Second Avenue
277-5400
140 E. 63rd Street at Lexington Avenue
750-4900
344 Amsterdam Avenue bet.
76th and 77th Streets
721-4200
2465 Broadway bet. 91st and 92nd Streets
799-1818
205 E. 85th Street bet. Second
and Third Avenues
439-8500
897 Broadway at 19th Street
780-9300
www.equinoxnyc.com

The Equinox clubs offer a few pre- and postnatal exercise classes but recommend using a personal trainer certified in pre- and postnatal fitness to work with you. There are many trainers available, but you must be a member of the club to hire one, and the cost is not included in the membership fee. Equinox is known for its outstanding instructors and offers a wide range of exercise classes, including spinning. Their locker rooms are immaculate. Baby-sitting for children 9 months and up is available at the 92nd Street Equinox through Playspace (769-2300). Cost is $21 for two hours. Kelly exercised at the E. 85th Street location before and after both her pregnancies and lost 25 pounds with Equinox after each birth. (She had gained 50-55 pounds with each baby.) The full service spa is great; it offers manicures, pedicures, facials, and massage.

Maternal Fitness
108 E. 16th Street, 4th floor, between
bet. Park Avenue and Irving Place
353-1947
www.maternalfitness.com

Developed by Julie Tupler, this unique fitness program physically prepares women for labor and teaches them to exercise safely throughout their pregnancies. All instructors are RNs and Certified Personal Trainers. Small groups or individual sessions focus on strengthening the abdominal muscles with the safe and effective "Tupler Technique" exercises. Kelly took five classes at the end of her first pregnancy and found them very helpful. Maternal Fitness offers a variety of other classes and services, including prenatal yoga, prenatal massage, infant massage, mother/baby exercise classes, and classes on breastfeeding and babycare. This program is also taught at Reebok Sports Club/NY, New York Sports Club, New York Health & Racquet Club, and other fitness centers. Individual sessions are $115 to $200, and a six-week workshop is $325.

Med Fitness

12 E. 86th St. bet. Fifth and Madison Avenues
327-4197
www.medfitnesstraining.com

Owner Michael Margulies has been voted top personal trainer at a U.S. personal training facility, and offers fantastic one-on-one training for pre- and postnatal women (not to mention everyone else). All the trainers here are certified with five or more years of experience. The space is small and unglamorous, but you'll be too busy working up a sweat to notice. A 10-pack training session is $650, which also allows you to use the gym for aerobic exercise when not training.

New York Health & Racquet Club

Various locations in all boroughs
(800) HRC-BEST to find the club nearest you.
www.hrcbest.com

New York Health & Racquet Clubs offer prenatal lectures and exercise classes through the Maternal Fitness program. Call Maryanne

Donner (802-5198) to find out when and where classes are available. Lectures are free to members, and the six-week workshop is $325 for members, $345 for non-members. Lecture topics include safe exercise during pregnancy, aerobic dos and don'ts, muscle strengthening, and flexibility. NYHRC offers baby-sitting at the York Avenue location only.

New York Sports Clubs

Various locations in all boroughs
(800) 796-NYSC to find the club nearest you.
www.nysc.com

The New York Sports Club offers two programs for new mothers, both taught by Maternal Fitness trainers. "Preparing for the Marathon of Labor" is a six-week prenatal class that helps women maintain their fitness during pregnancy. The cost is $325 for members, and $345 for non-members. A six-week postnatal class for new moms and their babies (from age six weeks to four months) focuses on light weights, dynabands, and exercises you can do with your baby. This class is $275 for members, and $295 for non-members. Many of the over 60 NYSC locations offer baby-sitting for a nominal fee. We like New York Sports because it provides more value than some of the more chic athletic clubs.

92nd Street Y

1395 Lexington Avenue at 92nd Street
415-5729
www.92ndsty.org

This is one of the most complete Y's in the city with everything imaginable! The Pregnancy Exercise class is an hour and fifteen minutes, helping moms-to-be ease the discomfort of pregnancy, develop body awareness, and maintain fitness through yoga and dance exercises. An eight-session class is $144 for nonmembers, and $112 for members. Prenatal Aquacise is also available, with a ten-session course costing $150 for nonmembers and $120 for members. Pick up a catalog, you will definitely want to sign up for a Mommy and Me class here as well. Baby-sitting fees are nominal.

Peggy Levine
212 W. 92nd Street bet. Broadway
and Amsterdam Avenue
362-5176
www.peggylevinefitness.com

Peggy Levine is a well-known name in women's fitness and her classes have an excellent reputation. Specialty pre- and postnatal classes (sixty-five to seventy-five minutes each) are $20 per session, or less for a series. Baby-sitting service is available for $2 to $3 per child, per class. Call 24 hours in advance if you require baby-sitting. Peggy also teaches prenatal classes at the Elizabeth Seton Childbearing Center (222 W. 14th Street bet. Seventh and Eighth Avenues).

Plus One Fitness Clinic
301 Park Avenue at 49th Street
355-3000, ext. 4970
One World Financial Center
200 Liberty Street
945-2525

Plus One is a personal training center. No group classes here. Prices are $50 for a half-hour session, and $90 for an hour. Certified exercise specialists are highly trained in pre- and postnatal fitness and offer both one-on-one and cross training. Baby-sitting is not available.

Reebok Sports Club/NY/Sports Club LA
160 Columbus Avenue at 67th Street
362-6800
330 E. 61st Street bet. First
and Second Avenues
355-5100
45 Rockefeller Plaza bet. 50th and
51st Streets, and Fifth and Sixth Avenues
218-8600

Reebok offers low-impact water aerobic classes and personal trainers who specialize in working with women during and after their pregnancies. Julie Tupler of Maternal Fitness, runs a six-week maternity workshop, open to all from 7:15 to 8:45 on Thursday evenings. The cost is $325 for members and $345 for non-members. Register as early as possible. Prenatal yoga is offered for members only on Thursday at 9:00 p.m. Maternal Fitness classes are available at various times throughout the year. Once your baby is six months old, you can leave him in the state-of-the-art Kids Club while you exercise. Mommy, Daddy and Me classes are held Sundays throughout the day. This is probably the largest and most expensive health club in the city; a yearly membership costs over $2,000. Pam, an exercise guru, has worked out and tried everything Reebok has to offer. And if her figure has anything to do with Reebok, they're doing something right!

Diana Simkin

348-0208

For 10 years, Diana was the pre- and post-natal exercise instructor for the Marymount Manhattan Fitness Certification Program, and she is also the author of *The Complete Pregnancy Exercise Program* and *Preparation for Birth*. She is a Certified Personal Trainer with a Master's degree in dance education and a specialty in pre- and postnatal exercise. She offers in-home, one-on-one fitness classes for women. Diane travels to Upper East Side and Upper West Side locations only.

Strollercize, Inc.

(800)Y-STROLL

www.strollercize.com

Created by Lizzy Trindade, Strollercize is a terrific way to meet other new moms, spend time with your baby and have a great workout all at once. This is a fun, interactive fitness program incorporating strollers and babies into the new mother's workout. Pre- and postnatal classes are held in various parks and gyms throughout the city, and personal training programs are also offered. Workouts are safe, tough and effective, and create a great atmosphere for both baby and mom. Strollercize offers 150 classes per month, year round, throughout Manhattan. Discounted memberships are available. Call for locations and times; and check out workshops and weekly new mother gatherings, "Margarita Moms."

Vanderbilt YMCA

224 E. 47th Street bet. Second
and Third Avenues
756-9600
www.ymcanyc.org

The YMCA's Vanderbilt location has a 45-minute prenatal exercise class, which includes a combination of aerobics and stretching and toning exercises. Classes are held twice a week; an eight-week series is free for members and $125 for non-members. A physician's approval is required. Individual membership to the Y is $888 a year with a one-time initiation fee of $125. Family memberships are also available.

YWCA

610 Lexington Avenue at 53rd Street
735-9750
www.ywcanyc.org

The YWCA offers a 40-minute Water Exercise for Pregnancy and Postpartum class twice a week, from 11:40 A.M. to 12:20 P.M. Mondays and Thursdays. The class is a combination of water aerobics and stretching. Price is $90 for a ten-class card, plus $60 for the annual YWCA membership. Individual classes are $10 for members, $15 for nonmembers. A doctor's note may be required.

Private Trainers

Here are four personal trainers who offer pre- and postnatal private training at your home, gym, or office: Jane Kornbluh, 677-6165; Ana Learner, 355-3109; Denise Marguiles, 737-9604; and Debby Peress, 249-3972. Their fees range from $60 to $75 per hour.

YOGA

There has been a huge yoga explosion since our first book. (Madonna's yoga practice throughout her pregnancies surely didn't hurt any.) But yoga is great exercise for pregnant women—aiding relaxation, maintaining flexibility, and providing an excellent way to workout without risking injury.

Many health clubs have yoga classes. If you have taken yoga before your pre-pregnant days and want to continue, do so. Make sure you tell your instructor you are expecting, however, and ask for alternatives that will be safer and more comfortable.

Yoga instructor Gayatri Martin tells us that prenatal yoga emphasizes the strengthening of pelvic floor muscles to get them ready for pregnancy and birth. Prenatal classes usually allow more time than traditional yoga for resting and relaxation. You'll learn breathing and postures that are helpful for birth and labor.

The following yoga instructors or studios specialize in pre- and postnatal yoga classes:

Mary Ryan Barnes
Yoga for Pregnancy
175 W. 93rd Street at Amsterdam Avenue
222-8597

A certified yoga and fitness instructor, personal trainer, and mother of two, Mary teaches Yoga for Pregnancy classes, couples workshops, and postnatal yoga at various facilities, including Maternal Fitness and Peggy Levine's. These classes help women strengthen their bodies and increase flexibility during pregnancy and teach breathing techniques for relaxation. You can also learn how to use yoga to ease labor and delivery. Mary will conduct private yoga sessions in your home for $550 for five sessions.

Beth Donnelly
718-604-0104

An Integral yoga instructor and co-author of *New York's 50 Best Places to Keep Your Spirit Alive*, Beth Donnelly teaches prenatal and postpartum yoga at a variety of locations in Brooklyn and Manhattan: Park Slope Yoga (792 Union Street, 2nd floor, bet. Sixth and Seventh Avenues), Yoga People in Brooklyn Heights, Brooklyn (157 Remsen Street bet. Court and Clinton Streets), and the Elizabeth Seton Childbirthing Center (222 W. 14th Street bet. Seventh and Eighth Avenues). Prenatal classes include movement, postures, chanting, breathing practices, relaxation, visualization, and meditation—all help moms-to-be maintain their balance during a time of intense physical, emotional, and spiritual change. The postpartum class is for moms and babies age six weeks to 16 months, and includes gentle stretches, breathing exercises, and singing; dads, nannies, and grandparents are welcome. Prices range from $12 to $15 per class.

Integral Yoga Institute
227 W. 13th Street bet.
Seventh and Eighth Avenues
929-0586
www.integralyogaofnewyork.org

The Integral Yoga Institute offers a multitude of classes for all levels, including prenatal and postpartum yoga, at various times throughout the week. The prenatal class focuses on movements, postures, and practices especially beneficial to pregnant women. Soothing and relaxation practices are emphasized. Postpartum classes are for moms and newborns ages one month to one year, and include one hour of gentle stretching, chanting, breathing, and a half hour of sharing and discussion. Each class is ninety minutes. A single class is $11; ten classes are $100; and twenty classes are $190.

Iyengar Yoga Institute of New York

27 West 24th Street, Suite 800,
bet. Broadway and Sixth Avenue
691-9642
www.yoga-ny.org

Iyengar Yoga Institute offers a Women's/Gentle Class that focuses on postures for the physical and psychological aspects of women's health, including pre- and postnatal. Prices per class range from $13 to $17.

Jivamukti Yoga Center

404 Lafayette Street, 3rd floor,
bet. Astor and 4th Streets
353-0214
853 Lexington Avenue, 2nd floor,
bet. 64th ad 65th Streets
396-4200
www.jivamuktiyoga.com

The Jivamukti Yoga Center offers two classes for soon-to-be and new moms. Prenatal Yoga meets Mondays through Thursdays from 10 A.M. to 11:30 A.M. Jivamukti focuses on breathing, stretching, and strengthening, as well as adapting yoga postures to the needs of the changing pregnant body. Baby and Me, a postpartum class for moms and dads with babies six weeks to 12 months, meets on Wednesdays from 3 P.M. to 4:30 P.M. This class emphasizes postures, and is designed to realign the inner body and tone the abdominal muscles. Special postures are taught for infants, and the class addresses postpartum issues. Each class costs $17, and is available as a series.

Peggy Levine

214 W. 92nd Street
362-5176 · www.peggylevinefitness.com

Peggy's yoga class is offered three times a week for seventy minutes and costs $20. Discounted series are available. A baby-sitter is provided during some classes for $2 to $3, per class, per child. Call twenty-four hours ahead if you need a sitter.

Gayatri Martin, R.N.

Choices for Childbirth
220 E. 26th St.
725-1078

Gayatri, a registered nurse, has been a Certified Childbirth Educator and yoga teacher since 1988. Her private classes emphasize "discovering your strengths, feeling your flexibility, and experiencing breath as the bridge between body, mind, baby, and heart." Gayatri is available for in-home instruction for a cost of $90 per hour.

Mikelle Terson

37 W. 76th Street bet.
Central Park West and Columbus Avenue

362-4288

Mikelle has been teaching privately for 15 years in conjunction with her work at the Reebok Sports Club and Chelsea Piers. She is available for private yoga instruction at your home for $150 per seventy-five-minute session. She is a wonderful instructor! Pamela's friend, Esther, took her yoga classes religiously through her pregnancy.

Yoga Zone
138 Fifth Avenue bet. 18th and 19th Streets
647-9642
160 E. 56th Street, 12th floor,
bet. Third and Lexington Avenues
935-9642
www.yogazone.com

All the teachers at Yoga Zone have been trained to work with pregnant woman. They offer a special hour-long pre- and postnatal yoga class on Tuesday and Thursday mornings at the 56th Street studio. Senior instructors prepare women for the deep internal work of pregnancy and postpartum life, concentrating on breath and unique physical characteristics. A single class is $20; three classes are $40, and 10 classes are $150.

Baby Om
Sandra Cameron Dance Center
20 Cooper Square bet. 4th Avenue
and East 5th Street
Locations in Upper West East Side,
Upper West Side, Downtown and Brooklyn
615-6935

www.babyom.com

A unique yoga class for moms and their babies. Moms (or dads) bring baby and participate in a yoga class run by Sarah Perron or Laura Staton, the founders of Baby Om. Baby Om is a challenging yoga class designed to stretch and tone the postpartum mom, while providing a playful and stimulating atmosphere for baby. Baby Om also offers prenatal yoga and toddler yoga classes.

MASSAGE

Many pregnant women suffer from back pain and strain, especially during the later months. Why not get a massage?

A massage therapist should be licensed by New York State, certified in prenatal massage, or have experience working with pregnant women.

Communication with your therapist is critical. If you feel lightheaded, short of breath, or uncomfortable, let the practitioner know. Many women feel uncomfortable lying on their backs after the fourth month (Remember, ACOG recommends that you do not lie on your back after this time), so prenatal massages are often given to a woman as she lies on her side with pillows between her legs. The Medical Massage Group has a special table with a cut-out middle so that you can lie on your stomach when you might be uncomfortable on your side.

Every massage therapist listed is licensed by the state of New York. Some specialize in prenatal massage, and many will come to your home for an additional fee. All work is by appointment only, so call ahead.

Carapan*
5 W. 16th Street bet. Fifth and Sixth Avenues
633-6220

Want a vacation right in the heart of the city? Try one of Pamela's favorite places. Carapan is a Zen-like massage center, with some practitioners experienced in prenatal massage. The atmosphere here is sublime. Fees are $95 for 60 to 75 minutes and $130 for 90 minutes.

Laura Favin
324 W. 89th Street bet.
West End Avenue and Riverside Drive
501-0606

Laura has been a licensed massage therapist for over 14 years, and labor support doula specializing in massage during pregnancy. Laura uses the bodyCushion™ system, which allows women to lie on their backs and face down safely and comfortably throughout their pregnancies. She charges $75 for a one-hour-and-fifteen-minute massage, $100 if she travels to your home or office. She also teaches infant massage—a lovely way to bond with your new child.

Sandra Jamrog
866-8257
e-mail: jjjamrog@aol.com

A mother of four, Sandra Jamrog has been teaching pre- and postnatal classes for more than twenty years. She offers parenting education classes and teaches postpartum movement, massage, and relaxation techniques.

The Quiet Touch
Various locations throughout the city
246-0008
www.massageinc.com

The Quiet Touch is a national service that provides licensed, insured, and fully equipped massage therapist at your door within a few hours. They have specialists in all types of massage, including prenatal. Massages are $100 per hour; membership packages are available for a discounted rate, and there is a 10 percent discount for first-time callers.

Skin and Body Contour
1100 Madison Avenue at 83rd Street
737-9604

Skin and Body Contour offers pregnancy massage and reflexology in a beautiful new spa environment. Other services include waxing, acupuncture, and microdermabrasion as well as the latest in endermologie—a technique that is supposed to reduce cellulite, exfoliate dead skin, increase circulation and help you lose inches. We haven't tried endermologie yet, but one of Kelly's friends swears by it!

Elaine Stillerman
108 E. 16th Street, Suite 401,
bet. Union Square East and Irving Place
533-3188

Elaine has been a licensed massage therapist since 1978 and began her pioneering work with expectant women in 1980. She is the author of *Mother Massage: A Handbook for*

Relieving the Discomforts of Pregnancy and *The Encyclopedia of Bodywork*, she also developed the course "Mother Massage®: Massage During Pregnancy," which certifies massage therapists and childbirth educators in prenatal massage. Elaine offers prenatal and postpartum massage therapy (and uses the bodyCushion™ system for moms-to-be). She offers baby massage classes and private labor support classes for partners. Each hour massage is $95.

Lisa Curry
Traditional Thai Massage
360-2319

Curry performs active massage, like assisted yoga, that can be done on one side. Many variations accommodate changes in the pregnant body.

The Medical Massage Group*
108 E. 66th Street, Suite 1A
328 E. 75th Street, Suite 3
472-4772
www.medicalmassagegroup.com

The Medical Massage Group has two new locations. Run by Donna and Harvey Manger-Weil, this practice is 90 percent pre- and postpartum medical massage and staffed with massage therapists who are also licensed physical therapists. The way it works is that your OB/GYN faxes over a prescription for lower back pain and other pregnancy related conditions, and they bill your insurance company directly.

The Stressless Step
115 E. 57th Street, 5th floor,
bet. Lexington and Park Avenues
826-6222
www.stresslessstep.com

This midtown spa has an entire floor in the Galleria building. They offer all types of massage, waxing, and facials in a totally tranquil environment with sauna, steam, and showers. They also offer some of the less expensive massages in town, and you can often get last minute appointments.

NUTRITION

You know that good nutrition is a critical part of producing a healthy baby, and there are many books available addressing this subject. Two of the best are: *What to Expect When You're Expecting*, the pregnant woman's bible which has an excellent section called the "Best Odds Diet," with guidelines on how to eat every day; and *What to Eat When You're Expecting*. Your OB or CNM should talk to you about nutrition, but if he doesn't, bring it up yourself.

If you are underweight, overweight, diabetic, or need extra help managing your diet, consult a nutritionist to set up a diet that meets your needs. Weight Watchers also offers a healthy plan for overweight pregnant women. You might want to keep them in mind for after the pregnancy, too . . . We did.

Eating Right While You're Pregnant
What you should know about nutrition and pregnancy:

Eat regularly and well. This is no time to diet. You will gain weight, and most obstetricians

today say a gain of 25 to 35 lbs. or more is normal. Increase your calorie intake by about 300 calories a day during the last two trimesters, as you will need more energy during this time.

❋ Eat healthy foods. That means ample daily servings of grains (cereal, whole grain bread, crackers), fruits, vegetables (steamed are best), protein (eggs, meat, fish, peanut butter), and calcium (milk, cheese, yogurt, tofu).

❋ Avoid junk food. When you want sugar, reach for fresh fruit, which will also help you avoid the ubiquitous affliction of pregnancy: constipation.

❋ Drink water. Your core body temperature is higher than normal when you are pregnant and you need to take in at least two quarts of liquid a day, especially before, during, and after exercise.

❋ Do not drink alcohol.

❋ Don't drink caffeinated beverages (coffee, tea, colas) during your first trimester, and restrict intake to one cup a day after that. Caffeine reaches the baby through the placenta.

❋ Listen to your body. Those infamous cravings for pickles and peanut butter may have a basis in physiology. Your body may need a little extra salt.

The following nutritionists have worked with pregnant women. Initial consultations cost around $100, with follow-up visits ranging from $35 to $75. You can also call the New York State Dietetic Association for certified dietitian nutritionists (C.D.N.) in your area at 691-7906. Or, send a self-addressed stamped envelope to the American Board of Nutrition (1675 University Boulevard, University of Alabama, Birmingham, Alabama 35294-3361; 205-975-8788). They can provide you with a listing of board-certified nutritionists with M.D.'s or Ph.D.'s in your area.

Erica Ilton, R.D., C.D.N.
529-0654

Joanne Diamond, R.D.
Women's Health Beth Israel
844-8620

Danielle M. Schupp, R.D .
Reebok Sports Club/NY
501-1401, ext. 3744

Danielle practices out of the Reebok Club on the West Side, but you don't have to be a member of the club to see her. She is terrific! Pamela liked her "never say diet" approach to sensible eating.

Bonnie Taub-Dix, M.A., R.D., C.D.N.
Practices in New York City
and Long Island: 737-8536;
516-295-0377

Elisa Zeid, M.S., R.D., C.D.N
575 Lexington Avenue, Suite 400,
bet. 51st and 52nd Streets
527-7557
www.nutritionmadeez.com

Elisa provides personalized nutritional counseling to women before, during and after pregnancy. She works with families to help all members—including infants and children—eat in a healthy and balanced way. Elisa also provides an individual 8-week weight management program to help women shed and keep off their postpartum pounds safely and sensibly.

3 · from health care to day care

Sometime toward the end of your pregnancy, you should begin searching for the people who will help care for your little one. *This* is a toughie. The very idea of entrusting your baby to another person can be terrifying. You'll feel more comfortable with the idea if you take the time to do the necessary research—scout around, ask questions, make phone calls, pay visits.

First, you will need to find a pediatrician. Your goal is to find one you and your husband or partner connect with and who can provide your baby with the best available medical care. But, that is just the beginning. You may wish to hire a baby nurse or doula (see page 47) to help out in your home the first few days or weeks after your baby is born. After that, your child-care needs depend on what else is going on in your life. If you are returning to a job after a maternity leave, you will probably require full-time help, either in your home or elsewhere. If you work at home or are involved in activities that will take you away from your child a period of time each day or week, you will need child-care part-time. Also, if you simply want to get out of the house now and then, *sans* baby, you should have one or two reliable baby-sitters to call upon. If you have family nearby, you may be lucky enough to have occasional free baby-sitting come your way.

We have each changed nannies several times since the first edition was published in 1997. The transitions were difficult both for our kids and ourselves, but we learned a valuable lesson: the most important person in your child's life is you, the parent. Kids eventually adjust to a new nanny or caregiver. That said, get the best nanny you can find, and keep looking until you find that person.

In this chapter, we'll show you how to find reliable child-care. To help get the ball rolling, we'll give you names and numbers and our impressions.

PEDIATRICIANS

You should begin looking for a pediatrician during the last few months of your pregnancy. Your baby's doctor will be noted on the record form that your obstetrician will send to the hospital about a month prior to your due date, and the pediatrician will then come by the hospital to examine your baby before the two of you are released.

Here's how to find one, and what you should look for:

Ask your obstetrician for a recommendation. If your doctor lives in the city, whom does she use for her own children? This is how Pamela found her pediatrician.

❋ **Ask relatives, neighbors, and friends about pediatricians they use.**

❋ **Call any of the hospitals in the city, and ask for a referral from the pediatric department.**

❋ **Go to the New York Public Library and look up listings in the American Academy of Pediatrics Directory. *New York* magazine's yearly edition of "The Best Doctors in New York" is a great resource as well.**

❋ **Consider location. Your newborn will be going to the doctor often, and having a pediatrician with an office near your home is practical, especially during an emergency or nasty weather.**

❋ **Consider whether you place importance on the doctor's age, type of practice (group, partnership, or solo practitioner), or gender (some parents prefer to have a pediatrician the same sex as their baby).**

Once you have the names of two or three pediatricians who sound promising, set up a consultation. Most will agree to make appointments in the early evening after regular office hours. Good doctors should be willing to take the time to meet with you and your husband or partner. Kelly requested consultations with five pediatricians. One did not conduct prenatal interviews; the other four were happy to meet with her and her husband to answer their questions and give them a brief office tour. It was time-consuming, but Kelly has been very happy with her pediatrician, and has never had to change. (If your prospective pediatrician is part of a group practice, it's a good idea to meet with most of the doctors; chances are each one will be treating your child at one time or another.)

Prepare a list of questions in advance and write down the doctors' answers. That way, you can compare pediatricians and discuss everything with your husband/partner who can't be with you at each consultation. And, while you are waiting, take a look around the waiting room.

Is it child friendly, with enough toys, pictures, and books to keep a baby or toddler busy during the wait to see the doctor?

❋ **Is the receptionist friendly, or does she seem curt and harried?**

❋ **If you're visiting during office hours, ask parents in the waiting room about their experiences with the doctor; have they been positive?**

❋ **Find out how long they typically wait to see the doctor. A forty-five minute wait with a sick toddler is no fun.**

✳ **Do sick and healthy children wait in the same waiting room? Kelly's pediatrician has eight examination rooms, and babies under one year old automatically go into one of these. The office tries to keep only healthy children in the waiting area.**

✳ **Is there an on-site lab for quick blood tests, ear-wave sonograms, etc.?**

When you sit down with the doctor, ask: **How does the doctor answer parents' non-emergency calls throughout the day? Is there a call-in hour or does the doctor take calls all day and return them intermittently between patients? Is there a nurse who can answer questions?**

✳ **How are emergencies handled? Is the doctor affiliated with a nearby hospital? Is the practice affiliated with more than one hospital? (A good pediatrician will meet you at the hospital or have a specialist meet you there in case of an emergency.)**

✳ **How does the pediatrician feel about breast-feeding? (Whether or not you choose to breast-feed, you will want a pediatrician who is supportive and encouraging of your decision.)**

✳ **What are the pediatrician's views on circumcision, nutrition, immunizations, and preventive medicine? (It is important that you and your doctor are in sync on most of these issues.)** ****If the pediatrician is a solo practitioner, who handles phone calls when she is on vacation?**

If you don't feel rushed during the consultation, and the pediatrician is patient with you,

these are good indicat
will be with your baby.
ask any questions. Eve
atrician don't be afr
many friends do ju
There are hundreas
York, so just persevere. Like all asp
care, the right one for you is out there.

BABY NURSES/DOULAS

Immediately after the birth of your baby, you may wish to have a baby nurse or doula.

Baby nurses usually come the day you bring the baby home and live with you in your apartment for a week or two or longer. An in-home nurse works twenty-four hours a day, seven days a week. She cares for the baby, gets up in the middle of the night to change and feed him or bring him to you for breast-feeding, and generally allows you to sleep late and rest up. Baby nurses are expensive, costing from $125 to $180 a day. Some live-out and work for shorter periods, (not a full day).

A doula comes to your home for a few hours each day and almost always lives out. She helps and pampers you: she does the grocery shopping, laundry, and fixes meals, so you have more time with your baby. She may also assist you in taking care of your baby by bathing or changing him, and she should be able to answer questions regarding breastfeeding.

When you hire a doula, typically you buy a set block of visits or hours with a fifteen-hour minimum. Each visit is at least three hours, and costs approximately $21 to $30 an hour.

he best way to find a baby nurse or doula hrough a trusted friend who has used one herself. Or call one of the many agencies that has baby nurse divisions. Kelly hired her nurse, Olga, through an agency and was extremely pleased. Olga had been taking care of babies for more than twenty years, and her references were impeccable. So good, in fact, that one family kept her for five years! Pamela hired a baby nurse that she found through a friend, and she is so great, she continues to works for the family one day per week.

An agency will send three or four candidates for you to interview while you are pregnant. You may then reserve the baby nurse or doula of your choice, and the agency will try not to place her for two weeks around your due date. If you are late or early, the nurse you've requested may be on another job, but this rarely happens. Agencies are very good at monitoring their baby nurses' schedules.

Baby nurses get booked way in advance, so plan early. Kelly started asking friends for recommendations when she was five months pregnant, and three of the names she received were already booked.

Of course, your mother or mother-in-law may offer to come stay with you. If you feel comfortable with a family member living in and helping out, great. However, we've found that many new parents prefer to hire short-term professional help which allows them to get the rest they need without having to impose on—or be nice to—a relative.

The following is a list of baby nurse and doula agencies in the New York area. We have had personal experiences with Avalon and In a Family Way. The owners are caring, responsible, and trustworthy.

Avalon Registry*
162 W. 56th Street, Suite 507
245-0250

Beyond Birth (Doulas)
1992 Commerce Street, Suite 40
Yorktown Heights, NY 10598
914-245-2229
(888) 907-BABY

Bohne's Baby Nursing
16 E. 79th Street, Suite G-4
879-7920

Doula Care
Ruth Callahan
70 W. 93rd Street
749-6613
www.webspan.net/~callahan
e-mail: callahan@webspan.net

Foley Nursing Agency
790 Madison Avenue, Suite 501
794-9666

Fox Agency
30 E. 60th Street
753-2686

In a Family Way
124 W. 79th Street, Suite 9-B
877-8112
www.inafamilyway.com

Mother Nurture
Doula Service
P.O. Box 284
Glen Oaks, NY 11004
718-631-BABY (718-631-2229)
www.mothernurture.com
e-mail: doulacomp@aol.com

All Metro Health Care
50 Broadway
Lynbrook, NY 11563
516-887-1200

NANNIES

Hiring someone to look after your child while you're at work or away is stressful and nerve-racking. You want someone who is good, kind, smart, honest, sober, reliable, loves kids, knows infant CPR, bakes cookies, and is going to think your baby is the most adorable child she's ever seen. You want another you.

Of course, you won't find another you, but if you're determined and keep your ears open, you will locate someone who will be an affectionate, caring, responsible child care provider for your youngster. Kelly conducted her own nanny search during the writing of this second edition, so we have up-to-date information to share.

You may want a nanny who lives with you or one who comes to your home each morning and leaves each evening. You may need this person's help on a part-time or full-time basis. There are several ways to go about finding her. As is true for so many services, *word of mouth is the best place to start.* Ask friends who have

Top Ten Things to Look For in a Caregiver

1. Track record and references (strong ones!) How long does she stay in a job?
2. The ability to speak and read English or your native language.
3. Personality—it's hard to be around someone who never smiles.
4. Experience—especially with children the same age as your own/same position as your own.
5. Honesty—this is fundamental to any relationship between employer and employee, and particularly in regard to someone hired to watch your children.
6. Patience.
7. Positive attitude.
8. Nice appearance.
9. Reliability and responsibility.
10. Instinct—trust your gut.

childcare whether their nannies have friends looking for work. When we were in search of help, we stopped nannies in the park, talked to mothers and nannies at the classes we took with our children, and looked at bulletin board notices in child- and religious-oriented institutions and at our pediatricians' offices. Many schools as well as the Parent's League also post nanny information on their bulletin boards.

If you get nowhere by word of mouth, try the newspapers. Many parents have successfully found child-care by advertising in newspapers or by answering an ad. We'll show you how to do that shortly. Finally, a number of agencies specialize in nanny placement. We list those agencies below.

We cannot sufficiently stress the importance of checking references and thoroughly questioning candidates. On more than one occasion, we have heard stories of falsified references in which nannies listed friends or relatives instead of former employers. Toward the end of this section, we'll give you a list of some of the most important questions to ask your future nanny. You may also want to read *How to Hire A Nanny* by Elaine S. Pelletier. This step-by-step guide helps you through the nanny search. Full-time (five days a week), live-out nannies with little experience usually start at around $350 a week. For an experienced, educated caregiver you can pay as much as $600 or $700. Live-in nannies, for which you provide room and board, start at $350 to $450-again, this is usually a non-American nanny with little work experience. Prices vary according to experience, education, checkable references, and legal status. Another excellent resource, written by two experienced British moms is *The Good Nanny Guide* by Charlotte Breese and Hilaire Gomer. Although geared to the English nanny system, it is full of practical advice and guidelines.

Newspaper Advertisements

Placing a classified ad can be an excellent way to find a nanny. The *Irish Echo*, the *Irish Voice*, and *The New York Times* are popular nanny-finding papers. A number of newspapers are published for various nationalities and many nannies look in them for jobs. Explore them if you would prefer a nanny from a specific country, would like your child to learn a foreign language, or if your spouse is from another country.

When you place an ad, be as specific as possible. If you must have a nonsmoker, live-in help, or someone with a driver's license, say so. If you need someone to work on Saturdays or stay late in the evening, state it. Check the classified sections to see examples of help-wanted ads, or follow our example:

Upper East Side Nanny Needed.
Live-in nanny needed for a two-year-old boy. Light housekeeping, shopping, and errands. Must have two years experience with toddlers and excellent checkable New York references. Nonsmoker. Must swim, drive, and cook. Must have legal working papers. Willing to travel with family. M-F, weekends off. Own room, TV-VCR, A/C. Call 555-5555.

When Kelly ran an ad similar to this one in two newspapers three weeks before Christmas, her phone began ringing at 6 A.M. the Wednesday morning the *Irish Echo* came out and she had received sixty calls by 11 A.M.

Interview candidates on the phone before you bring them to your home. Tell them about the job, find out what they are looking for, and ask about their past work experience. Screen them carefully; it will save you time later. Kelly needed a caregiver who could work on Saturdays and travel with the family, and she was able to eliminate a number of candidates who could not fill those requirements over the phone.

We recommend making a list of the three most appealing and the three least appealing aspects of your job. Discuss them with the applicant over the phone. Start with the three worst aspects: she must arrive at 7:30 every morning, she must baby-sit three nights a week, and she will be expected to work on Saturdays. If the applicant is still interested and if you are pleased with her responses to your key questions, proceed from there with an interview in your home or office.

The following four newspapers are reliable and frequently used. When you call, check their deadlines. Ads can be phoned or faxed, and can be paid with a credit card.

Irish Echo
309 Fifth Avenue
New York, NY 10016
686-1266

The *Irish Echo* comes out once a week on Wednesdays. Ads must be submitted before 2 p.m. the Friday before the ad is to run. Three lines cost $27 and each additional line is $9.

Irish Voice
432 Park Avenue South, Suite 1503
New York, NY 10016
684-3366

The *Irish Voice* comes out Wednesdays and accepts ads up to the previous Monday. Thirty words cost approximately $58.

The New York Times
229 W. 43rd Street
New York, NY 10036
354-3900
www.nytimes.com

An ad placed in the classified section of *The New York Times* can run in the Sunday edition only or in the Sunday edition plus two weekdays. Four lines on Sunday cost $149 plus $37.25 for each additional line; Sunday and two weekdays (Wednesday and another day of choice) cost $63 per line; one weekday costs $33.25 per line; and a weeklong ad costs $112.50 per line. Add an additional $10 if you wand the ad posted on the Internet.

The Polish Daily News
Nowy Dziennik
333 W. 38th Street
New York, NY 10018
594-2266, ext. 31

This daily paper (except Sundays) is written in Polish, but many of the classifieds are in English. Ads must be submitted by noon to run in the next day's paper. A thirty-five word ad running for one week costs $50; for Monday through Wednesday, $30; on Thursday, $12; on Friday, $13; and on Saturday, $18. For an additional $5, your ad is translated into Polish.

Agencies

On one hand, good word-of-mouth and a sterling reputation keeps a service business alive. On the other hand, the more people they place, the more money agencies make; high turnover is oddly beneficial to their business. This is contrary to what you are looking for-someone who will stay with you a long time. So, a few words of caution when using an agency. Although agencies claim they check references, many have been known to send a candidate on an interview with skimpy or weak references. Some have never even met the candidate face to face. Be on guard if, for example, a nanny's previous employer has moved and now has an unlisted phone number somewhere in Florida, or if the applicant hands you a hand-written letter of reference with grammatically incorrect sentences and misspelled words.

Although we can't personally endorse any of the agencies listed below, we know people who have found good help through them. We suggest you read the Department of Consumer Affairs' forty-two-page report on placement agencies entitled "Who's Watching Our Kids?" You can write to the Department of Consumer Affairs, 42 Broadway, New York, NY 10004, and request a copy. The report lists fifty agencies investigated by the department and any violations filed against them. You can also call their office, at 487-4444, to check whether a particular agency is licensed and whether it has received any complaints, or to file a complaint yourself.

A Choice Nanny
130 W. 57th Street
New York, NY 10019
246-KIDS (246-5437)

Best Domestic Services Agency
2 W. 45th Street, Suite 1000
New York, NY 10036
685-0351

The Fox Agency
30 E. 60th Street
New York, NY 10022
753-2686

Frances Stuart Agency
1220 Lexington Avenue
New York, NY 10028
439-9222

Domestically Yours
535 Fifth Avenue
New York, NY 10017
986-1900

The London Agency
767 Lexington Avenue
New York, NY 10021
755-5064

My Child's Best Friend Nanny Services
44 E. 32nd Street, 11th floor
New York, NY 10016
206-9910
www.nynannyservice.com

Nannies Plus
520 Speedwell Avenue, Suite 114
Morris Plains, NJ 07950

(800) 752-0078
www.nanniesplus.com

NY Nanny Center
31 Bayles Avenue
South Port Washington, NY 11050
516-767-5136

Pavilion Agency
15 E. 40th, Suite 400
New York, NY 10016
889-6609

Professional Nannies Institute
501 Fifth Avenue
New York, NY 10017
692-9510

Robin Kellner Agency
2 W. 45th Street
New York, NY 10036
997-4151

Town and Country
250 W. 57th Street
New York, NY 10019
245-8400

The Interview

Nothing is as important as the interview to determine whether a candidate is the right person to take care of your little one. Be conscious of the atmosphere you create. Are you interviewing potential nannies at your office, in your formal living room, in the playroom, family room, or at the kitchen table? Are you looking for someone to join the family, or will this person be more of an employee with a formal working arrangement?

Pamela always likes to interview nannies with her husband present. It's useful to get a second opinion, and to have another person asking questions you might forget to ask. It's also good to have your child nearby so you can see how the potential candidate interacts with him.

Here's our suggested list of interview questions:

* **Tell me about yourself. Where are you from? Where did you grow up? How many brothers and sisters do you have? Did your mom and dad work?**
* **Why do you want to be a nanny? What is it you like about being a nanny?**
* **What previous child-care experiences do you have? Tell me about those jobs.**
* **What was a typical day like? What did your duties/responsibilities include? (Look for someone who has held a child-care position similar to the one you are offering. If she cooked and cleaned on the last job and you are looking for light cooking and cleaning, she probably won't be upset if you ask her to grill a chicken breast or wipe off the kitchen counter.)**
* **How many children did you take care of in your previous positions? How old were they?**
* **Do you have children of your own?**
* **What did you like best about your previous jobs? What did you like least?**
* **Why did you leave your last job(s)?**
* **Did Mrs. X work? How did you two interact on a daily basis?**
* **Do you smoke?**

✳ Do you have CPR or first-aid training?

✳ Can you stay late during the week or work on weekends if necessary?

✳ Describe an emergency or stressful situation in your past job? How did you handle it?

✳ What are your child-rearing philosophies or views on discipline? Do you believe in spanking and time-outs?

✳ What are your interests? What do you like to do when you're not working?

✳ Do you have any health restrictions or dietary preferences I should know about?

✳ What are you looking for in a family?

✳ Would you travel with the family if needed?

✳ Do you know your way around the city?

✳ Do you drive, swim, bicycle, (or whatever else is important to you)?

✳ Do you like to read? What is your favorite children's book? (Some nannies can't read well in English.)

✳ When could you start? What are your salary requirements?

Checking References

Checking references with previous employers can be one of the most challenging parts of finding child-care. Who are you calling? How can you be sure the name you have been given is not a candidate's friend or relative? And then, some people just aren't very talkative on the telephone. They reveal very little that can help you reach a decision.

Use your common sense and intuition; be open and friendly; and identify yourself in detail. For example: "Hello Mrs. X, this is Mrs. Y, and I am calling to check a reference on Susan Jones, who told me she worked for you. My husband and I live in New York City on E. 53rd Street and we have a three-year-old daughter." Tell her a little about your family. This will help break the ice and allow you to ask about her family and work situations. It's important to know the kind of household in which your potential nanny has worked, because it may be very different from your own. If Mrs. X had a staff of three, and Susan had no household duties, she may not be happy in your home if you ask her to cook, clean, and do the laundry. Be realistic.

Here are some questions you may want to ask:

How did you meet Susan? (agency, friend, ad?)

✳ How long was Susan with you?

✳ Why did she leave?

✳ How many children do you have? How old are they?

✳ Do you work? What do you do? Were either you or your husband home during the day or was Susan pretty much on her own?

✳ What were Susan's responsibilities?

✳ What were her hours?

✳ Was there ever an emergency or difficult situation that Susan had to handle on her own?

✳ How would you describe her overall personality and attitude?

✳ Was it easy to communicate with her? Did she give you daily feedback on your children? Did she take direction/instruction well?

✳ Did she cook, clean, drive, run errands, swim, iron (or whatever you need most)?

✳ **Did you trust her? Did you find her reliable and honest?**

✳ **How did your children like her? Did you like her?**

✳ **Would you hire her again?**

Several agencies verify references on nannies. Documented Reference Check (800-742-3316, www.badreferences.com) investigates employment references and sends a report to you for $87.95. American International Security (703-691-1110) charges $95, for which you obtain a motor vehicle record, a New York City criminal convictions record, and a social security number track report. A credit check is an additional $35, and other services are available.

When the Nanny Starts

After you have found the right person, it is important to watch how she and your baby and/or children interact in order to make sure they are comfortable with each other. It's a good idea to have prepared a typewritten list of duties as well as what is expected of the nanny on a daily basis aside from child-care, such as cooking, cleaning, laundry and grocery shopping. Be specific. Sit down and go over everything again within the first few days to make sure she understands and accepts the responsibilities of the job. Set a date for a follow-up meeting in two weeks to discuss how things are going, what's working well, and what it not.

We are big on giving the nanny a "trial" period. We try her out for a week or so and see if it's a match hiring her full time. If you are going back to work, it is a good idea to have your new nanny begin at least two weeks before you start. This will give you an opportunity to observe her with your baby and to show her around your neighborhood. Take her to your supermarket, dry cleaner's (or to whatever other places she may need to visit while working for your family), as well as to the pediatrician's office so that she can feel comfortable going there without you if necessary.

You may also want your nanny to have a physical examination. Certainly, inquire about her health and vaccinations. Depending on where your nanny is from and how long she has been in this country, she may not be vaccinated against measles, mumps and rubella, or chicken pox. If she's not, arrange with your doctor for her to get these shots.

Once a nanny is on the job, you may want to monitor her activities in your absence. Parents who have had to hire a caregiver very quickly and have little time to train and supervise may find that this service provides peace of mind.

Care Check, created by Lori Berke and Gail Cohen, offers videotaping as a learning tool for better communication between you and your caregiver. Care Check has state of the art equipment and will rent or sell any customized surveillance system you need. A two-day video surveillance rental costs $229. Care Check can also help you with the prescreening process, including interview techniques and questions, and they will (for $200) conduct a check on your applicant, confirming previous employment, education, passport, and other records. International credit checks may cost more. Care Check can be reached at 360-6640; 1056 Fifth Avenue, New York, NY 10028.

Babywatch is a nationwide service that has been in business for eight years. The New York provider is Lori Schechter. With a wide variety of equipment available, Babywatch will install a monitoring device in your home to evaluate your nanny's performance. The cost is approximately $300 for a three-day rental, or you can purchase the equipment. She helps you find, hire, and train a nanny, and also sells a comprehensive guide to hiring nannies. You can reach Babywatch at 889-1494 or e-mail lorishecter@yahoo.com.

Finally, you may want to consider sending your new nanny to a one-day, six-hour training program called NannyWise (534-5623). Offered one Saturday per month, the course covers topics like the first year, how to handle tantrums, ways to promote emotional development, and guidelines for positive discipline. The price is $150. Owner Amy Hatkoff has been helping to train new nannies for years — making nannies better is her business.

The following is a list of additional companies that provide video surveillance and other nanny-related services.

Baby Safe
444 E. 86th Street
396-1995

Care Check
1056 Fifth Avenue
360-6640

Caring People, Inc.
718-591-0557

Kid-View, Inc.
299 East Shore Road, Suite 206
Great Neck, NY 11023
516-498-9300

Mind Your Business
P.O. Box 1390
Maplewood, NJ 07040
888-869-2462

Nanny Vision
677-2776

Taxes and Insurance

Remember that once you hire a nanny, you have become an employer. In a 1995 *New York* magazine article, C.P.A. Stuart Rosenblum, provided a list of responsibilities as an employer. You must:

1. **Apply for an employer identification number with the IRS using form SS-4.**
2. **File Schedule H (a tax form that replaced Form 942). Employers should report wages paid to household workers or nannies on their income tax returns. Schedule H, which is filed with your 1040, simplifies the work of calculating social security, Medicare, and federal income taxes.**
3. **Give your nanny a W-2 form, listing total wages and taxes paid, by January 31.**
4. **File a W-3, a summary of all your W-2s, by**

February 28. File quarterly and annual state reports.

Other forms to fill out include federal unemployment and state unemployment tax forms. These cover anyone who earns more than $100 a quarter. The federal unemployment tax form 940 can be obtained from the IRS; the New York State Labor Department supplies state unemployment forms.

Other areas of concern are compensation and disability policies. If you employ a childcare provider for more than forty hours a week, you should buy a workers' compensation and disability policy. These start at around $300. Call the State Insurance Fund for more information (312-9000). The IRS publishes two booklets to help employers through this maze: "Employment Taxes for Household Employers" (Book 926) and "What You Need to Know If You Hire Domestic Help" (Book 27). To receive these booklets, call the IRS at (800) 462-8100. Call the New York State Department of Labor (265-2700) to request the "Employer's Guide to Unemployment Insurance."

AU PAIRS

Hiring an au pair is a child-care option many parents find practical and economical.

Au pairs come to the United States from various countries, but they are usually European. They can remain in this country legally for one year and work a forty-five-hour week. Generally, an au pair has a weeklong orientation just after she arrives in this country, and takes one academic course during her stay. In addition, she is provided with support counselors and a health plan by her umbrella organization.

An au pair lives with you and is paid between $115 and $200 a week. Always interview a prospective au pair over the phone or in person if possible. Most agencies provide background information on several candidates.

Au pairs tend to be inexperienced childcare providers. They most often work in homes with stay-at-home mothers. They are not allowed to remain alone with children overnight, so an au pair is not a good option for parents who travel. Pamela's friend Margot has employed close to half a dozen au pairs in seven years. She was extremely satisfied with one out of six; the rest were mediocre to decent, but none fabulous. One drawback with au pairs is that they are young, and many of them want an active social life. In New York, that is not always compatible with child-care.

If you are interested in an au pair, contact the following agencies:

Au Pair America
102 Greenwich Avenue
Greenwich, CT 06830
(800) 9AU-PAIR (800-928-7247)

Au Pair USA/Interexchange
161 Sixth Avenue, 13th floor
New York, NY 10013
(800) AU-PAIRS (800-287-2477)

Au Pair Childcrest
6965 Union Park Center, Suite 100
Salt Lake City, UT 84047
(800) 574-8889

DAY CARE CENTERS

New York City has more than 2,500 day care centers where you can bring your child each morning and pick him up by 6 p.m. Centers must meet rigid requirements in order to be licensed by the State of New York.

One of the best professionally run day care centers we know is the Bright Horizons Center at 435 E. 70th Street (746-6543). This nationwide chain has an excellent reputation as a leader in upholding stringent day care standards. In addition, there are approximately 5,300 in-home care centers or family day care providers in the city. In family day care, an individual takes care of a few children (by law, no more than twelve) in her home. The provider must be licensed by New York State and must register with the Department of Health. Even so, be cautious. Pay a personal visit to the center, speak with other parents, and trust your instincts.

Investigate options offered by your employer. More and more companies are offering on-site day care, or are willing to contribute to day care costs.

For more information contact:

The Department of Health: This city agency regulates day care centers and will tell you whether a specific center is licensed. Call 442-9666, and ask for the childcare bureau.

✳ **The Daycare Council of New York: The Council will refer you to 25 centers free of charge. Centers are listed by zip code, and you can request referrals in three zip codes. The Daycare Council of New York is located at 10 E. 34th Street, New York, NY 10016. Their phone number is 213-2423. You probably want to look at centers that are in your home and office zip codes to compare and contrast.**

✳ **Child Care Inc.: Located at 275 Seventh Avenue, New York, NY 10001, 929-4999, this nonprofit organization serves as an information and referral resource for New York parents. Their excellent guides include "Choosing Child Care for Your Infant or Toddler," "Choosing an Early Childhood Program," and "In-Home Care." Other handouts cover finding and working with in-home care or nanny agencies, and they have samples of contracts for household employment. Child Care will also prepare lists of day care centers and in-home care providers by zip code.**

BABY-SITTING

You may be a stay-at-home mom who requires only a little childcare on a Saturday night or a few afternoons a week. The solution here is a baby-sitter. Ask your doorman, superintendent, or neighbor whether there are teenagers in the building available for baby-sitting, or check out colleges that have baby-sitting services or a baby-sitting agency. Each service works differently; often there is an initial registration fee between $15 and $45. Many require a two-hour minimum and have varying rates, starting at $6 an hour. Look for a sitter who has experience with children the same age as your child, and check references. Don't assume that just because someone is enrolled in a local college she is trustworthy.

Finally, tell everyone you know that you're looking for a sitter. Ask other baby-sitters or nannies for recommendations; check bulletin boards at your pediatrician's office and play spaces. Pamela has used Barnard Baby-Sitting Service and always finds the students reliable and competent.

You may want to consider having a sitter come for an afternoon when you are at home to watch how she interacts and plays with your child. It is better for your child to have regular sitters whom she knows and you trust.

The following is a list of baby-sitting services:

Avalon
245-0250

**Barnard Baby-Sitting Service/
Barnard College**
854-2035

Pinch Sitters
260-6005

Baby-Sitting Guild
682-0227

Beth Israel School of Nursing
614-6110
(Will post jobs on bulletin board for students.)

My Child's Best Friend Nanny Services (206-9910) has a temporary/on-call referral service called Instant Sitter. They can provide you with an instant sitter for your home, whether you need help for one evening or a week.

4 · adjusting to new motherhood

After you bring your newborn home, your bulging belly won't be the only thing missing—all semblance of control over your life will have vanished too . . . but that's OK.

The first few weeks at home are going to be turbulent. Many new mothers feel a bit blue or depressed. Having a baby is an emotionally draining experience, and to complicate things, those hormones really kick in after the birth. You may feel tired all day. Life will seem to be reduced to baby feedings, diaper changing, and laundry, laundry, laundry. The state of your apartment will deteriorate right before your very eyes.

Our advice? Let the place get messy. Use the time between feedings, changes, and naps to take care of yourself, rest and think about what an adorable child you have. Allow willing friends and grandparents to throw in a load of laundry for you or pick up your dry cleaning.

If you actually cook, forget about it now. Order in. New York is take-out heaven, and there is wonderful prepared food all around you. Come to think of it, order all your necessities! Most pharmacies will take phone orders and deliver. The big drugstore chains, such as Duane Reade and Rite Aid, all deliver formula by the case, disposable diapers and baby wipes by the package. Or get online and order formula and diapers from one of the sites listed in the Web directory. Have your food and supplies delivered from your local supermarket. Make it easy on yourself.

This book suggests dozens of places to meet new mothers and learn from the experts. We can't say enough about forming or joining a playgroup, or a group of moms with babies who are the same age as your own. Playgroups usually meet once a week in rotating homes. If you don't

Top Ten Things to Keep You Sane with a Newborn

1. Stock the freezer before the baby is born—lasagna, soup, etc.
2. Get help—a friend, mother, sister, or baby-sitter, if possible. Remember: any relief is better than no relief at all.
3. Sleep when the baby sleeps.
4. Order take-out food the first few weeks; it's too tiring to cook.
5. Buy in bulk and have it delivered—a case of formula, a box of diapers, and several packages of baby wipes will make life much easier.
6. Open up charge accounts at stores in the neighborhood that will deliver.
7. Let the house get messy.
8. Make friends with other new moms, and call them.
9. Try to go outside every day.
10. Attend a New Mother's Luncheon or class.

have friends with babies your age, don't worry, you'll meet some. Take a Strollercize class, attend a New Mother's Luncheon, sign up for a hospital class—before you know it, you will have friends all over town.

Joining a playgroup was a lifesaver for Pamela, whose children were both born in the winter. The women she met in Rebecca's group seven years ago are some of her best friends to this day. A playgroup should have four to six moms and babies and meet at a specific time each week. You can serve lunch, or just cold drinks, and let the babies do their thing while the moms discuss everything from breastfeeding to sleep deprivation and more. These get-togethers become vital to a new mother's sanity, and will become one of the highlights of your week.

NEW MOTHER CLASSES

Once your baby is a few weeks old and you have settled into something of a routine, you'll enjoy swapping baby stories with other mothers and sharing advice on how to care best for your infant.

A number of hospitals offer classes you can attend with your baby. They provide an opportunity to hear from pediatricians, child psychologists, child-safety experts, and other skilled professionals. Plus, you'll be able to ask questions and meet other new parents.

When Alexander was six weeks old, Kelly attended the five-week New Mother Discussion Group at New York Hospital. This class, led by Jean Schoppel, R.N. and Ronni Soled, became the highlight of her week. Pamela took the New Mother/New Baby class, for mothers with children newborn to twelve months, offered by the 92nd Street Y, and loved it.

Hospital Classes

The hospitals listed below offer new mother classes. Fees vary from hospital to hospital and change frequently; most range from $10 to $65 for one-time classes or workshops, and $100 to $200 for a series of classes or new mother support group meetings. Most hospital classes and support groups are open to all women, not just those who delivered at that hospital. So, if you want to take a class at New York Hospital but deliver at Beth Israel, just call New York Hospital to sign up. New moms are encouraged to bring their babies to all classes.

Beth Israel Hospital

16th Street at First Avenue
420-2000 (General)
420-2999 (Classes)

Beth Israel offers a variety of classes for the new mother, including a CPR course, a class in child safety, a breastfeeding class, and a New Mother's Support Group.

Columbia Presbyterian Hospital

Babies Hospital/Sloane Hospital for Women
Broadway at 166th Street
305-2500 (General)
305-2040 (Parent Education Program)

Columbia Presbyterian offers classes in breastfeeding, baby care, and parenting.

The Mount Sinai Medical Center

One Gustave L. Levy Place
Klingenstein Pavilion
Fifth Avenue at 98th Street
241-6500 (General)
241-7491 (Women & Children's Office)
241-6578 (Breastfeeding Warm Line)

Mount Sinai offers classes in caring for newborns, CPR, and breastfeeding, and has a New Mother's Support Group that meets once a week.

New York Hospital/
Cornell Medical Center

525 E. 68th Street
746-5454 (General)
746-3215 (Preparation for Parenthood Office)

New York Hospital offers "Adapting to Parenthood," which can be taken before or after a baby is born, a baby care class, and a New Mother's Discussion Group that meets once a week. The Preparation for Parenthood staff maintains a telephone information line for new mothers.

New York University Medical Center

560 First Avenue at 32nd Street
263-7200 (General)
263-7201 (Classes)

New York University Medical Center offers a breastfeeding support group for new mothers that meets once a week.

Roosevelt Hospital

1000 Tenth Avenue at 59th Street
523-4000 (General)
523-6222 (Parent/Family Education)

Roosevelt Hospital offers classes in baby care, infant CPR, child CPR, breastfeeding, and has a New Mother's Support Group.

St. Luke's Hospital
1111 Amsterdam Avenue at 114th Street
same phone numbers as Roosevelt Hospital

All classes are given at Roosevelt Hospital.

St. Vincent's Hospital and Medical Center
153 W. 11th Street
604-7000 (General)
604-7946 (Maternity Education)

St. Vincent's offers classes in newborn care and breastfeeding and has a Breast-feeding Support Group.

Other Classes, Groups, and Seminars

There are excellent non-hospital based support and discussion groups throughout the city. Many of them, like the hospital classes, teach infant CPR, which every new parent should learn. Some of the classes listed are fun to take with your child.

Schedules and fees are always subject to change. Call for the most up-to-date information.

BabyWise
Amy Hatkoff
534-5623

The BabyWise seminar is designed to give expectant and new parents access to the leading research on infant development. Topics include: what infants know, the importance of early bonding, how to promote a secure attachment, the dangers of stress for infants, and adapting to new parenthood. Director Amy Hatkoff has worked with children and families for years.

Save-A-Tot
317 E. 34th Street
725-7477

Save-A-Tot offers private or group infant/child CPR at your home or in midtown Manhattan. The cost is $60 per person and $100 per couple. Private childbirth education classes are also available.

Tot-Saver
5 E. 98th Street
241-8195

Conducted at Mount Sinai Hospital, these classes teach CPR techniques for infants and children as well as safety and injury prevention. The fee is $60 per person or $100 per couple for this two-session course.

The Fourth Trimester
Dr. Donna Steinberg
182 E. 79th Street
348-6308

The Fourth Trimester is a small mother's support group that meets to discuss the range of issues facing new mothers, including returning to work, postpartum blues, and infant development. There are day and evening groups available to accommodate any new mom's schedule. The cost is $25 per group meeting.

Ann Profitt, M.A
Battery Park City
938-0139

Ann Profitt holds private individual and/or couples seminars for new and expectant parents. Discussion topics include the practicalities of parenting, changes in marital relationships, and work issues. Seminars are $100 per person and $125 per couple.

The Parent Child Center
247 E. 82nd Street
879-6900

The Parent Child Center, affiliated with the New York Psychoanalytical Society, offers weekly learning-while-playing groups to parents and children (from birth to three years). These groups are limited to seven or eight families in order to provide an intimate and cohesive environment. This side-by-side program costs about $650 for 18 classes (from either September through February or February through June).

Parenting Horizons*
Julie Ross
765-2377
Central Presbyterian Church
593 Park Avenue at 64th Street
765-2377

Julie Ross teaches "Practical Parenting," which covers how to handle tantrums, and how to help children sleep at night, learn to brush their teeth, get dressed for school, and perform other daily tasks. Julie works to build parental confidence and gives practical examples of what to do when a particular situation arises. Kelly and Pam have both had wonderful experiences with Julie Ross. She is an excellent resource. Classes meet weekly for eight weeks, three semesters per year. Fees are $350 per person and $625 per couple. This is an excellent class for parents of toddlers. Private instruction is also available.

The SoHo Parenting Center
568 Broadway, Suite 205
334-3744
www.sohoparenting.com

The Parenting Center, a respected downtown resource for new moms, organizes various mother/infant support groups during the day and in the evenings. The center offers a second-time mother's group and both private and group parent counseling sessions. It also offers mother/toddler programs, sleep counseling, and pre- and post-natal yoga. The directors of the center—Jean Kunhardt and Lisa Speigel—along with Sandra K. Basile, have written *The Mother's Circle*, about the first year of motherhood.

Elizabeth Bing Center for Parents
164 W. 79th Street
362-5304

The Elizabeth Bing Center conducts several classes for new moms and dads, including seminars on parenting, baby safety, and breastfeeding. Elizabeth is a much loved teacher who has been doing this for over 30 years. Each seminar is approximately one and one-half hours and costs approximately $75 (varies by seminar). The center also offers a Lamaze refresher class for second-time parents for $250.

The Early Childhood Development Center
163 E. 97th Street
360-7803

The center conducts one-hour weekly meetings to discuss sleeping, feeding, crying, and other early child-raising issues. Twenty sessions cost $400.

Educational Alliance Parenting and Family Center at the Sol Goldman YM-YWHA*
344 E. 14th Street bet. First and
Second Avenues
780-0800, ext. 239

The Educational Alliance, a nonprofit organization, is a great city resource with a variety of wonderful workshops for parents and classes for children of all ages. For new moms, the Alliance offers New Parents Stroll In, an open discussion led by the director of the Parenting and Family Center, Kiki Schaffer. The group meets on Tuesdays (newborn to six months), and Wednesdays (six months to one year). Each session is $12 for nonmembers, $10 for members. (Ms. Schaffer, a CSW, is available for private counseling sessions as well. She can be reached at 529-9247.) The Alliance also offers a workshop entitled Preparing Your Marriage for Parenthood, counseling groups for mothers suffering from postpartum depression and mothers returning to work; classes in infant massage, postnatal exercise with baby; and Postpartum Poetics—in which new moms and the writer-in-residence work together to "write the motherhood experience." Kiki Schaffer is a consummate profes-

sional, and we only wish we lived closer to the Sol Goldman Y.

Fatherhood Forum
724-2652

Charles A. Bonerbo, CSW, and Lee Welch, CSW, offer father support groups and workshops as well as monthly lectures and group discussions at an Upper West Side location.

The Jewish Community Center on the Upper West Side
15 W. 65th Street, 8th floor, bet.
Columbus Avenue and Central Park West
580-0299

The JCC offers a wide range of classes for new parents, including New Moms, New Babies, Infant/Child First Aid/CPR, Baby Teeth Basics, Postpartum Depression, and Massage for Babies: Connecting to Your Child. The JCC is a valuable local resource for parents. Their new 120,000 square foot home at 76th Street and Amsterdam, will offer even more for young families.

Mother-Baby Discussion and Play Groups
Parent-Infant Program of Columbia University
560-2444

These groups meet once a week to help new mothers learn more about early childhood and interact with child development, parenting specialists and other new parents. Private consultations are also available in several Manhattan locations. Meetings are held at the Elizabeth Bing Center for Parents at 164 W. 79th Street bet. Columbus and Amsterdam.

Mothers & More

614-0163

www.mothersandmore.com

This mother's group meets twice a month and features guest speakers or topics for discussion. They also have a book club, a mom's movie club, mom's night out, and play groups. Meetings are on the Upper East side, and events take place throughout the city. Call to get on the mailing list to receive the monthly newsletter. Membership is $45 a yar.

Kiki Schaffer, CSW

Mother/Infant Counseling

529-9247

Kiki offers short-term psychotherapy for new moms and their babies to promote healthy interaction and to safeguard the relationship from potential early problems. She also will counsel women on postpartum depression.

92nd Street Y "New Parents' Get Together"*

92nd Street YM-YWHA

1395 Lexington Ave.

996-1100

www.92ndsty.org

"New Parents' Get Together" features speakers who discuss topics including working and parenting, childcare, sleep, babies, and your marriage. (Free for members of the Y's Parenting Center, $5 for nonmembers; annual membership is $175.) There is a New Parents' Get Together on Sunday mornings for moms and dads who can't make it during the week. Other classes for new moms include postpartum exercise, caring for a newborn, and a breastfeeding workshop. The Y also offers a New Mother/New Baby class that tackles different topics each week. The Y offers baby-sitting for children four months to four years; $8/hour for nonmembers and $6/hour for members. For more information on the parenting center call 415-5609 or 415-5611.

Rhinelander Children's Center

350 E. 88th Street bet. First

and Second Avenues

876-0500

The Rhinelander Center is part of the Children's Aid Society. For expectant or new moms, classes include Enhanced Lamaze, Lamaze Refresher, and Infant Massage. Parenting classes include "Tired of Nagging and Yelling," and "Nurturing Your Child's Self-Esteem." For parents of older children, there are daytime and evening discussion groups, with topics that include gaining cooperation, calming temper tantrums, learning to share, and reducing sibling squabbles. Kelly has had positive experiences over the years at Rhinelander.

Mom and Tot Get Together in NYC

Jean Ellen Connelly

614-0163

Bernadette Depaz

982-3504

www.femaleNYC.com

This non-profit organization meets twice a month in the evenings to discuss child/home/work issues. This support group is good for moms who have left the work force, and will help set up playgroups. Membership is $24 for a year and includes a weekly newsletter from the New York chapter. There are East Side and West Side groups.

New Mother's Luncheons
1 West Side and 2 East Side locations
Ronni Soled*
744-3194
ronninml@aol.com

Ronni Soled, a mother and former teacher, holds a bi-weekly luncheon series on the East Side, usually on Tuesdays and Thursdays from 11:30 A.M. to 2:30 P.M. at the Hi-Life Restaurant, for mothers and babies ages newborn to six months and has added another location in the Carnegie Hill area on Mondays. The sessions include a little playtime, lunch, and a guest speaker, anyone from a baby-proofing expert addressing home-safety issues, to a pediatrician discussing eating schedules and sleeping patterns. Lunches cost $30 for the first one, or you can purchase a series of five for $105. Ronni is an invaluable source of information for New York moms and often serves as a convenient play date matchmaker.

The New Mother's Luncheon opened an Upper West Side outpost in January 2000. This luncheon is run jointly by Ronni and Pamela. Pamela is there each week and Kelly is a frequent guest speaker. The luncheons meet on Wednesdays from 11:30 A.M. to 2:00 P.M. at various West Side restaurants.

New Mommies Network
Lori Robinson
769-3846
www.newmommies.com

Lori Robinson organizes lunches, brunches, and occasional dinners several days a week at different restaurants. They range in price from $10 to $30, last two hours, and attract 20 to 25 moms with babies (newborn to one year). Lori holds separate events for moms of toddlers (10-24 months) called the Graduate Group and also organizes events for working mothers and expectant parents. Past speakers have addressed sleep problems, second babies, pediatric care, and eating habits, and schedules. Dads are always welcome.

The Parent's League*
115 E. 82nd Street
737-7385

The Parent's League, a nonprofit organization founded thirty years ago, is a vital resource for New York parents. For a $75 annual fee, you'll have access to lectures, literature, and counseling services, plus a calendar and guide to citywide events and programs for children, a birthday party reference guide, a list of emergency telephone numbers, a newsletter, and information on schools and after-school activities. The league maintains an advisory service for schools and camps, as well as a listing of nannies, mother's helpers, and baby-sitters. You'll also receive the Parent's League Toddler Book, which contains information on classes you can take with a toddler.

The Parent's League publishes and sells a guidebook to private schools that describes all of the Independent Schools Admissions Association of Greater New York (ISAAGNY) member schools.

The Parenting Program
Temple Shaaray Tefila
250 E. 79th Street at Second Avenue
535-8008, ext. 248

The Parenting Program provides social interaction for you and your toddler (dads and grandparent, too). There are daytime classes for parents and toddlers, evening classes for toddlers and employed mothers, and evening playtimes for dads and toddlers. Classes offer children between ages 16 and 36 months (classes are divided by age) developmentally appropriate challenges that foster self-confidence and curiosity in the world around them. This unique program also incorporates Sabbath celebrations, Hebrew songs, and holiday rituals. Classes cost about $40 per session.

Elizabeth Silk, M.S.S.W., C.S.W., B.C.D.
235 W. 71st Street, 2-Unit 1
873-6435

Elizabeth Silk, a psychotherapist with expertise in womens' reproductive issues, postpartum depression, and mothering, holds weekly groups for new mothers. The women focus on adding new dimensions of motherhood to their identity.

Màire Clements, R.N., I.B.C.L.C.
595-4797

Màire Clements (pronounced "Moira"), R.N., is a breastfeeding expert and lactation consultant who teaches women how to breastfeed correctly. She gives breastfeeding classes at St. Luke's Roosevelt Hospital and other locations. She also sponsors luncheons where she speaks, offering mothers additional support and guidance about breastfeeding and other issues concerning new mothers. Màire offers a working mother's group and a breastfeeding Toddler Teas group, all of which she personally caters at mother's homes (locations rotate).

Phyllis LaBella, C.S.W., B.C.D.
Adoption Specialist,
Domestic and International
987-0077

Phyllis treats an entire range of emotional problems and issues affecting adopted children, adoptive couples, and birth moms.

Nancy Samalin, M.S.
787-8883
www.samalin.com

Nancy has worked with parents, educators and health care professionals since 1976, teaching positive discipline and improved communication skills for toddlers through teens. She is also a prolific author of parenting books such as *Loving Your Child is Not Enough: Positive Discipline that Works*. She is a frequent contributor to *Parents* magazine, and a wonderful speaker on children's issues.

Lisa Schuman, C.S.W., C.A.S.A.C.
590 West End Avenue, Suite 1A

874-1318

Lisa Schuman is a psychotherapist who specializes in family issues. She works with couples, individuals, and groups on child-rearing issues, relationship difficulties, and a wide range of parenting questions. She also works with parents in the area of infertility and adoption.

Jan Wenk, IBCLC
917-313-1085

Jan Wenk and her partner Emily Pease, R.N., IBCLC, are both board certified lactation consultants in private practice, meeting women in their own homes to help them with any breastfeeding needs. They are also associated with Elizabeth Seton, where they meet women one-on-one for breastfeeding consultations and run a weekly breastfeeding support group for moms-to-be as well as new mothers. They also teach prenatal breastfeeding classes. Medicaid clients are accepted.

HOTLINES, WARMLINES, AND OTHER SPECIAL HELP

There may be times during your baby's first few weeks or months when you need more specialized help or support than your pediatrician, mother, or friend can provide.

During these weeks it is a good idea to keep handy the telephone number of the nursery of the hospital in which you delivered. Often, the nurses can easily answer your questions and help you through a minor crisis. Some hospitals also have special telephone numbers set up to assist new moms. Inquire about your hospital's policy for new mother call-ins. Following are a variety of additional support groups and referral programs, as well as some important numbers to have in case of an emergency.

Adoption
Adoptive Parents Support Group
475-0222

A support group for adoptive parents.

Adoptive Parents Committee
304-8479

An adoptive parents support group with chapters in New York, Long Island, and Westchester.

At-Home Moms
American Mothers at Home
(800) 223-9260

A nationwide organization for stay-at-home moms. The membership fee of $25 includes a bi-monthly magazine and a resource guide that puts you in touch with support groups in your area.

Breastfeeding
La Leche League
794-4687

A worldwide volunteer organization founded by a group of mothers to support other moms who chose to breastfeed their babies. La Leche's services are free, nonsectarian, and supported by membership fees ($30 per year).

La Leche has group leaders in various parts of New York who run monthly meetings to discuss breastfeeding. They also provide a valuable telephone help service. When you call, a recording gives you the name and number of a woman who can be reached that day. A new mother who couldn't figure out how to work her electric breast pump called La Leche, and a volunteer spent twenty minutes on the phone explaining it to her.

Beth Israel Medical Center
Lactation Program
420-2939

A warmline to answer breastfeeding questions and provide support for nursing mothers.

Mothers Network
875 Avenue of the Americas, Suite 2001
New York, NY 10001
239-0510

A membership organization giving new mothers the opportunity to network with other new moms. They offer workshops, phone support, tips on childcare, shopping trips, activities, and more.

The National Association of Mothers Centers
Levittown, NY
516-520-2929

A referral service for mothers' groups in your area.

Hotline Help

Child Abuse and Maltreatment Reporting Center
(800) 342-3720

A hotline to report cases of suspected child abuse.

Emergency Children's Service
341-0900 (general)
966-8000 (nights, weekends, holidays)

Emergency assistance for abused, assaulted, mistreated, or neglected children.

National AIDS Hotline
(800) 342-AIDS

Trained specialists answer questions about HIV infections and AIDS.

New York Foundling Hospital Crisis
Intervention Nursery
472-8555

An emergency placement for a preschool child whose parent is under stress. This free service provides a cooling-off period for parents for as long as two days.

Poison Hotline
340-4494/764-7667

A service that offers immediate advice and direction in cases of poison ingestion.

Premature Infants

The best place to get advice and counseling or to find out about support groups for parents of premature babies is through your hospital's

Intensive Care Nursery. Many ICNs automatically provide such support. If yours does not, ask the staff to direct you to a group in your area.

National SIDS Resource Center
(800) 221-SIDS (800-221-7437)

This center provides Sudden Infant Death Syndrome (SIDS) information to parents.

Single Parents
Parents Without Partners
(800) 637-7974

A self-help group providing support and information about single parenting issues.

Single Mothers by Choice
988-0993

A support group for women who have had a baby on their own.

Single Parent Resource Center
947-0021

A clearinghouse of information on single parent programs in the United States and abroad.

Single Parents Support Group
780-0800 ext. 239

This group meets at the Educational Alliance on Monday nights from 6:15 P.M. to 7:45 P.M. Baby-sitting is available with advance reservation.

Twins or More
M.O.S.T. (Mothers Of Super Twins)
631-859-1110

A support group for parents of triplets, quadruplets, or quintuplets.

National Organization of Mothers of Twins Clubs, Inc.
877-540-2200

This club provides information on local twin, triplet, and quadruplet (or more) support groups.

Special Needs Groups
The Lighthouse/New York Association for the Blind
821-9200

The Lighthouse works with blind children throughout the city and provides comprehensive services and resources for them and their families.

Cerebral Palsy
United Cerebral Palsy of New York City
677-7400

This organization offers comprehensive services for children and their families, beginning at infancy.

Cystic Fibrosis Foundation
986-8783

A foundation providing advice, counseling, and hospital referrals for families of children with Cystic Fibrosis.

National Down Syndrome Society
460-9330

This society offers general information, parent support, and assistance with identifying programs at local hospitals for Down Syndrome babies and children.

League for the Hard of Hearing
(917) 305-7700

Provides information on speech and hearing programs and clinics.

Pregnancy and Infant Loss Center
(Bereavement Group)
612-473-9372

This center provides information on local support groups for women or couples recovering from a miscarriage or the loss of an infant.

Educational Alliance
780-0800

Educational Alliance runs workshops to help parents through pregnancy loss.

**Resources for Children
with Special Needs**
677-4650

An information, referral, advocacy, and support center for parents of children with special needs.

Spina Bifida Information and Referral
(800) 621-3141

Williams Syndrome Hotline
www.williams-syndrome.org
(248) 541-3630

YIA Early Intervention Program
418.0335

IMPORTANT SUPPLIES
Diaper Services

In our environmentally conscious age, the use of cloth, instead of disposable diapers, is gaining popularity. Below is a list of diaper services that deliver in the New York City area. Most offer identical services, with little variation in price. Diaper pails can be purchased from all these companies for about $12. In all instances, eighty newborn diapers are delivered to your house once a week and the soiled ones are picked up.

Nature Baby Diaper Service
48 Harold Street
Tenafly, NJ 07670
(800) 344-3427

The price is $15.75/week.

Special Deliveries Diaper Service
47 Purdy Avenue
Port Chester, NY 10573
(800) 582-7638

The price is $15.95/week. This company produces a monthly newsletter listing baby items available through their service.

Tidy Diapers
50 Commerce Street
Norwalk, CT 06850
(800) 732-2443

$15.95/week, or $95 for five weeks.

Diapers Direct (800) 515-3427, is a delivery service featuring Tender Touch disposables. Diapers Direct is a wholesaler, and sells at a deep discount. Newborn diapers are delivered in cases of 288 for $49.

Breast Pumps

For breastfeeding working moms or other women who would like their husbands or care-givers to feed baby an occasional bottle of breast milk, an electric breast pump is a won-derful convenience. Electric pumps are faster and easier to use than manual or battery-oper-ated pumps. If you plan to breastfeed for three months or less, we recommend renting an electric, hospital-grade pump. Pumps can be rented by the day, week, or month. They can also be purchased through The Right Start Catalog. Buying is a good idea if you plan to breastfeed for an extended time or if you are planning to have more children. The Medela Lactina is a good one to rent or purchase. For the nearest outlet, call Medela at: (800) TELL-YOU. The La Leche League, 794-4687, can also tell you where to rent a breast pump.

Prices for pump rental range from $50 to $80 per month. Most places sell an accompa-nying kit that contains sanitary accessories to be used with the pump. The kit is priced at about $30 for the single pump and $40 for the double. The single pump allows you to pump milk from one breast, and the double from both breasts at the same time.

Breast pumps can be rented at the follow-ing locations:

UPPER EAST SIDE
Calagor Pharmacy
1226 Lexington Avenue at 83rd Street
369-6000

Clayton & Edwards Pharmacy
1327 York Avenue at 71st Street
737-6240

Falk Drug
259 E. 72nd Street at Second Avenue
744-8080

Goldberger's Pharmacy
1200 First Avenue at 65th Street
734-6998

Kings Lexington Pharmacy
1091 Lexington Avenue bet. 76th
and 77th Streets
794-7100

Timmerman Pharmacy*
799 Lexington Avenue bet. 61st
and 62nd Streets
838-6450

UPPER WEST SIDE
Apthorp Pharmacy*
2211 Broadway at 78th Street
877-3480

Chateau Drug
181 Amsterdam Avenue bet.
68th and 69th Streets
877-6390

Regine Kids
2688 Broadway bet. 102nd
and 103rd Streets
864-8705

Sandra Jamrog
Home delivery
866-8257
jjjamrog@aol.com

Suba Pharmacy
2721 Broadway at 104th Street
866-6700

MIDTOWN
NYU Medical Center
560 First Avenue at 32nd Street
263-BABY

Elizabeth Seton Childbearing Center
222 W. 14th Street bet. Seventh
and Eighth Avenues
367-8500

St. Lukes Roosevelt Hospital Center
1000 Tenth Avenue at 58th Street
523-4000

Westerly Pharmacy
911 Eighth Avenue at 54th Street
247-1124

DOWNTOWN
Barren Hospital Medical Center
49 Delancey Street bet. Eldridge
and Forsyth Streets
226-6164

C.O. Bigelow Apothecaries
414 Sixth Avenue bet. 8th and 9th Streets
533-2700

Elm Drugs
298 First Avenue bet. 17th and 18th Streets
777-0740

Kings Pharmacy
5 Hudson at Reade Street
791-3100

Little Folks
123 E. 23rd Street bet. Park
and Lexington Avenues
982-9669

Miriam Goodman
Home Delivery
219-1080

5 · entertainment for kids and moms

You've survived the first couple of months; you have packing the diaper bag down to a science, you're getting a handle on this motherhood business—it is time to venture out with your little one and have some fun!

You and your baby can roll around on a mat together at the 92nd Street Y, get some culture at the Temple of Dendur at the Met, relax at an outdoor cafe, or stroll to a neighborhood playground and meet other moms and their babies.

In this chapter, we'll give you a rundown of the Mommy and Me classes and activities available in the city. (Unless otherwise indicated, caregivers, dads, or grandmas are also welcome to take their young charges to these classes.) Then we'll turn to New York's playgrounds and parks, museums, indoor play spaces, child-friendly restaurants, and other special spaces where you and your baby can have a good time.

Given our considerable experience with all of these classes and activities, we have a few thoughts on monitoring your child's schedule. With our first kids, we both overdid it with classes. Beginning at three months old, Rebecca and Alexander "learned" music, art, gym, French, ballet, tumbling, soccer, swimming—you name it. You get the idea; we overbooked them. The second time around, we were smarter and realized that playgroups and time with mom in the park are just as valuable as Gymboree.

Once Benjamin was a year old, he and Pamela began a gym and music class. It paid to wait because he enjoyed it much more at one year than Rebecca had at six months. Angela took her

Top Ten Things to Do with Your Family on the Weekend

1. Visit Chelsea Piers (skating, gymnastics, bowling, etc.).
2. Go to Central Park to watch the roller-bladers and feed the ducks (mid-park at 72nd St.).
3. Go to dinner at the restaurant at the 79th Street boat basin cafe (79th St. and the Hudson River). Eat good food in a kid-friendly environment and watch the boats.
4. Go down to Battery Park City. Stroll by the water, eat ice cream cones, and people-watch.
5. Visit the Brooklyn Botanic Garden. They have a great kiddie area with all types of hands-on activities.
6. Invite a few other families to a potluck picnic in Central Park. Bring bubbles, balls, and blankets.
7. Take a drive out into the country for fall apple-picking/pumpkin-picking.
8. Visit the penguins in the Central Park Zoo (infants love to look at black and white).
9. Form a "daddy" playgroup—dads get to bond with other dads and babies, and you get some time off.
10. Go to a playground in a neighborhood

first music class with Kelly at age one and she is more advanced and talkative now at age two than her brother was at that age, although he had been introduced to everything under the sun by age two.

MOMMY AND ME CLASSES AND PROGRAMS

As your child grows, she is going to learn to run, jump, tumble, sing songs, and scribble pictures all on her own. But classes can help her develop social skills, learn how to function in groups, be disciplined, and acquire a host of other skills. Above all, children enjoy themselves in these programs, and it's nice to have some places to go during New York winters.

All these places and programs offer classes for children age three and under. Some take babies as young as three months. However, you and your child will find an organized class much more enjoyable if she is able to sit up on her own, so it's a good idea to wait until your baby is at least six to nine months old before signing up.

Here are some guidelines to follow as you check out these programs:

Take a trial class or attend an open house before you sign up. You may have to pay for it, but you'll have a better sense of what you are getting into.

※ Look for classes with children the same age as your own.

※ Look for big, open, clean rooms with plenty of space and light, accessible by elevator or ramp. You should not have to walk up five flights of stairs carrying your baby, diaper bag, and stroller.

❉ Equipment should be scaled down to small-child size, and any gymnastic-type facilities should include lots of mats and other safety features.

❉ Small to medium size classes are best. Do not be too concerned if a class is very big on the first day, because everyone is not there every week. Illnesses, naps, and vacations normally account for a quarter of a class being absent in any given week.

❉ The teacher makes all the difference, some are better than others. The other children and their mothers and nannies also can affect the atmosphere of a class. If you are the only mom in attendance, for example, you may feel awkward spending time with ten nannies every Thursday afternoon at two o'clock. (You can always ask to switch to a class with more moms.)

❉ Location is important. Enroll in a class near your home. If you can push your baby in a stroller less than ten blocks, you will be more likely to attend and to make it there on time.

Prices and schedules change almost every semester, so call ahead for the latest information. Classes often run in sessions of seventeen to nineteen weeks; prices range from $275 to $400. During the summer, many places—Jodi's Gym and the 92nd Street Y, for example—offer four-, six-, and nine-week sessions that cost from $95 to $200.

Applause! Kids
181 E. 73rd Street,
#19A (mailing address)
472-0703
www.applauseny.com
Age: 6 months to 4 years

Run for 6 years by Audrey Kaplan and Pamela Fisher, Applause! Kids has recently begun offering a "Broadway Babies" class on Tuesday and Wednesday mornings, a Mommy and Me class with a Broadway twist. Each week children learn songs and stories from different Broadway shows through puppetry, movement, and storytelling. Locations are on the Upper East and West sides.

Asphalt Green Inc.
The A.G.U.A. Center
1750 York Avenue at 91st Street
369-8890
Age: 4 months and up

Swimming classes for young children at Asphalt Green, a huge fitness and sports complex, are held in the warm water teaching/exercise pool (not the Olympic-sized pool) under excellent supervision. Water Babies is for four- to eighteen-month-olds. It accustoms them to being in the water through soothing games and songs. Water Tots, for children eighteen to thirty-six months, teaches kicking, arm movements, prone floating, and safety jumps. The curriculum incorporates the teaching methods of both the American Red Cross and the American Swim Coaches Association. Adults must go in the water with children under three.

Asphalt Green also hosts parties and offers delightful puppet shows for children 11 months and older, as well as various art and fitness classes such as Toddlercise, Tumble Tots, and Kindermusik. This is one of the best places for swimming lessons in the city, and parents travel from across town to downtown so their kids can swim here. Book your classes early!

Baby Fingers
164 W. 79th Street, Suite 1D,
bet. Columbus and Amsterdam Avenues
317 E. 89th Street, lower level,
bet. First and Second Avenues
874-5978
www.mybabyfingers.com
Age: newborn to 3

A unique program for children one month to three years offering sign language instruction through the arts. Classes involve music, signing and singing. Founder Lora Heller is certified in early education, special education and speech therapy. She is also a musician with a magical voice.

Bloomingdale School of Music
323 W. 108th Street bet. Broadway
and Riverside Drive
663-6021
www.bloomingdalemusic.org
Age: 6 months and up

Bloomingdale's preschool programs are an ideal way to introduce children to the world of music. Baby's First Music Class offers a wealth of fun activities like singing, dancing, rocking, and exploring instruments, and shows adults how to help their children develop musically. While Music and Movement encourages children age 18 months to 3 years to improvise and stretch their imaginations through music. A number of classes are offered for older kids, too, without parents or caregivers, including Musical Adventures, Dalcroze Eurythmics, Guitar, Keyboard, Violin, and more.

C.A.T.S. (Children's Athletic Training School)*
593 Park Avenue bet. 63rd
and 64th Streets
The Jewish Center
131 W. 86th Street, 5th floor,
bet. Amsterdam and Columbus Avenues
235 E. 49th Street (bet. 2nd and 3rd Avenues)
Ages: 1 year and up

CATS is the only comprehensive children's sports training program for one- to ten-year-olds in the United States. Baby CATS and Kiddie CATS meet once a week in a large auditorium-like space; children under two years play on gym equipment such as slides and tunnels. Classes are large, eighteen toddlers with moms or caregivers, with three coaches for each session. Many children stay with the program for years, going on to take lessons in tennis, soccer, golf, hockey, basketball, dance, and martial arts. Alexander loved CATS and even participated in CATS summer programs for two years.

Chelsea Piers
Pier 62, 23rd Street at Twelfth Avenue
336-6500
Age: 15 months and up

In addition to their extensive adult offerings, Chelsea Piers, the largest sports complex in New York, offers programs and facilities for very young children. Pier Play, for ages fifteen months to three years, uses directed play such as games, art, and drama to encourage children to share and ask questions. For physical activity, enroll your child in the preschool gymnastics program (seventeen months to five years), or take her to the Toddler gym, where she can crawl, roll, and jump on mats and equipment designed to help develop basic skills. Chelsea Piers also offers an excellent introduction to soccer for 3 to 5 year olds. Benjamin is currently enrolled. He is learning all the soccer moves and about teamwork. Two hours at the Toddler Gym is $10; call for other prices.

Child's Play

Central Presbyterian Church
593 Park Avenue at 64th Street
838-1504
Rutgers Presbyterian Church
236 W. 73rd Street at Broadway
877-8227
Age: 6 months to 5 years

Child's Play offers a combination of storytime, gym play, singing, and art projects for parents and children (no caregivers). Babyplay is for children four to twelve months old; Playgroup, the toddler class, is for children twelve to thirty months old. They also offer a nursery program for 3- to 5-year-olds, where parents stay with the children. A program is available for children being home schooled as well, providing a forum for parents to exchange ideas and a place for children to interact.

Children's Tumbling

Suellen Epstein
9-15 Murray Street at City Hall
233-3418
Age: 2 years to 10 years

Downtown moms think highly of this tumbling and gymnastic program for children over eighteen months. Classes are a special combination of dance, gymnastics, and theater. The culmination of each semester is a show, with dramatic lighting and music and, a recent addition, stilt walking, in which the children showcase what they've learned. Classes for toddlers are kept small (six or seven children), last an hour, and meet once a week.

Church Street School for Music and Art

74 Warren Street at W. Broadway
571-7290
Age: 2 years and up

This well-regarded program teaches music, movement, art, and instruments. Toddler classes (for two- and three-year-olds) run forty minutes with ten children, a teacher, instructor, and mommies or caregivers. Church Street School features the Dalcroze method of music instruction, which combines music awareness and movement.

Circus Gymnastics

2121 Broadway at 74th Street
799-3755
Age: 6 months and up

Mommy & Me is a forty-minute class that includes circle games, supervised instruction on gymnastic equipment, a parachute, a ball pit, and a trampoline. The classes are for children ages six months to three years. All instructors are particularly skilled in working with young children. You and your little one can have a great time here.

Columbus Gym*
606 Columbus Avenue bet. 89th
and 90th Streets
721-0090
Age: 12 months and up

The facilities at Columbus Gym are some of the nicest and cleanest in the city; there are tunnels, trampolines, balance beams, and hills to climb over and through. Gymnastic classes for toddlers twelve to eighteen months are with mom or caregiver. For older toddlers, there's P.E.P. (Preschool Enrichment Program), a ninety-minute mini-preschool class including gym, arts and crafts, painting, music, and storytime. Pamela and Rebecca (and then Pamela and Ben) took the P.E.P. class for a year and enjoyed it tremendously.

Create a Day
57 E. 75th Street at Park Avenue
452-2560
Age: 2 years to 5 years

Create a Day is a brand-new program that challenges your child's imagination through art, creative play, and wonderful props. This class changes its theme every week and takes your child on exciting adventures by creating a new

look every time. One week the room may be set up to resemble the moon and your child is an astronaut, and the following week, a circus featuring your child as an acrobat, or maybe the rainforest with your child as a tour guide. Ages 2 to 5, with a maximum of eight children in each class. Owner Candace Sands also carries clothing for children (The Best Dressed Kid).

Diller-Quaile School Of Music
24 E. 95th Street bet. Madison
and Fifth Avenues
369-1484
Age: 1 year and up

Diller-Quaile is a New York institution. There are music classes for toddlers and moms, as well as private instruction on different instruments. Classes begin in September and run until June. Music Babies, for those aged twelve to fifteen months, teaches lullabies, finger plays, nursery chants, and a variety of playful rhythmic activities. Music for Nearly Twos uses movement activities, games, and percussion instruments to guide classroom play. There are ten to twelve children in a class, with three instructors for children under eighteen months. Note: The application process begins one year in advance of classes. Call for more information. Classes start at $1,000 for about thirty sessions.

Discovery Programs
251 W. 100th Street at West End Drive
749-8717
Age: walking to 12 years

Gym for Tots takes place in a gymnastic

playroom where children are encouraged to run, jump, climb, balance, bounce, roll, and swing, with a parent or caregiver. Music, Dance and Storytime is a program of movement games, action songs, finger play, and friendship. In the toddler art classes, children use brushes, finger paints, sponges, and other materials to explore the world of shape, color, and texture. There is also an On My Own Preschool Program for two- to four-year-olds. Classes are two hours daily and individual schedules are developed.

The Early Ear
48 W. 68th Street bet.
Central Park West and Columbus Avenue
353 E. 78th Street bet. First
and Second Avenues
110 W. 96th Street bet. Amsterdam
and Columbus Avenues
877-7125 (for all locations)
Age: 4 months to 4 years

The Early Ear is a highly regarded introduction to music for babies as young as four months. Each class has ten children, with two teachers, one to accompany and another to demonstrate. Classes are forty minutes and incorporate sing-a-long, games, play activities and mini musical instruments. The cost of each fifteen-week session is $345 with a registration fee of $30. From Pamela's own experience with Benjamin, it's best to start when the child is a year old.

Educational Alliance Parenting and Family Center at The Sol Goldman YMHA*
344 E. 14th Street bet. First
and Second Avenues
780-0800 ext. 239
Age: newborn to 36 months

The Educational Alliance Parenting Center offers Mommy and Me, Two x Two play classes that concentrate on play, music, and art, and Tykercise, a sensory-movement course for children three to 18 months. There is also a variety of multi-cultural classes, such as Chinese for Children (ages 3-4) for adopted children, French lessons, Judaica programs, and even a Japanese Parenting Center. Classes last from forty-five minutes to two hours and are limited to twelve children and adults. They also have a monthly Daddy and Me group (birth to one year), a three-session workshop for new parents called From Pair to Parent, evening groups for working and single parents, and other parenting classes. You can join the new 14th Street Y for a yearly fee, which entitles you to program discounts, special events, priority registration, and pool and gym facilities. Classes have member and non-member fees. Kiki Schaffer, the director, creates a special sense of community and is an encyclopedic resource for the downtown parent.

Funworks for Kids
201 E. 83rd Street at Third Avenue
759-1937/(917) 432-1820
Age: 9 months to 3 years

Funworks has been around for fourteen years and offers sixty- or ninety-minute classes—a preschool-type program—of combined music, art, and movement. Classes feature free play that includes a ball pool and air mattresses, and circle time with singing, dancing, and the use of many props such as puppets, parachutes and balls. Plus there's an art project and story time. This program has a loyal following and moms praise the extended program, especially the one for toddlers. Funworks also hosts birthday parties and play time hours.

Free to Be Under Three
253-2040

This very popular class was started a few years ago by Joe Robertson. It incorporates music, storytime, and free play hour in a preschool like environment. There are at least two teachers—with high energy and an understanding of early development issues—in each class. Register at birth, as the wait list is long and it can take a year or more to get a spot.

Gymboree
401 E. 84th Street at First Avenue
50 Lexington Avenue at 24th Street
30 W. 68th Street bet.
Central Park West and Columbus Avenue
210 W. 91st Street bet. Broadway
and Amsterdam Avenue
64 W. 3rd Street bet. LaGuardia
and Thompson Streets
877-496-5327
Age: 3 months to 4 years

These popular, organized playgroups are

the original "mommy and me" classes. Gymboree features circle games and songs, free play on gymnastic-style equipment, exercise games, and parachute play. There are about twelve children to one teacher in each class. Classes meet once a week for forty-five minutes. Join Gymboree at any time, and they will pro-rate their fees. Check out the location you're interested in; facilities vary somewhat.

Gymtime/Rhythm and Glues
1520 York Avenue at 80th Street
861-7732
Age: 6 months to 12 years

Gymtime offers organized play classes that feature songs, games, and circle time for mother and child in clean, bright rooms with gymnastic-style equipment. You'll also find a variety of classes, including cooking, sports, Tae Kwon Do, and art for toddlers. There can be up to ten children in a class with two instructors; classes meet once a week for forty-five minutes to one hour. Gymtime will pro-rate their prices for latecomers.

Hands On! A Musical Experience, Inc.
1365 First Avenue bet. 73rd and 74th Streets
628-1945
529 Columbus Avenue bet. 85th
and 86th Streets
496-9929
Age: 4 months to 4 years

Samari Weinberg (no relation to Pamela), a seasoned, early-childhood music teacher uses a specially formatted program, Hands On! to present musical activities that also enhance other types of learning such as the acquisition of language, listening skills, auditory discrimination, social understanding, and personal discovery. Young students learn to listen and sing everything from popular American folk songs to Broadway tunes. Classical themes are introduced as well. Classes are approximately $350 for a 15-week session, plus a $30 yearly fee. Samari is a former Early Ear instructor, and is wonderful with children.

JAMS
Ansche Chesed Synagogue
W. 100th Street bet. Broadway
and West End Avenues
Stephen Wise Free Synagogue
30 W. 68th Street bet.
Central Park West and Columbus Avenue
595-0563
www.jamsnet.com
Age: newborn to 5 years

JAMS is offered for children ages newborn to 5 years old. Founded by Jay Danzig, a music teacher with 20 years of experience, JAMS helps to cultivate a love and understanding of music in a unique way. Your child will be introduced to international songs, dances, chants, rhythms, and more. Jewish JAMS is also offered, with an emphasis on teaching children Jewish songs and dances.

Jodi's Gym*
244 E. 84th Street bet. Second
and Third Avenues
772-7633
Age: 6 months to 12 years

Classes in this brightly colored, well-padded facility feature free play time, singing, stretching, and an obstacle course. Jodi personally trains all her instructors, who are certified by the USA Gymnastic Federation. Classes for children under three feature slides, ladders, tunnels, balls, and parachutes that are just right for tiny hands and feet. Classes are forty minutes, and there is a maximum of sixteen children to a class with two instructors.

Judy Stevens Playgroup*
77 Franklin Street at Church Street
941-0542
judy.stevens@mindspring.com
Age: 2 to 3 years

Judy Stevens, an artist and a mother, started forming playgroups for downtown moms more than fourteen years ago. And what special play groups they are! Judy does art projects and activities with lots of music, movement, and free play in a warm, child-friendly loft. There are only six toddlers in a class. Classes meet two to four times a week and lunch is served. There is always a waiting list.

Kids Co-Motion
West Park Presbyterian Church
165 W. 86th Street at Amsterdam Avenue
Rebecca Kelly Dance Studio
579 Broadway bet. Prince and Houston Streets
The Soundings
280 Rector Place
The Maternal Fitness Studio
108 E. 16th Street bet. Park Avenue
        and Irving Place

431-8489
www.rebeccakellyballet.com
Age: 12 months to 6 years

Choreographer Rebecca Kelly and her husband, dancer Craig Brashear, founded this popular, unique and creative program in 1991. It provides a joyous atmosphere with motion, tumbling, song, and music for young children with their caregivers. Kids Co-Motion emphasizes a productive, positive learning experience. Classes run in twelve-week sessions, in fall, winter, spring, and in an extended summer program. Class prices vary with the length of the session. There is a one-time registration fee of $20 per family.

Kindermusik
The Greenwich Village Center
(a.k.a. The Children's Aid Society)
219 Sullivan Street at W. 3rd Street
864-2476
Age: newborn to 7 years

Kindermusik is an international music program with more than 2,100 teachers. This introductory music class gets toddlers singing, chanting, dancing, and playing simple instruments like rhythm sticks, bells, and drums. The sessions are forty-five minutes to an hour long, and children can participate with either a parent or caregiver. Kindermusik also holds classes at Asphalt Green.

The Language Workshop for Children
888 Lexington Avenue at 65th Street
396-0830
Age: 12 months to 5 years

François Thibaut created the Language Workshops for small children in 1973, and today they are more popular than ever. In the Just for Tots program you'll find a variety of forty-five-minute classes for toddlers, including arts and crafts, music and movement, and gymnastics, in addition to the French and Spanish language workshops.

Life Sport Gymnastics
West Park Presbyterian Church
165 W. 86th Street at Amsterdam Avenue
769-3131
Age: 18 months to adult

Rudy Van Daele has been teaching gymnastics for twenty years. Classes here are small, with seven to eight students, and include activities on mats, trampolines, beams, and horses. Children are encouraged to try whatever interests them, from cartwheels to flips and more. Yoga classes are also offered.

**The Lucy Moses School
for Music and Dance**
129 W. 67th Street bet. Broadway
and Amsterdam Avenue
362-8060
Age: 12 months and up

In Music Mates, toddlers sing, dance, and learn about different instruments with teachers Anna Rodriguez and Michael Glick. The school offers a class that combines rhythm games, creative movement, and dramatic play; and there are a number of music, movement, and dance classes for older preschoolers as well. Children attend with parents or caregivers.

Mary Ann Hall's Music for Children*
The Church of Heavenly Rest
2 E. 90th Street bet. Madison
and Fifth Avenues
203-454-7484/(800) 633-0078
Age: infants, toddlers, and up

Mary Ann Hall's Music for Children is nationally acclaimed. This early childhood program nurtures young children in a musical environment, "connecting the art of the music with the heart of the child." Children discover, explore and develop natural musical abilities. Mary Ann and Emily Hall play the piano as children walk, march, gallop, and run to the appropriate accompaniment. They lead the group in various songs and free play with a variety of musical instruments. Weekly forty-five minute classes, not exceeding ten children, run from October to May. Kelly has used this program with both of her children.

Mary Copeland's Dancing Adventures
Peggy Levine
212 W. 92nd Street bet. Broadway
and Amsterdam Avenue
362-5176; 718-601-9639
Age: 3 years to 8 years

Imagine climbing a steep mountain into a deep, dark forest with lantern in hand and backpack secured. Branches brush your face as you push them aside, mud clings to your feet as you sink into wet ground. A bear lumbers forth out of hiding while an owl hoots, searching for a plump green frog to gobble up. You've just entered the exciting and fanciful world of Mary Copeland's Dancing Adventures. Let your moving monkey take a walk on the wild side. Classes are grouped by age and run 45 minutes to one hour. Birthday parties are also available.

Mommy and Me
The Greenwich Village Center
(a.k.a. The Children's Aid Society)
219 Sullivan Street at W. 3rd Street
254-3074
Age: 10 months to 3 years

Children play outdoors, in an enclosed playground, singing songs, listening to stories, and doing art projects. Toddler Time, Toddler Gymnastics, and Kindermusik are among the featured classes. There is also a variety of classes for children up to five years old, in subjects such as woodworking, pottery, ballet, and Kung Fu. There are ten children and two teachers in every class.

Music Together*
Over twenty locations in Manhattan
and Brooklyn
244-3046 (for all East Side locations)
219-0591 (for all West Side locations)
358-3801 (for all Lower Manhattan locations)
(718) 369-3099 (for Brooklyn location)
www.musictogether.com
Age: birth to 4 years

Music Together is a forty-five minute class for mommies and children (or caregivers/fathers), where they sing, dance, chant, and play with various instruments. At the beginning of the program, parents receive a cassette tape, a compact disc, and a charming illustrated songbook. They are encouraged to play the tape at home and children come to know and love the songs. Music Together has ten to twelve children per class. There are classes for babies and toddlers separately and classes for infants and toddlers mixed together. Tuition is $185 ($175 for returning families) for ten weekly 45-minute classes. Additional siblings are $150 each. Pamela has taken many classes at various Music Together locations with Rebecca and Ben. Instructors do vary with each location, so we recommend a trial class before signing up.

Musical Kids

122 E. 88th Street bet. Lexington
996-5898
Age: Newborn to 7 years

Music classes with two teachers and a pianist leading children in singing, dancing and playing musical instruments.

Rhinelander Children's Center

350 E. 88th Street bet. First
and Second Avenues
876-0500
Age: 6 months to 4 years

Rhinelander is a very popular Upper East Side community center. Mommy and Me classes, early childhood development programs, and evening parenting seminars are all taught here. The Baby Fingers class teaches sign language to six- to twelve-month-olds. Children twelve to eighteen months old can enjoy Steppin' Out, an hour of free play, music, art, stories, bubbles, and snacks. Toddler Time, for eighteen- to twenty-four-month-olds and thirty- to thirty-six-month-olds, and Kiddie Crafters, an art class for toddlers age two and one-half to three and one-half years, are also offered. Classes usually have fifteen children with two instructors. Classes fill quickly, so apply promptly.

Seventy-Fourth Street Magic

510 E. 74th Street bet. York Avenue
and the East River
737-2989
www.seventyfourthmagic.com
Age: 6 months and up

Seventy-Fourth Street Magic is held in a clean, bright, and large play space made up of two gyms. The gym for children over one year has padded tunnels, bridges, and houses, while the baby gym, for children under a year, is filled with a bubble pen and big balls. Classes focus on music, art, and gymnastics, and run from forty-five minutes to an hour. They usually have ten children with two instructors. Seventy-Fourth Street Magic also offers a large variety of cooking, drama, and science activities.

Sokol New York Gym

420 E. 71st Street bet. First
and York Avenues
861-8206
Age: 10 months and up

Founded in 1867, Sokol New York offers Mommy and Me classes for infants, and a toddler gym class for one-, two-, and three-year-olds. Classes consist of free play, circle time, parachute play, bubbles, and more, with a different theme every few weeks. This is one of the most reasonably priced programs in New York-$385 for a once-a-week, forty-five-minute class-and it runs from September through May.

The Sunshine Kids' Club:
A Preschool of Music
230 E. 83rd Street bet. Second
and Third Avenues
439-9876
Age: 6 months to 3 years

The SKC strongly believes that music expands a child's horizons intellectually, and strives to provide a curriculum that uses music to promote each child's individuality. Children are divided into six age groups and each class is limited to ten children. Classes are 45 minutes and a parent or caregiver must accompany children. The space is small, but founder Trish Bolton is a gifted and talented teacher, and spent many years at Diller-Quaile. These classes are hot right now, and tough to get into, so reserve your place early.

Sutton Gym
20 Cooper Square at 5th Street
533-9390
Age: 18 months and up

Classes in this large, clean gym emphasize stretching and strengthening. The small beams, barres, and mats are perfect for toddlers. There's a tumbling track as well. The friendly and helpful staff encourages visits before signing up. Classes run for seventeen weeks and have six children per instructor.

Take Me to the Water
828-1756
www.takemetothewater.com
Age: 6 months and up

Heather Silver teaches private, semiprivate, and group swimming classes. Classes at Take Me to the Water can be as small as three babies and mothers with one instructor, and are taught at various public and private pools around the city, including 74th at York, 48th at Broadway, 91st at Columbus, and in Battery Park. Classes parallel the school year; none are held in the summer. You can take as few as four classes for $150.

Tumble Town
118 E. 28th Street bet. Lexington and Park Avenue South, Room 708
889-7342
Ages: 6 months to 6 years

Tumble Town is a gymnastics program for children six months to six years old. They offer mommy and me tumbling classes for the three and under set, and afterschool gymnastics classes for children three to six years old.

Turtle Bay Music School
244 E. 52nd Street bet. Second
and Third Avenues
753-8811
Age: 18 months to adult

Turtle Bay, founded in 1925, is a full-service music school offering private music classes in all instruments. Music and movement classes start for toddlers at eighteen months, and there are programs for two-and three-year-olds as well. The Mommy and Me classes focus on movement, song, and percussion instruments. This warm and friendly school is ideal for midtown families.

YWHA 92nd Street*
1395 Lexington Avenue at 92nd Street
415-5600
www.92ndsty.org
Age: Newborn to adult

The 92nd Street Y's Parenting Center has a variety of activities and outstanding programs for parents and children, making it a nationwide model. Classes include Lamaze, Caring for a Newborn, Breastfeeding, Baby Massage, Rock N' Roll Baby, Little Explorers, Kids in the Kitchen, and Parkbench. A $175 membership in the Parenting Center allows you priority registration, special prices for every class, invitations to New Parent and Toddler-Parent Get-Togethers, members' rates for babysitting ($7/hour), and special discounts at children's stores around the city.

For West Side parents, the 92nd Street Y offers a limited number of classes at the Spanish-Portuguese Synagogue at 70th Street and Central Park West.

Each of the following Y Associations offers a variety of classes for your baby, from gymnastics to music to swimming. Call your nearest Y for information, or go to www.ymcanyc.org.

THE Y ASSOCIATIONS
YWCA of the City of New York
610 Lexington Avenue at 53rd Street
755-4500

Vanderbilt YMCA
224 E. 47th Street bet. Second
and Third Avenues
756-9600

YMCA
5 W. 63rd Street bet.
Central Park West and Broadway
875-4112

McBurney YMCA
215 W. 23rd Street at Seventh Avenue
741-9210

PLAYGROUNDS

New York's parks and playgrounds provide just about every activity you can think of. The park is a great place for your baby or toddler to explore, swing, slide, and climb, and for you to meet other moms with children close in age to yours. And when the weather's nice, you'll love going out, enjoying a change of scenery, and taking in some fresh air.

The Department of Parks and Recreation oversees some 1,578 parks and 862 playgrounds around the city. In the past few years, many playgrounds have been renovated and now have soft rubber mat surfaces, brightly colored metal bars for climbing, and sprinklers for cooling. One of the city's most original playgrounds is the Rustic Playground at E. 67th Street, a perfect stop before or after a visit to the Central Park Zoo.

You can call the Parks Department at 360-8111 (www.nycparks.org) for information on events in any of the city's parks. For older children, call the department's recreation office at 16 W. 61st Street, 408-0243, to find out about playground programs, sports, and Arts in the Park, a summer series of free activities and performances for children. Playground Partners is a wonderful organization dedicated to fund-raising to help maintain the playgrounds within Central Park. Their annual spring parties in the Park are not to be missed!

Central Park

You can easily spend a leisurely day in Central Park. Walk around the Boat Pond (72nd Street at Fifth Avenue), or sit in an outdoor cafe and watch the miniature boat enthusiasts sail their remote-controlled beauties across the pond. Run through the Sheep Meadow (69th Street at mid-park) or Strawberry Fields (72nd Street at Central Park West); bring a ball for a game of catch and some nibbles for a picnic lunch. Or buy one from a nearby concession stand.

Some of our favorite Central Park spots are:

Alice in Wonderland statue (74th Street at Fifth Avenue). As soon as your youngster is moving around comfortably on her own, this huge, bronze statue, full of nooks and crannies to climb on will captivate her. There are always lots of kids, with moms and caregivers sitting on the nearby benches keeping an eye on things.

James Michael Levin Playground (77th Street at Fifth Avenue). This newly renovated playground has a padded gym/slide good for eighteen-month-olds and up; space to run, play, or ride a tricycle; an enclosed swing area; a big, roomy sandbox; and a toddler-friendly water sprinkler system for hot summer days.

Spector Playground (85th Street at Central Park West). A West Side favorite, this playground has an area for children under two, with a sandbox, slides, climbing equipment, and a blacktop space for tricycles and toy cars. For children over two, a sandy section of the playground has tire and rope swings, climbing chains, and more.

Adventure Playground (next to Tavern on the Green, W. 67th Street at Central Park West). Divided into two sections, a lower play area has baby swings, a sandbox, slides, and a bridge, while the hilltop playground, for older kids, resembles an Egyptian park. Perfect for "imagination" games!

Diana Ross Playground (81st Street at Central Park West). This is the perfect place to go with your new baby or visiting five-year-old niece; it has baby swings as well as great climbing equipment for older kids.

E. 96th Street Playground (at Fifth Avenue). This large, well laid out playground is the East Side stomping ground for the 4- to 6-year-old set. After pre-school it is the place to meet, complete with swings, sandbox, climbing gym, and fort.

You'll undoubtedly find your own favorite parts of Central Park. And, of course, you'll pay many visits to these two special attractions:

The Central Park Carousel
Middle of Central Park at 64th Street
879-0244

The Central Park Carousel is one of this country's great antique carousels. Each ride lasts about five minutes and is accompanied by calliope music. Your baby can ride with you on a horse that moves up and down, on a stationary horse, or in one of two chariots. Each ride costs one dollar per person.

Central Park Wildlife Conservation Center (Zoo)
Fifth Avenue at 64th Street
861-6030

Officially called the Central Park Wildlife Conservation Center, this recently renovated zoo provides natural habitats for mostly small (with the exception of the polar bear) animals. Visit the rain forest, complete with monkeys; the penguin house; and, of course, the sea lions' circular pool with see-through sides. The daily sea lion feedings are sure to delight your youngster. You'll find plenty of places to sit, as well as a cafeteria.

There are scheduled tours and activities each day (story hours, arts and crafts, and animal feedings), so call ahead. Adult admission is $3.50, $1.50 for seniors, children three to ten years pay fifty cents, and children under three are free. These prices include admission to the newly renovated Tisch Children's Zoo's Enchanted Forest and Domestic Animal Area.

Other Parks
While Central Park is the biggest and best, New York has a variety of parks where your child can have some outdoor fun. Here are some favorites, by neighborhood:

EAST SIDE (EAST RIVER)
*Carl Schurz** (East End Avenue at 84th Street). This popular Upper East Side park has something for everyone: for infants, there is a play area with swings, bridges, and slides; for toddlers, there is an enclosed sandbox with climbing and sliding jungle gyms; and for adults, there is a superb riverside promenade. A paved pavilion with a sprinkler fountain running in the summer is used for ball play and tricycles in the fall and spring.

*John Jay** (FDR Drive at 76th Street). This big, clean enclosed playground has slides and moving bridges, a good central sprinkler system, a sandbox with swings for all ages, and benches all around. From the Fourth of July to early September, a large swimming pool is open from 11 A.M. to 7 P.M., and there are free swimming lessons for children ages three and up. Sign up early; the playground and pool get busy and crowded in the summer months.

You might also check out these parks:
St. Catherine's Playground
(First Avenue at 67th Street).
Sutton Place Park
(FDR Drive at 57th Street).

MacArthur Playground
(FDR Drive at 48th Street).

WEST SIDE/RIVERSIDE PARK

Hippo Park Playground at Riverside Drive and 91st Street. * This is one of our favorites, with adult and baby hippo statues ideal for climbing. It's extremely clean, and monitored by a parents' association as well as by the Parks Department. Picnic tables, benches, slides, a sandbox, seesaws, swings, and climbing equipment are shaded by fifty-year-old oak trees. This playground was specially designed for kids ages two to seven.

PS 87 Playground at 77th Street and Amsterdam. This playground was completely gutted and redone within the past two years. What a clever place! Lots of interesting structures to climb on, monkey bars for all size kids-even pretend kiosks for kids who want to play "store."

Riverside Drive at 76th Street. * Here you'll find nicely divided sections for infants and toddlers, plenty of climbing equipment, swings, and a gentle circular sprinkler system. There is a separate sandbox, a nice grassy area, and a basketball court for older children nearby. Bring your sunscreen; there isn't a lot of shade.

River Run Playground at 83rd Street and Riverside. * This is Pamela's favorite "new" place. This playground was recently renovated, and true to its name has a "river" running through the center (with about an inch of water in it). The water is turned on in this park if the temperature reaches 75 degrees. The playground also features a sandbox with faces sculpted into the perimeter, tons of climbing equipment for all ages, a mini carousel, and swings for all sizes.

A friend of Pamela's held her daughter's third birthday party here this summer, and the kids had a blast! You must call the Parks Department for a permit, but it's free, and there are three picnic tables there to hold your pizza and cake. And remember this is New York—you can get pizza delivered directly to the playground!

Other Riverside Park playgrounds are located at:
Riverside Drive at 97th Street.
Riverside Drive at 110th Street.
Riverside Drive at 123rd Street.

DOWNTOWN

Hudson River Park Playground * (Chambers at Greenwich Street). A thriving downtown favorite, this clean, enclosed playground sits across from the esplanade of the Hudson River. All the equipment is labeled by age group, and there's a separate section for tables. There are swings, a sand table, a sliding bridge, climbing structures, sprinklers, and some of the most imaginative play equipment in the city.

Battery Park * (Battery Park City). Located at the tip of Manhattan, this park attracts a number of tourists. While the swings and slides (across from the entrance to the Staten Island

Ferry) are old and outdated, the grassy park itself has a fabulous view and is a pleasant place for picnicking.

Also for downtown parents and tots:
PS 40
(Second Avenue at E. 19th Street).
Union Square Park
(Broadway at E. 16th Street).
Washington Square Park
(W. Fourth and MacDougal Streets).
Duane Park
(East Stuyvesant High School).
Abingdon Square Park
(Bleecker and Bank Streets).
James J. Walker Park
(Leroy Street and Seventh Avenue).

PUBLIC LIBRARIES

Beginning at six months, children are good candidates for short library visits. Sit and relax while your toddler listens during story time, watches a short film with popular characters, or participates in an art and crafts project.

The New York Public Library system puts out a free booklet every month listing each branch's activities for children, but proximity to your home is the key in choosing what to do. Stop in or call and see what's going on.

Library branches with children's activities are listed below, by neighborhood.

UPPER EAST SIDE
96th Street
112 E. 96th Street bet. Park
and Lexington Avenues
289-0908

67th Street
328 E. 67th Street bet. First
and Second Avenues
734-1717

Webster
1465 York Avenue bet. 77th and 78th Streets
288-5049

Yorkville
222 E. 79th Street bet. Second
and Third Avenues
744-5824

UPPER WEST SIDE
Bloomingdale
150 W. 100th Street at Amsterdam Avenue
222-8030

Columbus
742 Tenth Avenue bet. 50th
and 51st Streets
586-5098

Riverside
127 Amsterdam Avenue at 65th Street
870-1810

St. Agnes
444 Amsterdam Avenue at 81st Street
877-4380

MIDTOWN

Donnell Library Center

20 W. 53rd Street bet. Fifth and Sixth Avenues

621-0636

This special branch boasts the largest collection of children's and young adult books in the city. Moreover, it houses Christopher Robin's original Winnie-the-Pooh stuffed animals (Pooh, Tigger, Eeyore, Piglet, and Kanga), who live in the second floor children's room.

Epiphany

228 E. 23rd Street bet. Second
and Third Avenues

679-2645

Kips Bay

446 Third Avenue at 31st Street

683-2520

DOWNTOWN

Hudson Park

66 Leroy Street at Seventh Avenue

243-6876

Jefferson Market

425 Sixth Avenue at 10th Street

243-4334

Lower East Side

New Amsterdam

9 Murray Street bet. Broadway
and Church Streets

732-8186

Tompkins Square

33 E. 10th Street bet. Avenues A and B

228-4747

OTHER ACTIVITIES FOR YOU AND YOUR CHILD

Everything in this section is worthy of a gold star.

The Bronx Zoo

185 Street at Southern Boulevard

718-220-5100

At the Bronx Zoo, the largest in the United States, animals roam in large, natural settings. The Sky Ferry takes visitors through the park-a nice rest for a tired toddler and his exhausted parent. Visit the children's area, a petting zoo where youngsters can pet and feed some smaller animals and go on rides. Admission is $9 for adults and $5 for children two to twelve. Children under two are free and Wednesdays are free for everyone. Admission to the children's zoo is an additional $3.

The Children's Museum of Manhattan

212 W. 83rd Street bet. Broadway
and Amsterdam Avenue

721-1234

This interactive museum allows young children to explore, touch, and investigate its various exhibits. Its size has doubled since our first edition and the museum offers more than ever before for children of all ages. The Creative Corner is an early childhood center (for ages four and under) where children can paint, color, and play with educational toys in a specially designed kids' room. Exhibits change yearly, but you will always find something geared toward the under two set here. Story hours, puppet shows, and other activities are offered throughout the museum. They also offer terrific birthday parties that are popular for two and three olds. Admission is $6 for adults and children over one; children under one are free; seniors 65 and over are $3. Strollers or carriages must be folded up and checked at the door.

The Children's Museum of the Arts
72 Spring Street at Broadway
274-0986

You can spend an entire afternoon at this hands-on museum, which offers exhibits as well as activities for children. You and your child can do arts and crafts, make a poster for Dad, or create a T-shirt design. Slides, climbing equipment, and a dress-up corner are also available. Two- and three-year-olds love this museum. Ages eighteen months and over: $4 per person on weekdays and $5 per person on weekends.

The American Museum of Natural History
79th Street at Central Park West
769-5100

Even when the Museum of Natural History fills with toddlers and their parents, it's so huge and full of hands-on exhibits and fascinating things to see that you'll hardly notice the crowd. Little children stare in wonder at the lifelike dioramas and those spectacular dinosaurs. Parents love bringing their children to the Whale's Lair, where little ones can run around on the huge floor under the giant blue whale. And for your convenience, there's a child-friendly cafeteria, located in the basement. Adult admission is $6, children are $3, and seniors and students are $4.

Metropolitan Museum of Art
Fifth Avenue at 82nd Street
535-7710

There are times you just need a good place to take a sleeping baby while you stroll around by yourself or with a friend. And even when your toddler is awake, the Met does have some open spaces, such as the reflecting garden, where the little one can roam. Strollers are not allowed on Sundays, but the museum will provide you with a backpack for your child when you check your stroller. We found that our toddlers were good for about an hour. Suggested donations are $8 for adults and $4 for students and seniors, but you can give whatever you want. Children under twelve are admitted free.

Barnes & Noble/Barnes & Noble Junior
Locations throughout the city.

These are more like community centers than bookstores. Introduce your children to the kids' sections, where they can listen to you read a story or lie on the floor to look at books by themselves. In addition, the stores have special scheduled readings, Gymboree story time, and bedtime stories. Schedules change weekly, so call ahead or drop by for a listing of events. Most Barnes & Noble stores are open from 9 A.M. to 11 P.M.; all events are free.

Scandinavia House
58 Park Avenue bet. 37th and 38th Streets
879-9779
www.amscan.org

As we were going to press, we found out about the new Scandinavia House and its Heimbold Family Children's Center, which offers regular programs and activities for children and families. Scandinavia House provides a cultural link between the U.S. and five Nordic countries. Though this place is not tried and true like our other listings, it's definitely worth checking out.

INDOOR PLAY SPACES

This section was a lot bigger in our first edition, but since then many play spaces closed and have not been replaced. Some classes such as Funworks and Child's Play do offer drop-in hours where you can use the classroom facilities like a play space. Indoor play spaces are a child's dream: places to run, jump, and climb with lots of other kids on a variety of playthings. Our experience is that it's usually better to go early in the day when the facilities tend to be less crowded and cleaner. No matter how many attendants are on duty, keep a careful eye on your child. And wash your little one's hands when you leave (kiddie colds spread like wildfire).

Playspace
2473 Broadway at 92nd Street
769-2300

Playspace is a big indoor playground with tubes and tunnels to climb through, an Olympic-sized sandbox, slides, a little-kid climbing wall, a tree house, ride-on toys, puppets and costumes. Children from six months to six years are welcome, and there's a separate area for children under two, so they're safe from big-kid play. An adult must accompany all children, although the staff monitors children's activities at all times. The cost is $5.50 per person; the second parent is free. A cafe is open until one hour before closing; no outside food is allowed in. Birthday parties are popular here, too.

Rain or Shine
202 E. 29th Street bet. Second
and Third Avenues, 4th floor
532-4420

This space is designed to resemble a natural rain forest, and accommodates children from 6 months to 6 years. There is a dress-up stage and a large play house with a fully equipped wood kitchen, as well as pop-a-shot basketball, large ride-on toys, a rock climbing wall, soft blocks, and more. Adults enter free and children are admitted for $6.95 for two hours. Times vary so call ahead. Downstairs is a store with toys, cribs, linens, and clothing—just about anything a child might want or need. Rain or Shine also hosts a variety of birthday parties, and offers many unique classes for children ages 9 months to 5 years, including yoga, cooking, drama, gymnastics, and music.

CONCERTS, SHOWS AND SPECIAL EVENTS

When your child is between two and three years old, he may be ready to enjoy one of the city's many shows, concerts, or special events that are produced especially for children. Watch for:

Performances of The Big Apple Circus (at Damrosch Park behind Lincoln Center from October through December), Sesame Street Live (at The Theater at Madison Square Garden in February), the Madison Square Garden Ice Shows (throughout the winter), and Barney, Baby Bop, and the gang (at Radio City Music Hall in January). Blues Clues, Rugrats, and Pokemón at Radio City at various times during the year. Call Ticketmaster or Telecharge for ticket prices and purchases.

Children's theater shows are offered throughout the year by The Puppet Company (741-1646), Puppetworks (718-965-6058), TADA! (627-1732), The Paper Bag Players (362-0431), and Tribeca Performing Arts Center (346-8510).

❋ Call for prices, schedules, and information; some shows are for children age three and over.

❋ The Lolli Pops Concert Series introduces children to classical music and the orchestra at hour-long concerts. Produced by The Little Orchestra Society (971-9500), the concerts are wonderful for children ages three to five.

❋ The Swedish Cottage Marionette Theater produces children's classics at the theater in Central Park at W. 81st Street (988-9093). Kid favorites here have included *Cinderella*, *Rumpelstiltskin,* and *Gulliver's Travels*. Tickets are $4 for children, $5 for adults. Call ahead for reservations.

❋ New York Theater Ballet's "Once Upon a Ballet" Family Series at the Florence Gould Hall (355-6160) is ballet made for children. Though the offerings change each year, *The Nutcracker* is always included in the package.

6 · after-school activities

Preschoolers are tremendously curious about the world and have great capacity to learn. Today many children ages 3 and younger are enrolled in programs designed to expand creativity, enhance social skills and improve fitness. They might take violin lessons, attempt computer games, or plunge into the muddy delights of clay. Many toddlers enjoy tumbling or the challenge of martial arts classes, while others study languages, take ballet and learn to swim.

Never before have there been so many choices for your child. But a word of caution: beware of over-scheduling. Every city baby, no matter how bright, needs free time to play with friends or simply to be alone.

CHOOSING A PROGRAM

The hardest part of choosing a program is determining the best, most wonderful activity for your child when there are so many great options available. It's easy to become overzealous in your approach to your child's happiness and well-being, but you have to keep your perspective. Remember to be light-hearted about your child's free time. You're not sending him off to become a neurosurgeon or master violinist, but exposing him to activities that may or may not become large parts of his life. Finding a program ultimately should be a child-directed process. Rebecca tried ballet, gymnastics, soccer, and modern dance before falling in love with ice skating; now she's been skating for three years. Alexander tried acting, soccer, and Taekwondo, among other activities, and still hasn't settled on one "thing." Ideally, you want your child to experiment and learn, and have a great time, too!

Most classes are offered once a week on a year-long, semester-long, or per class basis. A more intensive class, like a violin class, might meet twice a week. Our kids have enjoyed taking up to three or four classes per week, but don't push; you don't want to force anything, or you'll end up making a chore out of what should be a fun, passion-driven experience. In this chapter you'll find classes in art, dance, music, pottery, and theater, as well as a number of sports and personal enrichment programs, language and computer classes, and other programs like chess.

Whatever you choose, be sure to take convenience into account. We recommend choosing classes within ten blocks of your home.

Here are a few more things to think about when choosing a class or program:

How long has the school/gym/academy been in business?

✳ **How large are classes?**

✳ **How many teachers/coaches are there?**

✳ **Must you commit to a full year, by the semester, or by the class?**

To make the process as easy as possible for you, we have listed classes in every subject appropriate for your city baby. Our kids and our friends' kids have tried many of these programs with happy results. But be sure to check out each program carefully yourself. Notice how the afternoon is structured, and how the teachers interact with the children.

You can also contact the Parent's League (at 737-7385) for more information on after-school activities available throughout the city. Good luck—and remember to have fun!

ONE-STOP SHOPPING: AFTER-SCHOOL INSTITUTIONS

Our "after-school institutions" really are one-stop shopping meccas, offering a multitude of programs for children of all ages-everything from art, music, gymnastics, and cooking, to science and Jewish culture. As your child gets older, he can even join a swim team or basketball league. These all-purpose after-school institutions make your life easy (always a plus for City Moms), provide everything your child could need. The following are the best of these super schools with programs for children up to 3 years old.

Asphalt Green
90th-92nd Streets at York Avenue
369-8890 for catalog
www.asphaltgreen.com

This huge, modern fitness complex has an extensive Youth Aquatics program for children 4 months and up; the instructor ratio is 5:1. There is also a variety of gymnastics, indoor/ outdoor soccer, and basketball classes, as well as instruction in karate and chess. This is one of the best pools in the city for learning to swim.

Chelsea Piers
Pier 62, 23rd Street and Twelfth Avenue
336-6500
www.chelseapiers.com

This enormous sports complex has it all: huge, two-level gym, an entire track, a sand volleyball court, a climbing wall, a three-level driving range, twin hockey rinks, soccer fields, roller hockey rink—you name it. Tumbling classes are offered for children ages 3 and up.

Discovery Programs

251 W. 100th Street at West End Avenue
749-8717

Discovery Programs offers a range of interesting, creative classes for children from toddlers to age 7. The Young Leonardos class brings together artistic creativity and scientific problem solving by exploring the outside world, while the Young Explorers class learns about cultures throughout the world. Taekwondo, ballet, and acting classes are also offered.

The Jewish Community Center of the West Side

15 W. 65th Street, 8th floor, bet.
Columbus Avenue and Central Park West
580-0099
www.jjcnyc.org

A wonderful resource for Upper West Side parents, The JCC offers several classes for kids, including the popular Art-N-Orbit classes (described on page 104), and basketball and soccer. There are also many toddler and Mommy and Me classes, as well as great programs in family health and education.

92nd Street Y

1395 Lexington Avenue at 92nd Street
996-1100
www.92ndsty.org

Here classes include tennis, circus arts, chess, cooking, computers, science, soccer, Taekwondo, gymnastics, swimming, music (including guitar and piano instruction), and dance (including ballet, Isadora for Children, and modern dance classes). Art classes include Learning from the Masters, in which kids create original artwork based on the media and techniques of famous artists; and A Course of a Different Color, in which children explore their ideas, dreams, and fantasies through mask making, book making, clay sculpting, painting, collage, and more. Kelly and Alexander have taken many classes here over the years.

Rhinelander Children's Center

350 E. 88th Street bet. First
and Second Avenues
876-0500

In Rhinelander's After School Arts & Smarts club, kindergartners and first-graders take part in the KinderClub, exploring art, music, and computers, and engaging in dramatic play, dance, outdoor play, and cooking. In The After School Visual & Performing Arts Program, kids can take classes in art, music, fashion design, cooking, singing, dance, computers, ceramics, pottery, sculpture, woodworking, chess, and more.

74th Street Magic

510 E. 74th Street bet. York and the river
737-2989

74th Street Magic offers a wealth of activities for kids. There are music classes that explore the sounds of reggae, jazz, and more; science and exploration classes; Kindermusik classes that take kids on musical adventures with song, dance, stories, and games; various Tumble Time classes that provide gymnastics instruction for kids of different ages; and Magical Movement classes that integrate dance! Your child can also take art and music classes, as well as classes that incorporate stories, puppets, science activities, games, and more.

THE ARTS
Arts Classes

After-School Art, Inc.

510 E. 74th Street (at 74th Street Magic)
bet. York Avenue and the East River
718-941-4885

In Mark Rosenthal's After-School Art program, children explore different media, create their own projects, work on fine motor skills, and have fun in general. A professional painter and former medical illustrator, Mark has taught art for over 20 years. He often tells fairy tales and myths during class. This is Rebecca's favorite art class. Each class is limited to fifteen children, and with ten or more children a second teacher is present.

Art-N-Orbit

Reebok Sports Clubs, East and West
160 Columbus Avenue at 67th Street
330 E. 61st Street bet. First and
Second Avenues
Jewish Community Center

of the Upper West Side
15 W. 65th Street, 8th floor, bet.
Columbus Avenue and Central Park West
The Children's Museum of Manhattan
212 W. 83rd Street bet. Broadway
and Amsterdam Avenue
420-0474

Art-N-Orbit offers art and science programs for children ages 18 months to 10 years old. Classes last between forty-five minutes to an hour once a week, and are offered on a semester basis (September to December, January to March, April to June); summer classes are offered as well. Classes are $450 per semester, and are limited to 15 children. Rebecca really enjoyed the class she took here. Art-N-Orbit also does fabulous birthday parties.

Create a Day

57 E. 75th Street bet. Park
and Madison Avenues
452-2560

Create a Day stretches imaginations with art, creative play, and wonderful props. The theme changes every week and takes your child on exciting adventures by creating a new look every time. One week the room may be set up to resemble the moon and your child is an astronaut, and the following week, a circus featuring your child as an acrobat, or maybe the rainforest with your child as a tour-guide. Ages 2 to 5, with a maximum of eight children in each class. The cost is $385 per 10-class session. Reservations are recommended, though not required.

Gymtime/Rhythm & Glues
1520 York Avenue at 80th Street
861-7732

Kids can take art, music, cooking, and dance classes, as well as combination classes like music/art, music/cooking, gym/cooking, and music/gym in this popular East Side program.

Hi Art!
362-8190
www.hiartkids.com

Hi Art! is an ambitious ten-week series of workshops designed to introduce children ages 2 to 12 to "real" art in highly imaginative and creative ways. Classes are held in galleries and museums throughout the city as well as in a midtown studio, where children study opera, ballet, theater, and symphonies, and engage in ongoing art projects designed to help them understand how actual artists work. Each class series is centered around a contemporary musical work.

Dance Classes

The Ailey School
211 W. 61st Street, 3rd floor,
bet. Amsterdam and West End Avenues
767-0590, ext. 506

The official school of the Alvin Ailey American Dance Theater offers a First Steps Program for children ages 3 to 6. Ballet is taught in graded levels, and classes incorporate other forms of dance (Dunham, Graham-based modern, Horton, and Limon techniques; West African, Spanish, and East Indian dance,

mime, and floor gymnastics for boys) as children progress through the curriculum.

American Youth Dance Theater
434 E. 75th Street, #1C, bet. First
and York Avenues
717-5419

Kids 2 and older learn ballet and creative dance, tap, and jazz.

The Bridge for Dance
2726 Broadway, 3rd floor, at 104th Street
749-1165

Children ages 3 and up learn expressive movement, while ages 6 and up begin studying ballet, tap, and pre-jazz.

Broadway Dance Center
221 W. 57th Street at Broadway
582-9304, ext. 25
www.bwydance.com

Broadway Dance Center offers children ages 3 to 14 fun, creative, and challenging classes in ballet, tap, jazz, hip-hop, creative movement, pre-dance, voice, acting, and theater performance. They also have a youth performance company, A.I.M., or Arts in Motion—providing an opportunity for young dancers to perform in the community. Past students at the Broadway Dance Center have performed in *Miss Saigon, Annie Get Your Gun, Lion King*, and other Broadway plays.

Chinese Folk Dance Company
New York Chinese Cultural Center

390 Broadway, 2nd floor, bet. Walker
and White Streets
334-3764

In this Chinatown cultural center, children ages 3 ½ and older can study Chinese language, Chinese dance, Chinese acrobatics, Chinese opera, and Chinese painting. All nationalities are welcome.

Dance for Children
Murray Street Studio
19 Murray Street bet. Broadway
and Church Street
608-7681

Children ages 3 to 5 explore the basic vocabulary of movement in the Creative Movement class, exercising their imaginations through ideas, images, and stories.

Djoniba Dance and Drum Center
37 E. 18th Street, 7th floor, bet.
Broadway and Park Avenue South
477-3464
www.djoniba.com

Children 3 to 16 can take classes in African dance, African drums, Capoeira, and ballet at this downtown studio.

The School for Education in Dance and the Related Arts
254-3194

Taught in schools and day care centers throughout the city, this is an interrelated arts program that includes movement, music, theater games for self esteem, exposure to visual quality arts, and tumbling as it applies to dance-all combined in one class. The purpose is to deal with the creative process at the earliest possible moment of a child's development, for lifetime use. If this program is not available in your child's school, you can call to discuss ways to bring it into your child's school.

In Grandma's Attic
Studio Maestro
48 W. 68th Street bet. Columbus Avenue
and Central Park West
The Basement Space
102 W. 75th Street at Columbus Avenue
Peggy Levine
212 W. 92nd Street bet. Broadway
and Amsterdam Avenue
Playspace
2473 Broadway at W. 92nd Street
The Ward Studio
145 W. 28th Street, #8F, bet.
Sixth and Seventh Avenues
Civic Center Synagogue
49 White Street bet. Church Street
and Broadway
726-2362

This is a fantasy-based creative dance program for children ages 2 to 12. In Budding Ballerina (2 years) children dance to nursery rhymes and favorite stories; in Fairies and Fantasy (3-6 years) children revisit favorite fairytales and learn new tales and stories.

Greenwich House Music School

46 Barrow Street bet. Bleecker
and Bedford Streets
242-4770
www.gharts.org

Greenwich House Music School has been providing high quality, affordable music education since 1902. Children ages 2 to 7 can choose from classes in music, art, ballet, and musical theater.

Judy Lasko Modern Dance

Alexander Robertson School
3 W. 95th Street bet. Central Park West
and Columbus
864-3143

This school offers modern dance classes for children ages 3 and up. Judy Lasko has been teaching for 35 years, and is both a dancer and Orff music teacher.

Kids Co-Motion

West Park Presbyterian Church
165 W. 86th Street at Amsterdam Avenue
Rebecca Kelly Dance Studio
579 Broadway bet. Prince and Houston Streets
The Soundings
280 Rector Place
The Maternal Fitness Studio
108 E. 16th Street bet. Park Avenue
and Irving Place
www.rebeccakellyballet.com
431-8489

Choreographer Rebecca Kelly and her husband, dancer Craig Brashear founded this unique creative program in 1991. Kids Co-Motion emphasizes a productive, positive learning experience. In the after-school program kids ages 3 to 7 are introduced to ballet and modern dance with emphases on creative movement and active listening to music.

Kinderdance®

579-5270
www.kinderdance.org

Kinderdance® is a developmental dance, movement and fitness program for children ages 2 to 8. Classes are a combination of warm-up, motor skills, ballet, gymnastics, creative movement, and tap dance. This is a popular program taught in 30 different elementary schools throughout the city; outside students are accepted at some Upper West Side and Chelsea locations. You can also call about getting Kinderdance® into your own child's school.

Manhattan Ballet School

149 E. 72nd Street bet. Lexington
and Third Avenues
535-6556

At this 40-year-old neighborhood school children are taught classical ballet in a traditional manner. Children from ages 2 to 6 study creative movement and pre-ballet.

The Lucy Moses School for Music and Dance

129 W. 67th Street bet. Broadway
and Amsterdam Avenue
362-8060

For almost 50 years, The Lucy Moses School has offered a variety of classes in dance, music, theater, and the visual arts for children ages 12 months and up. A nurturing faculty makes learning the arts a positive experience for children.

Perichild Program
132 Fourth Avenue, 2nd floor,
bet. 13th and 12th Streets
505-0886
www.peridance.com

Located at the Peridance Center, the Perichild Program offers technique classes in ballet, modern, jazz, tap, hip-hop, and Taekwondo for children ages 2 and up.

Shake, Rhythm and Roll
West Side Dance Project
348 W. 42nd Street bet. Eighth
and Ninth Avenues
563-6781

The West Side Dance Project offers dance and music education programs for children ages 3 and up. Classes are offered in instrumental music (on all instruments), music introduction, voice, creative movement, classical ballet, modern jazz, and tap. Classes are also held at an Upper West Side location.

Music Classes
Bloomingdale School of Music
323 W. 108th Street bet. Broadway
and Riverside Drive
663-6021

www.bloomingdalemusic.org

Bloomingdale School of Music offers a variety of children's classes, including, keyboard, guitar, violin, recorder, chamber music, and Musical Adventures and More Musical Adventures, in which kids develop music skills through song, creative movement, listening, and playing.

Campbell Music Studio
305 West End Avenue at 74th Street
436 E. 69th Street bet. York
and First Avenues
496-0105

Felicia and Jeffrey Campbell have been teaching music to children for almost 20 years. Music classes for children ages 18 months to 5 years include live music, singing, movement, solfege, stories, notation, and original songs (Felicia writes them all).

Church Street School for Music and Art
74 Warren Street bet. W. Broadway
and Greenwich Street
571-7290

This school offers a variety of classes in music and art for children ages 22 months and older. Classes are offered in everything from Music and Movement to Visual Art, with an emphasis on the process of making art in a relaxed setting. A children's chorus, private lessons, and music therapy are also available.

Diller-Quaile School Of Music
24 E. 95th Street bet. Madison

and Fifth Avenues
369-1484
www.diller-quaile.org

Diller-Quaile is a New York institution. Through their Early Childhood Program this family-based school offers a number of music classes for children from 2 to 7 years, including Music and Movement, Dalcroze Eurythmics, Story Dramatization, Chorus, Creative Movement, Meet the Instrument, and Instrument Making. Classes meet for a full year. A 45-minute Rug Concert is given once a month, on Friday afternoons and Saturday mornings, for children both enrolled and not enrolled in school; concerts introduce children to all the instruments of the orchestra, plus additional instruments (a tabla player comes once a year), and all kinds of singing voices. The concerts also involve singing, movement, and the opportunity for audience members to play rhythm instruments. This is one of the most established music schools on the Upper East Side.

Family Music Center

Asphalt Green
555 E. 90th Street at York Avenue
275 W. 96th Street at Broadway
864-2476

Colleen Itzen was the first Kindermusik® teacher in Manhattan, and still offers the program to children ages newborn to 7. In these music and movement classes children enjoy singing, rhyming, instrument playing, dancing, and composing. Private instruction on the piano is also available.

The French-American Conservatory of Music

154 W. 57th Street, Suite 136
(Carnegie Hall), at Seventh Avenue
246-7378
www.sacmusic.org

The French-American Conservatory of Music, located in the historic Carnegie Hall studios, offers Kindermusik® classes for children ages 3 and up, as well as private instrumental and vocal instruction for ages 4 and older.

Greenwich House Music School

46 Barrow Street bet. Bleecker
and Bedford Streets
242-4770
www.gharts.org

See entry on page 107.

Mary Ann Hall's Music for Children

2 E. 90th Street bet. Fifth and
Madison Avenues
(800) 633-0078

These creative classes for kids ages 2 to 8 weave music in and out of poetry, books, dance, drama, and art. Kelly has taken many classes here with Alexander and Angela, and always finds them to be warm and upbeat.

Mozart for Children

129 W. 67th Street bet. Broadway
and Amsterdam Avenue
15 Gramercy Park on 20th Street
off Park Avenue
120 E. 87th Street bet. Lexington
and Park Avenues

942-2743

Debbie Surowicz's popular classes introduce children ages 1 1/2 to 7 to classical music through singing, rhythmic instruments, and choreographed dances. Classes include live music and visits from various musicians. Private mini-group classes are also available at your own location.

Music, Fun & Learning

339 E. 84th Street bet. First and
Second Avenues
263 W. 86th Street at West End Avenue
717-1853

At Music, Fun & Learning children 4 months to 6 years enjoy instruments, movement, stories, and singing in spirited classes featuring live music and colorful props (toddlers come with a parent or caregiver). Teacher and director Barbara Frankel helps kids develop their imagination, coordination, and listening skills while learning about different musical qualities. She also offers private classes in piano and flute, provides entertainment at birthday parties, and demonstrates instruments and songs from around the world in a participatory song and story hour called Tuneful Tales, held several times a year. Call for details.

The School for Strings

419 W. 54th Street bet. Ninth
and Tenth Avenues
315-0915

This Suzuki-based school teaches violin, cello, and piano to children ages 3 and up.

Beginners take a full course of study, which includes a weekly individual lesson, musicianship class, group class, and parent class (in which parents learn the rudiments of the child's instrument). After the first year, parents are no longer required to take classes, but are expected to remain actively involved in the child's instruction. As children advance, study of orchestra and, eventually, chamber music is incorporated into their routine. The School for Strings is also one of the leading teacher training schools for violin, cello, and piano in the U.S.

Third Street Music School Settlement

235 E. 11th Street bet. Second
and Third Avenues
777-3240

This school was founded in 1894 as a settlement house for anyone interested in art and music, regardless of talent or ability to pay. In addition to being a fully licensed pre-school with an arts focus, the school also offers a variety of music classes in voice, and various instruments and forms of performance (chamber music, ensemble, etc.) for children ages 18 months and up. Some dance and art classes are also offered.

Turtle Bay Music School

244 E. 52nd Street bet. Second
and Third Avenues
753-8811

Turtle Bay, founded in 1925, is a full-service music school that offers private music classes in all instruments for children ages 18 months and older. This warm and friendly school is ideal for midtown families.

Pottery

Greenwich House Pottery
16 Jones Street bet. Bleecker
and W. Fourth Streets
242-4106

This long-established school offers classes exclusively for children, and also classes in which children ages 2½ to 5 collaborate with parents or caregivers to create imaginative clay works.

SPORTS
Gymnastics

Gymnastics is a popular after-school activity, especially for girls. If your daughter is an avid gymnast, many of these facilities also offer gymnastics teams.

Asphalt Green
555 E. 90th Street bet. York
and East End Avenues
369-8890 for catalog
www.asphaltgreen.com

Chelsea Piers
Pier 62, 23rd Street at Twelfth Avenue
336-6500
www.chelseapiers.com

Circus Gym
2121 Broadway, 2nd floor, at 74th Street
799-3755

Columbus Gym
606 Columbus Avenue bet. 89th
and 90th Streets
721-0090

Gymtime Gymnastics
1520 York Avenue at 80th Street
861-7732

Jodi's Gym
244 E. 84th Street bet. Second
and Third Avenues
772-7633

Life Sport Gymnastics
West Park Presbyterian Church
165 W. 86th Street at Amsterdam Avenue
769-3131

Sokol New York
420 E. 71st Street bet. First and York Avenues
861-8206

Sutton Gymnastics
20 Cooper Square (Third Avenue at 5th Street)
533-9390

Tumble Town Gymnastics
Baruch College, Room 1125
17 Lexington Avenue at 23rd Street
802-5632

**Wendy Hillard Foundation-
Rhythmic Gymnastics NY**
792 Columbus Avenue,
Suite 17T, at 100th Street
721-3256

Swimming

These locations offer individual and group lessons. A special favorite here is Take Me to the Water; many New Yorkers have taught their children to swim through this program.

Asphalt Green
555 E. 90th Street bet. York
and East End Avenues
369-8890 for catalog
www.asphaltgreen.com

This huge, modern fitness complex has an extensive Youth Aquatics program for children 4 months and up; the instructor ratio is 7:1 for kids 5 and up, and 5:1 for younger.

New York Health and Racquet Club
24 E. 13th Street bet. Fifth Avenue
and University Place
924-4600
1433 York Avenue at 76th Street
737-6666

Private swim classes.

Take Me to the Water
10 locations
828-1756
www.takemetothewater.com

YWCA
610 Lexington Avenue at 53rd Street
655-4500

Yoga

As yoga gains popularity with moms and dads, kids want to join in the fun, too. Here are some studios that offer yoga for kids.

B.K.S. Iyengar Yoga Association
27 W. 24th Street, Suite 800,
bet. Broadway and Sixth Avenue
691-9642

Goodson Parker Wellness Center
30 E. 76th Street, 4th floor,
at Madison Avenue
717-5273

Next Generation Yoga
200 W. 72nd Street, Suite 58,
bet. Broadway and West End Avenue
595-9306
www.nextgenerationyoga.com

Through movement, music, crafts, games, storytelling, and laughter, kids discover the art of yoga. Baby Yoga, Yoga Therapy, Toddler Classes, Mommy & Me, Daddy & Me, and Family Yoga are among the classes offered.

PERSONAL ENRICHMENT PROGRAMS
Computer Classes
Futurekids Computer Learning Center
1628 First Avenue bet. 84th and 85th Streets
717-0110
www.futurekidsnyc.com

At Futurekids Computer Learning Center, children ages 3 to 15 learn the latest technology. Children are introduced to animation, graphics, operating systems, word processing, the Internet, and more—all incorporated with themes and subjects kids love.

The Techno Team Lab
Reebok Sports Club
160 Columbus Avenue at 67th Street
501-1425

Provided by Radicel Education Technology, these classes introduce children ages 3 and older to the use of computers in daily life, and focus on enhancing and enriching academic and creative skills. Classes are small with individualized programs for each child.

Etiquette Classes
Nicole De Vault, Etiquette Consultant
415 E. 37th Street, Suite 22J,
bet. First Avenue and the FDR
481-7280

Nicole De Vault offers private lessons for children ages 3 and older, and will make house calls to work with families in their homes. Parents and children can formulate their own curricula, focusing on table manners, social skills (introductions, eye contact, posture, conversation), phone manners, cross-cultural etiquette, or any combination of the above.

Language Programs
China Institute in America
125 E. 65th Street bet. Park
and Lexington Avenues
744-8181, ext. 142
www.chinainstitute.org

Children ages 3 to 10 gain familiarity with Chinese language and culture through active classroom instruction. Songs, games, and art add to the linguistic and cultural experience.

La Croisette French Language Center
861-7723

La Croisette offers three separate programs in which children learn French through a range of fun, creative activities. In the regular classes, children ages 2 $1/2$ to 9 learn through songs, poems, creative projects, stories, games, and educational videos, while in the Art/French class kids ages 5 to 7 focus on painting, collage, printing, stencils, and more. A Puppetry at La Croisette class centers around puppet making, puppet "discussions," and a small puppet show kids put on for parents-all in French, of course!

Language Workshop for Children
888 Lexington Avenue at 66th Street
396-0830

Children ages 3 to 10 learn French or Spanish in an active environment, filled with songs, play, sports, gymnastics, cuisine, and dance.

7 · kid-friendly restaurants

Yes, dining out with your new baby or toddler can be an enjoyable experience; the choice of restaurant is critical and must meet your needs. They are as follows:

When your child is still an infant, under one year, you want a restaurant that provides stroller or carriage space and a staff that doesn't mind babies.

When your child is a toddler, an understanding staff is even more important since your youngster may knock over a glass of water, rip up the sugar packets, or throw flowers on the floor. Also, the restaurant should provide adequate booster seats and quick service (so you can be in and out of the restaurant in an hour).

Certainly, if you have favorite neighborhood spots with food you already love, you can always look around to see if children are dining there and whether there is adequate space next to tables for a stroller holding a sleeping infant.

But what do you do when you are in an unfamiliar neighborhood? Look for kid-friendly clues: paper rather than cloth table covering, crayons, children's menus, booster seats, highchairs, and interesting sights such as fish tanks, rock pools, gardens, shopping areas, and the like. New York's ethnic restaurants can be wonderful for children. The owners usually like kids; waiters will bring them something to eat right away; and these places can be quite flexible about menu offerings. Coffee shops are good, too, but not necessarily during a frantic lunch hour.

But what about the food? We are not restaurant critics, but we do know what we like where family dining is concerned. Good food for everyone is integral to the dining experience. Out of two zillion options, we are including our favorites for you to dine *en famille*.

Before you go out, consider your child's ability to sit still and eat in a somewhat mannerly fashion. Some days it might be better to stay home and order in.

UPPER EAST SIDE
Barking Dog Luncheonette
1453 York Avenue at 77th Street
861-3600
1678 Third Avenue at 94th Street
831-1800

These are cozy spots with cozy food like meat loaf, pot roast, mashed potatoes, and all-day breakfast stuff. The decor is comfortable, too, with a dog motif.

California Pizza Kitchen
201 E. 60th Street bet. Second
and Third Avenues
755-7773

With all of the great New York pizza in this city, who would have thought that California Pizza Kitchen would be so popular? People like California Pizza Kitchen for its unique style of pizza and for their tremendous variety of toppings. The restaurant is kid-friendly and offers yummy pizzas and pastas for the little ones, as well as high chairs and crayons.

China Fun
1239 Second Avenue at 65th Street
752-0810
1653 Broadway at 51st Street
333-2622
246 Columbus Avenue at 71st Street

580-1516

These restaurants are big and noisy and just our style, with inexpensive generous portions that kids love. In fact, we know a couple of kids hooked on the steamed vegetable dumplings.

Hi Life Bar and Grill
1340 First Avenue at 72nd Street
249-3600
477 Amsterdam Avenue at 83rd Street
787-7199

Yummy bar food and burgers, and now sushi, too! The food here is reasonably priced, and the waitstaff friendly. Take advantage of the kid-appealing early bird specials every weeknight until seven. Don't forget to try the fries—they're fabulous!

Il Vagabondo
351 E. 62nd Street bet. First
and Second Avenues
832-9221

Haven't been here for a while? Remember the bocce court? Kids love it, of course. They don't have to concentrate on eating but can look at an actual ball rolling on a floor really made of dirt . . . in a restaurant! This restaurant is crowded and loud, with Italian fare everybody likes.

Serendipity
225 E. 60th Street bet. Second
and Third Avenues
838-3531

A classic. You're not a New York kid until you've had a foot-long hot dog (which you'll never finish) and a frozen hot chocolate (which your mother will finish quite easily). Lots of great stuff to look at here, from the offerings near the front door to the giant clock and colorful stained glass lampshades. It's also fun to walk up and down the spiral staircase. No strollers or carriages!

Tony's Di Napoli
1606 Second Avenue at 83rd Street
861-8686

This spacious Italian restaurant is a favorite of East Side families, with enormous portions served family style. Strollers are not permitted at the tables, so bring a car seat. Families should come early for best service.

UPPER WEST SIDE
Avenue Bistro
520 Columbus Avenue at 85th Street
579-3194

Scott and Linda Campbell, owners of this French-American bistro, have changed the lives of Upper West Side dads, moms, and babies by introducing Baby Fine, natural and freshly made baby food in flavors such as carrot, tomato potato, sweet pea, pear, and banana. You can order it right off the menu or take a jar home for the little one or yourself—and, believe us, it's that good. The grown-up food is great, too. Avenue Bistro is open for all three meals, and dinner can be crowded and noisy—not ideal for a maneuvering a sleeping baby in a stroller—but it's worth it.

The Boulevard Cafe
2398 Broadway at 88th Street
874-7400

Every Monday night is an all-you-can-eat chicken and ribs night for you, plus a kid's menu. Kid platters come with French fries in a little Chinese take-out carton. There are crayons on the table to occupy young artists while you're waiting. This place is noisy, with lots of room between tables downstairs. Sit upstairs for a great view of Broadway.

Gabriela's
685 Amsterdam Avenue at 93rd Street
961-0574
315 Amsterdam Avenue at 75th Street
875-8532

It's big, bustling, open all the time from breakfast until dinner so you can eat at odd hours, and the place is filled with kids of all ages. Authentic Mexican fare (downright cheap) from tacos, quesadillas, enchiladas, rice and beans for the kids, to more exotic house specialties for you. Be extra early for dinner, or you'll wait.

Josephina

1900 Broadway bet. 63rd and 64th Streets
799-1000

If you're near Lincoln Center and if you're in the mood for healthy, organic California-style eating, this is the place. It's airy, roomy, and kids like it.

Louie's Westside Cafe

441 Amsterdam Avenue at 81st Street
877-1900

This comfortable neighborhood place will prepare anything your kids want. They're happy to push tables together for bigger parties.

Polistina's

2275 Broadway bet. 81st and 82nd Streets
579-2828

Ever since Polistina's opened on the Upper West Side a few years ago, it has been a major hit with neighborhood families. Crayons and coloring books for kids, delicious pizzas, and a comfortable, relaxed atmosphere make this place a winner.

Popover Cafe

551 Amsterdam Avenue at 87th Street
595-8555

Children love the teddy bears that live all around this restaurant; kids can "adopt" one while you enjoy the wonderful food. Freshly baked popovers with strawberry butter are the main attraction here, and well worth waiting for.

MIDTOWN EAST AND WEST
Broadway Diner

590 Lexington Avenue at 52nd Street
486-8838
1726 Broadway at 55th Street
765-0909

This upscale diner is better than most but remains easy on the pocket. The food is typical American fare, including sandwiches, salads, grilled burgers, eggs, and pancakes. This is a good choice if you're in a hurry; you'll have no problem getting in and out in less than an hour.

Ellen's Stardust Diner

1650 Broadway at 51st Street
307-7575

This '50s-style diner features milkshakes, burgers, chicken, and tuna melts, as well as some Mexican dishes and an assortment of salads. The waiters sing and entertain; the kids will enjoy it as much as you will.

Hamburger Harry's*

145 W. 45th Street bet. Broadway
and Sixth Avenue
840-0566

Known for big burgers, Harry's is casual and friendly. The menu has chicken and eggs, too, but this is a place for a burger fan.

Metropolitan Cafe

959 First Avenue bet. 52nd and 53rd Streets
759-5600

Metropolitan is large, busy, and kid-friendly, and its main attraction is the beautiful outdoor garden. The menu reflects Indonesian, French, and Chinese, but mostly American influences.

CHELSEA/FLATIRON

America

9 E. 18th Street bet. Fifth Avenue
and Broadway
505-2110

On weekends this huge, friendly restaurant sets up a kids' reading area with little tables, chairs, and books. A balloon artist wanders through on Saturday and Sunday afternoons making balloon hats and animals. There are lots of highchairs and good food that appeals to the whole family.

Chat 'n Chew

10 E. 16th Street bet. University Place
and Fifth Avenue
243-1616

It feels like you're in a tiny town in the South in the 1950s, but you could only find a place like this in New York. There's plenty to look at in this crowded restaurant, from antique advertising signs to old jukeboxes. If you can take it, there are great deep-fried dishes, too. Chat 'n Chew is best for booster-seat kids.

WEST VILLAGE

Arturo's Pizzeria

106 W. Houston Street at Thompson Street
677-3820

Here's a neighborhood place with a low-key atmosphere friendly to kids. The brick oven pizza, their specialty, is delicious, and the service is quick. Arturo's also serves all types of salads, pastas, and chicken dishes.

Cowgirl Hall of Fame

519 Hudson Street at 10th Street
633-1133

Lil' pardners from all over come to see the Western memorabilia in this cool little shop that stocks everything from sheriff badges to squirt gun holsters to bandanas to rawhide vests. The food appeals, too, with a perfectly messy Frito pie (a bag of chips split open, topped with chili) and a baked potato dessert (vanilla ice cream rolled in powdered cocoa and topped with "sour cream," or whipped cream that sits on a hot fudge pond).

EAST VILLAGE

Miracle Grill

112 First Avenue bet. 6th and 7th Streets
254-2353
415 Bleecker Street between Bank Street
and W. 11th Street
924-1900

This comfortable and reasonably priced restaurant serves excellent black bean soup, lamb, and pork chops. Dine in the garden, if possible—it's beautiful; a nice place to relax when you've been on the go all day.

Two Boots

37 Avenue A bet. 2nd and 3rd Streets
505-2276

Two Boots to Go-Go

74 Bleecker at Broadway
777-1033

Two Boots to Go West
201 W. 11th Street at Seventh Avenue
633-9096
Two Boots Pizzeria
42 Avenue A at 3rd Street
254-1919

The "boots" of Italy and Louisiana kick in for great pizza with creative toppings. Great decor, lots to look at, and a great party atmosphere that's enhanced by lively music.

CENTRAL VILLAGE/NOHO
Noho Star
330 Lafayette Street at Bleecker Street
925-0070

A standard for some Manhattanites, this restaurant has a casual and comfortable atmosphere that easily accommodates kids. You'll find interesting Chinese and Thai food here, as well as kid favorites like pasta, burgers, salad, and chicken.

TRIBECA
Bubby's
120 Hudson Street at North Moore Street
219-0666

The menu at this child-friendly restaurant is standard diner fare but better, with a gourmet twist. Bubby's is best known for its delicious breakfasts; it's a popular brunch spot on weekends.

The Odeon
145 W. Broadway bet. Duane and Thomas Streets
233-0507

Popular with celebrities for years, this restaurant has gained a following among downtown families. It is a cozy spot, with great food and good people watching. Don't skip the fries! The Odeon gives out crayons, proving that kids are welcome.

SOHO
Tennessee Mountain
143 Spring Street at Wooster
431-3993

Be prepared for messy fingers and faces at this BBQ joint. Bringing your children is encouraged here—they get a chef's hat and crayons. You can find some of the best barbecue ribs in the city here; and parents will go for it, too.

The Chains

Somedays you will just need a reliable restaurant where you can have a decent meal with the kids. Special menus, reasonable prices, and highchairs are all to be expected at local and national chains. Popular national chains include Pizzeria Uno and T.G.I. Friday's.

Carmine's
2450 Broadway at 91st Street
362-2200
200 W. 44th Street bet. Broadway and Eighth Avenue
221-3800

Popular, family-style southern Italian food is the specialty here. Carmine's is bustling, fun, and noisy, but the wait can be excruciatingly long. If you go with at least six people, you can make a reservation (and you'll be able to sample more dishes).

Dallas BBQ

1265 Third Avenue at 73rd Street
772-9393
27 W. 72nd Street bet. Columbus Avenue and Central Park West
873-2004
132 Second Avenue at 8th Street
777-5574
132 W. 43rd Street between Sixth Avenue and Broadway
221-9000
21 University Place at 8th Street
674-4450

Inexpensive, big portions of kid favorites from ribs to burgers to corn on the cob make this a great standby.

EJ's Luncheonette

1271 Third Avenue at 73rd Street
472-0600
447 Amsterdam Avenue bet.
81st and 82nd Streets
873-3444
432 Sixth Avenue bet. 9th and 10th Streets
473-5555

Tons of families come for the children's menu featuring everything from PB&J to scrambled eggs. Breakfast is served all day long, an interesting concept. (We call it brinner.) Lines are long for weekend brunch.

Jackson Hole Burgers

1611 Second Avenue bet. 83rd and 84th Street
737-8788
232 E. 64th Street bet. Second and Third Avenues
371-7187
517 Columbus Avenue at 85th Street
362-5177
521 Third Avenue bet. 34th and 35th Streets
679-3264
1270 Madison Avenue and 91st Street
427-2820

This traditional burger joint has every kind of burger and topping you could ever want, as well as great fries, salads, omelets, Tex-Mex stuff, and fantastic chocolate cake and sundaes. Kids love it!

John's Pizzeria

260 W. 44th Street bet. Broadway and Eighth Avenue
391-7560
408 E. 64th Street bet. First and York Avenues
935-2895
48 W. 65th Street bet.
Central Park West and Broadway
721-7001
278 Bleecker Street bet. Sixth and Seventh Avenues
243-1680

Some New York parents we know swear these thin-crust pies from a wood-burning oven are the best in the city. The service is fast;

there's pasta for the rare child that does not eat pizza; there's plenty of room around the tables; and it's noisy, so your child won't stand out among the loud voices of all the other children. Another plus: your child can watch the chefs prepare your pizza.

La Cocina
217 W. 85th Street bet. Broadway
and Amsterdam Avenue
874-0770
2608 Broadway bet. 98th and 99th Streets
865-7333
762 Eighth Avenue bet. 46th and 47th Streets
730-1860

La Cocina features moderately priced but quite generous single tacos, burritos, enchiladas, and more, including large, well-deserved margaritas for the adults. There's plenty of room around the tables. Kids get to choose a marble to take home for their collections.

Ollie's Noodle Shop & Grille
200 W. 44th Street at Seventh Avenue
921-5988
1991 Broadway bet. 67th and 68th Streets
595-8181
2315 Broadway at 84th Street
362-3712
2957 Broadway at 116th Street
932-3300

Early every evening, Ollie's is filled with children who love the soups, noodles—from soft to crispy; from hot to cold—and all the other classic Hong Kong style dishes. Huge portions, moderate prices, and the fastest service a parent could ever hope to find are all huge plusses.

Theme Restaurants
The West 50's now offer big blaring restaurants of all varieties and gimmicks that are sure to attract visitors. Amid the tourists, you won't find a whole lot of New York parents popping in (waiting in line is more like it) as their first choice for dining. However, you may find yourself in that neighborhood or planning a birthday party, and these places do come up in conversation. So here goes:

Hard Rock Cafe
221 W. 57th Street bet. Broadway
and Seventh Avenue
489-6565

Harley Davidson Cafe
1370 Sixth Avenue at 56th Street
245-6000

Jekyll & Hyde
91 Seventh Avenue South
bet. W. 4th and Barrow Streets
989-7701

Mickey Mantle's
52 Central Park South bet. Fifth
and Sixth Avenues
688-7777

Planet Hollywood
140 W. 57th Street bet. Sixth
and Seventh Avenues

333-7827

Coffee Bars

Now that life seems to imitate episodes from *Seinfeld*, it is amazing that we once lived without double iced-mocha lattes. Even more important, that hit of caffeine, administered at opportune moments during the day, does a lot for a mother who has been called into action during the wee hours. Here are two of our favorite places to swill coffee, accompanied by babies and toddlers.

DT:UT

1626 Second Avenue bet. 84th
and 85th Streets
327-1327

This coffee bar/lounge has plenty of space for strollers. The coffee, including delicious lattes and cappuccinos, is good, and the food selection is appealing. Menu items include sandwiches (ham & cheese, tuna fish, and more), as well as gourmet offerings. Lots of quiet corners and tables with sofas and comfortable chairs make this feel like your own living room. A relaxing place for breakfast, lunch, or just a snack—the staff never rushes you.

Starbucks

For branches, call 613-1280.

Although Cooper's, Timothy's (especially the 72nd Street location, where the people-watching and sunshine make it a favorite), and New World (our favorite for food) are cozy, atmosphere and ample space at Starbucks make it a good choice for a group of stroller-clad moms. You can sit for hours and chat over a coffee. (That is, if your munchkin will allow it.) And, if you're hungry, Starbucks offers a nice selection of breakfast foods all day, plus prepared sandwiches for lunch. We couldn't live without our their tall skim lattes. In fact, we wrote the bulk of City Baby at various Starbucks around town.

A FEW WORDS ON BATHROOMS...

We can't even begin to tell you how important this topic is. Once you begin to venture into the word with your child, you'll soon realize the challenge of finding a decent bathroom in the city. New York can frustrate even the most formidable city moms searching for a clean place to change a diaper. To aid you in this important mission, here are some good bathrooms in a variety of neighborhoods. Keep them in mind in case you suddenly find yourself in a bathroom bind. We've noted the best places for diaper changing and nursing; all bathrooms include a handicapped stall unless otherwise noted.

Barnes & Noble

Locations throughout the city.

All the Barnes & Noble stores have bathrooms, and the stores with a Junior section have an oversized stall with a changing station inside.

Starbucks

Locations throughout the city.

All Starbucks have large bathrooms. Most have a diaper deck inside.

See the lists below for some of the nicest spots in town, but remember any hotel will suffice! If you are desperate McDonald's and Burger King have bathrooms, but they are rarely the cleanest. We suggest scoping out your neighborhood for kid-friendly restaurants that will let you use their bathrooms when needed. This will come in handy for potty training, too!

EAST SIDE

If you're anywhere in midtown on the East Side, you're near a number of department stores that provide comfortable, clean bathrooms. Barney's (Madison Avenue at 61st Street), Bergdorf Goodman (Fifth Avenue at 57th Street), Bloomingdale's (Third Avenue at 59th Street), Bendel's (Fifth Avenue at 55th Street), Lord & Taylor (Fifth Avenue at 39th Street), and Saks Fifth Avenue (Fifth Avenue at 50th Street) all have bathrooms with enough stalls so that there's usually not a lineup; all include diaper changing areas and/or couches or chairs nearby or in the stalls that are suitable for diaper changing or nursing.

Here are some other facilities you'll want to know about:

EAST SIDE
FAO Schwarz
767 Fifth Avenue at 59th Street
644-9400
Location: second floor

The New York Palace Hotel*
455 Madison Avenue at 50th Street
888-0131
Location: second floor (take stairs up one flight or the elevator)

The Hotel Pierre
2 E. 61st Street bet. Madison and Fifth Avenues
838-8000
Location: main floor

The Regency Hotel
540 Park Avenue at 60th Street
759-4100
Location: main floor lobby

Tiffany & Company*
727 Fifth Avenue at 57th Street
755-8000
Location: mezzanine

The Waldorf Astoria
301 Park Avenue at 50th Street
355-3000
Location: main floor lobby

WEST SIDE
Manhattan Mall
100 W. 32nd Street at Sixth Avenue
465-0050
Locations: second, fourth, sixth, and seventh floor

The Empire Hotel
44 W. 63rd Street bet. Broadway
and Columbus Avenue
265-7400
Location: mezzanine

New York Hilton
1335 Sixth Avenue at 53rd Street
586-7000
Location: second floor on
the 54th Street side of hotel

Macy's
151 W. 34th Street at Herald Square
695-4400
Locations: cellar, second, sixth,
and seventh floors

The Mayflower Hotel
15 Central Park West at 61st Street
265-0060
Location: lobby

DOWNTOWN
ABC Carpet & Home
888 Broadway at 19th Street
473-3000
Location: second and fourth floors

Bed, Bath & Beyond
620 Avenue of the Americas at 19th Street
255-3550
Location: main floor

Millennium Hilton
55 Church Street bet. Fulton and Dey Streets
693-2311
Location: third floor

SoHo Grand Hotel
310 W. Broadway bet. Grand
and Canal Streets
965-3000
Location: main floor

South Street Seaport
(The Fulton Market) 11 Fulton Street
732-7678 (general information)
Location: mezzanine

Tribeca Grand Hotel
2 Avenue of the Americas
bet. White and Walker Streets
519-6600
Location: lower level past the concierge desk

World Financial Center
The Winter Garden
West Street bet. the World Trade
Center and the Hudson River
945-0505
Location: main floor

PART TWO

shopping for your city baby:

everything you need to have

8 · the big firsts

A baby is to celebrate! First you mark the new arrival with a printed birth announcement, something special, of course, but where do you find exactly the right thing? In the ensuing months, as you watch your baby grow, there will be many joyful and singular moments to celebrate. We call them "the big firsts." For each, New York can provide an expert who will help you make the most of these once-in-a-lifetime occasions. This chapter lists what we've discovered to be the best stationers for buying ready made or personalized birth announcements; the most fun and unusual party places; the absolute best bakeries for ordering that first—and second, and third—birthday cake; the most skillful and entertaining hair cutters, the most reliable shoe stores, and the most artful photographers for that important first portrait.

Of course, you will be taking hundreds of your own photos as your child grows. For Rebecca and Alexander, we always had a camera at hand to record such things as haircuts and parties. But with the second and third child, we found it was easy to overlook either photographing or videotaping their big firsts. To make sure you never miss a special moment, do what lots of moms do: keep a disposable camera in your stroller.

You will be amazed at how fast your baby grows. Just when you are wondering when your baby will ever have enough hair to warrant a real haircut, it will be time to consider another important first: preschool. This is a rite of passage in New York, or anywhere, and we conclude with a few suggestions on how to start exploring the options.

BIRTH ANNOUNCEMENTS

Even in this day of e-mail and Web sites, printed birth announcements are still the most popular way to get the word out about the new addition to your family.

There are several options available. You can purchase ready-made cards at a stationery or party store and fill in your new baby's name, weight, size, and birth date.

Or you can order through a catalog, such as H & F birth announcements-(800) 964-4002. The price for 100 announcements and plain envelopes is $62; envelopes printed with the return address are an additional $12.50. Most parents we know order pre-printed cards. Another alternative, economical too, is to buy plain cards and print announcements from your computer at home. If you have a digital camera, you can even print a snapshot of your little bundle of joy on the card. Kelly did this the second time around, believing that everyone who knew her well already knew about Angela's arrival, and that it was unnecessary to spend hundreds of dollars on birth announcements.

It's a good idea to choose your announcements a month or so in advance of your due date. If you are ordering from a store or catalog, plan on two weeks for printing. Get your envelopes early, and address them in advance. Then, after the baby is born, call the shop with all the details, such as height, weight, sex, and date and time of birth.

New York stationers have everything you could possibly want, and they will ship your selection directly to you. Below, we list the best. These are also great sources for special birthday party invitations for the years to come.

Berkeley Stationers, Inc.
19 W. 44th Street bet.
Fifth and Sixth Avenues
719-5181

Berkeley carries a line of announcements in all price ranges, some discounted, including Crane's, Elite, Encore, Regency, and William Arthur, and many others. Nina, the owner, will work with you to choose exactly what you need. An order of 100 cards can cost anywhere from $50 to $500, with an average of $150 per order. Kelly got Alexander's birth announcements here.

Blacker & Kooby
1204 Madison Avenue at 88th Street
369-8308
www.blackerandkooby.invitations.com

With more than seventy companies to choose from, the selection at Blacker & Kooby is outstanding. It ranges from well-known lines like Crane's, Regency, and William Arthur, to smaller, more creative ones like Blue Mug and Stacy Claire Boyd. At this Carnegie Hill spot, an order for 100 baby announcements starts at $150.

FranMade
250 W. 89th Street bet. Broadway
and West End Avenue
799-9428

Fran Goldman is an advertising executive by day and a card designer by night. Fran's cards are hand-drawn and hand-colored, and can be customized to your specifications. She can also create something entirely new. An order of 100 announcements costs $190. There is an additional fee for new designs. Pam had Rebecca and Benjamin's announcements designed by Fran.

Hudson Street Papers

357 Bleecker Street between 10th
and Charles Streets
229-1065

Hudson Street Papers is a legendary West Village shop where parents can create the announcements of their dreams. In addition to name-brand cards like William Arthur, they offer a choice of 450 varieties made from their unique in-store computerized lettering and design system. With a turn-around time of one week, they are a terrific alternative to more traditional cards. One hundred birth announcements range from $180 to $250.

Hyde Park Stationers

1070 Madison Avenue at 80th Street
861-5710

In comfortable surroundings, you can sit and look at a variety of manufacturer's lines, including Crane's, William Arthur, Chase, Elite, and Regency. Prices for an order of 100 cards range from $75 to $700.

Jamie Ostrow

876 Madison Avenue at 71st Street
734-8890

Beautiful announcements, as well as personal stationery and invitations, designed by Jamie Ostrow fill this lovely store. There are many other lines to choose from, including Crane's. An order of 100 announcements starts at $170.

Kate's Paperie

561 Broadway at Prince Street
941-9816
8 W. 13th Street at Fifth Avenue
633-0570
1282 Third Avenue at 74th Street
396-3670

These crème de la crème of paper stores carry an outstanding selection of baby announcements, including unusual and hard-to-find manufacturers, such as Sweet Pea, Indelible Ink, Blue Mug, and Stacy Claire Boyd. Working with an experienced staff person, customers can also design their own cards and choose from dozens of papers and type styles. Announcements can then be printed by letterpress if so desired. An order of 100 cards starts at $150. Kate's hands-on approach and the store's welcoming atmosphere make new moms feel right at home.

Laura Beth's Baby Collection

300 E. 75th Street, Suite 24E
717-2559

Laura Beth, a former buyer in the Baby Department at Barney's New York, meets one-on-one with stylish Moms-to-be to help them select their birth announcements as well as linens and accessories. She offers high-end cards, both whimsical and classic, at prices 20 percent below retail-or 100 cards for $125. Lines include Stacy Claire Boyd and Blue Mug Designs.

Lincoln Stationers

1889 Broadway at 63rd Street
459-3500

Lincoln Stationers is a wonderful resource for the Upper West Side. They carry all major brands, or you can create your own with the staff.

Little Extras

676 Amsterdam Avenue at 93rd Street
721-6161

Little Extras carries many of the top lines, such as Stacy Claire Boyd, Regency, Sweet Pea, Encore, Indelible Ink, and Lalli, all discounted. Orders of $200 or less are discounted 10 percent, and orders over $200 are discounted fifteen percent. An order of 100 cards costs a little over $100. This comfortable store delivers for free if you live on the Upper East or Upper West Side.

Paper Emporium

835A Second Avenue at 44th Street
697-6573

Paper Emporium has a small, quality selection including Crane's, Regency, William Arthur, and Carlson Craft. This store has one of the fastest turnarounds: three days on most orders. The price range for 100 cards is from $100 to $400.

Papyrus Cards & Stationery

1270 Third Avenue at 73rd Street
717-1060
852 Lexington Avenue bet. 64th
and 65th Streets
717-0002
107 E. 42nd Street at Lexington
Avenue (Grand Central Station)
490-9894
2157 Broadway bet. 75th and 76th Streets
501-0102
www.papyrusonline.com

Papyrus is an upscale chain of fine papers and cards, with lines like William Arthur, Crane's, Stacy Claire Boyd, Cross My Heart, and Carlson Craft. An order of 100 announcements costs between $240 and $500, and is usually shipped to the customer between seven and ten days. Papyrus can be found in malls around the Tri-state area. This is also a great place to find special gift items.

Rebecca Moss, Ltd.

510 Madison Avenue at 53rd Street
832-7671

This handsome store sells some prepackaged birth announcements, but focuses on big manufacturers' books, including those of Crane's, William Arthur, Stacy Claire Boyd, and Cross My Heart. An order of 100 announcements costs approximately $150.

Mrs. John L. Strong
Barney's

660 Madison Avenue at 61st Street, 2nd floor
833-2059

Elegant and exquisite, this stationer is one of the few in New York that still practices the art of hand engraving. Prices start at $500 for 100 announcements and go up according to style and detail. Mrs. John L. Strong is the engraver of choice to the city's socially prominent; she is a favorite of *Martha Stewart Living*. You may see her showroom by appointment. Some of her cards are also sold at Barney's.

Tiffany & Co.
727 Fifth Avenue at 57th Street
755-8000

Tiffany & Co. has a large stationery department offering both the Tiffany brand and some Crane lines. The Tiffany cards are simple, elegant, engraved, and costly. The average price for 100 announcements is more than $500. They have recently introduced new lines of cards that are a bit more fun.

Venture Stationers
1156 Madison Avenue at 85th Street
288-7235

One of the most popular East Side shops for stationery and announcements, Venture carries a large selection of manufacturers, including Stacy Claire Boyd, Sweet Pea, Crane's, Lalli, and Regency. The average price for 100 announcements is $150. Venture is also a great place to pick up a quick birthday gift, with a nice selection of craft kits and other items. Pamela often shops here when she is in the neighborhood.

BIRTHDAY PARTIES

Many parents love extravagant birthday parties, especially their child's first one. When your baby hits the magic age of one, the birthday party is mostly for Mom, Dad, grandparents, and friends. A cake and a few balloons will make most one-year-olds very happy, and you'll get great photos of your baby mushing up his icing.

We like the idea of having the first birthday at home, but this may not be possible if you have a big family, many friends, and a small apartment. Happily, New York is full of places that organize parties for one-year-olds. Keep this list handy for future reference-two through six-year-olds can have even more fun at a party place.

Most of these sites will host a party seven days a week. They offer catering services that supply everything down to the cake and party favors, though all will let you bring your own. Prices are noted, but this is New York, so they may change over time. Call ahead. The Parent's League at 115 E. 82nd Street (737-7385) has more party information; however, you must be a member ($75 annual fee) to use their files. Many of the below listings are great for older birthdays, too. We've had and attend-

The Five Best Places To Have a Two-year-old's Party

1. Your home, if you have room, or a common space in your apartment building.
2. Any place with Bobby DooWah, the children's musical entertainer (914-366-8291).
3. Columbus Gym (721-0090).
4. Jodi's Gym (772-7633).
5. Children's Museum of Manhattan (721-1234).

ed many 2nd, 3rd, 4th, and even 7th birthdays at several of the places mentioned below.

Chelsea Piers Gymnastics*
Pier 62, 23rd Street at Twelfth Avenue
336-6500
www.chelseapiers.com

Little ones, ages 6 months to 3 years, spend thirty minutes in a party room and an additional hour or more in the baby gym, where they can crawl, explore, play in a ball pit, and be entertained by an instructor. For $350, ten kids can play for one and one-half hours ($15 for each additional child, per hour). Older children, ages 3 and 4, have a more advanced gymnastic experience in which they play on rope swings and a trampoline. Chelsea Piers also offers theme Barbie or Batman party packages. For older kids, Chelsea Piers offers parties of all types, including bowling, ice-skating, roller-blading, and basketball. Catering is additional. Kelly went to a great 7th birthday at the bowling lanes this year!

Child's Play
Central Presbyterian Church
593 Park Avenue at 64th Street
838-1504

For $100 for two hours, you can rent space here and have your own party. The rental includes a playroom with toys and books, a large kitchen with a small table area, two climbing slides, two long tables with twenty chairs, a tape player, and a coffee machine. The space is available all day Tuesday, Friday, Saturday, and Sunday from September to June, and on Sunday afternoons in the summer. Best for children 2 and under. This is one of the best deals in the city!

Circus Gymnastics
2121 Broadway at 74th Street
799-3755

Circus Gym offers fun gym-based parties for kids age one and up. Children can jump on the trampoline, go through obstacle courses, and play on and under a parachute. Each party is one-and-a-half hours long, and includes at least two instructors for the group. Circus Gym provides coffee for the grown-ups, and you provide everything else-paper goods, food, drinks, cake, etc. A party for 10 children is $350 ($12 for each additional child). Pamela held Rebecca's 1st birthday party here with much success. Catering from Fairway (downstairs) makes it easy. Space is available Friday afternoons, Saturday, and Sunday.

Eli's Vinegar Factory*
431 E. 91st Street at York Avenue
987-0885, ext. 4

Eli's Vinegar Factory offers a wide variety of party options in their own setting on the second floor of the store. Spacious and comfortable, this is a terrific place to hold large birthday parties for any age. The basic party package costs $25 per child (with a minimum of 25 kids), and another $250 for staffing. Clearly this is not a bargain, but we've never tasted better food at a birthday party! This price includes a two-hour party, tables and chairs, balloons, snacks, juice, and two kiddie entrees-with options like chicken fingers, mini pizzas, and PB&J. Eli's does not provide entertainment, but you are free to hire your own entertainers and have them perform in the space. For an additional charge, Eli's will host a pizza-making party or a cookies and cake-decorating party. Eli's offers a full adult catering menu as well, so if you'd like to offer food for adults, they can do it all.

Gymtime*
1520 York Avenue at 80th Street
861-7732

Partygoers can play in the padded big or minigym spaces. Kids enjoy tumbling and crawling in the gym spaces, and participating in activities involving a trampoline, a parachute, a ball pit, and bubbles. There are also circle songs. Helium balloons are provided, along with coffee and tea for adults. The space is available Friday, Saturday, and Sunday during the school year, and Monday and Wednesday in the summer. The cost is $400 for ten children ($15 for each additional child) for one and one-half hours.

Jodi's Gym*
244 E. 84th Street bet. Second
and Third Avenues
772-7633

Jodi's Gym is very popular among the 2 through 4 crowd. This bright and spacious facility provides a young child with gym equipment all scaled down to just the right size. Birthday party kids play for forty-five minutes with an obstacle course, air mattress, balance beams, bars, mats, slides, parachutes, bubbles, and much more. They then have thirty minutes for cake and ice cream. A party for 10 children costs $375 ($13 for each additional child). Food packages are available, including cake, juice, and paper goods for $5 per person, or $7 per person for all of the above plus pizza. Jodi's is available Monday through Friday in the summer, and Monday, Friday, Saturday, and Sunday during the school year.

Linda Kaye's Birthday Bakers PartyMakers
195 E. 76th Street bet. Third
and Lexington Avenues
288-7112
www.partymakers.com

Linda Kaye offers children's birthday parties at a most unique location, The Central Park Wildlife Center. For children ages 1 to 4, she offers two themes: Animal Alphabet Safari, where children learn about animals through the alphabet and Breakfast with the Penguins, where children enjoy a party meal in the Penguin House. The cost for 15 children in the Animal Alphabet party is $460; Breakfast with the Penguins for the same number is $700. Linda Kaye offers an extensive party selection for older children as well, both at the Zoo and at the Museum of Natural History.

Party Poopers*
104 Reade Street at Broadway
587-9030
www.partypoopers.com

Party Poopers creates zany and original theme parties at their various locations throughout the city. They have a large selection of costumed characters to choose from, as well as magicians, clowns, storytellers, puppeteers, and other entertainers. For Rebecca's 5th birthday, Party Poopers provided the Spice Girls to entertain the gang. Prices start at $229 for one character at your own location for half an hour, and go up to $2,000 and more for full-service party packages at their place that include costumes, dancing, snacks, soda and juice, balloons, and paper goods. Kids can also have fun with a closet full of costumes, a tiny castle, toys, a moonwalk, and face painting. Check out their online store, Pooper Cavern, or their Reade Street location, both of which offer paper goods, balloons, favors, costumes, and everything else you could need for parties.

Playspace*
2473 Broadway at 92nd Street
769-2300

Parties last for two hours here, during which a staff member helps children explore a playground with riding toys, building blocks, a slide, a huge sandbox, xylophones, trains, basketball hoops, and a dress-up theater with costumes. After playtime, refreshments are served in a party room. The cost is $239 for ten children during the week and $319 on weekends ($19.95 for each additional child). This includes juice, coffee for adults, and a helium balloon for each child. For $319 for ten children during the week or $399 on weekends ($14.95 for each additional child), you get all of the above, plus invitation cards and envelopes, paper goods, pizza, a personalized

Carvel cake, and a Playspace gift T-shirt for the birthday child.

Seventy-Fourth Street Magic*
510 E. 74th Street bet. York Avenue
and the East River
737-2989
www.74magic.com

Seventy-Fourth Street Magic has a big and beautiful indoor play space, and holds parties on Friday, Saturday, and Sunday. Toddlers spend one hour in the baby gym with a supervisor/teacher who helps them with the equipment, swing, and ball pit, and then another thirty minutes in the party room. One and one-half hours for twelve children costs $400 ($15 for each additional child), and includes balloons, as well as coffee and tea for the grown-ups.

If you're having a party at home and want to hire entertainment, check these out:

Bobby DooWah* (music with instruments and dancing or a puppet show; fabulous for first and second year birthdays! A favorite of Pamela and Kelly's-between the two of us, we've used him 5 or 6 times), 914-366-8291 or through 772-7633 (Jodi's Gym).

Cynthia's Musical Parties (music and instruments), 717-6141

Hollywood Pop Gallery (all kinds of costumed characters), 777-2238
www.hollywoodpop.com

Arnie Kolodner (best for 3 and up; most popular with the 4 to 6 year crowd, with wonderful Cinderella and Peter Pan parties!), 265-1430

Madeline the Magician 475-7785

Marcia the Musical Moose (costumed moose character, puppet show, and sing-along; did Alexander's second birthday with great success), 567-0682 or 914-358-8163

Magical Musical Marion (costumed character and music), 917-922-9880

Only Perfect Parties (variety of theme characters and shows), 869-6988 www.nycparties.com

Send in the Clowns* (variety of theme characters and shows; Kelly has used Gary for years and has had Barney, Baby Bop and BJ, Batman and Robin, and the Power Rangers come visit her!), 718-353-8446

Silly Billy (magic, comedy and fun; he's a legend among kids ages 4 to 7), 645-1299

Ronni Soled, Parties Perfect (Ronni, of New Mother's Luncheon fame, also provides entertainers who do magic shows, clown shows, trivia shows, and holiday parties for ages 3 and up.), 744-3194

Tilly the Clown (funny magic, face-painting, storytelling, and games), 721-1867

Central Park Parties

Central Park offers a myriad of party opportunities and is reasonably priced! Hurray! Here you are only limited by your imagination. To begin, for parties of more than 20 people, you need a permit from the City Parks and Recreation Department (360-8111 or www.nyc.gov/parks). A permit costs $25, payable to the city by check or money order.

Central Park parties have to be planned with a rain date or a back-up (indoor) plan in case of inclement weather. That aside, plan for lots of outdoor games, such as circle time for younger kids, hot potato, freeze dance (bring batteries for your portable radio), or have a friend (or Bobby Doowah) play guitar. Any entertainers you would hire indoors can be hired outdoors as well. Clowns, costumed characters, and even the Spice Girls have made it to Central Park parties.

Pamela's friend Esther planned a softball party for her son's sixth birthday, and it was a huge success. She got a permit for a softball field, provided each child with a team T-shirt, and had a real game!

Some popular party locations in Central Park include:

The Great Lawn: mid-park, between 79th and 86th Streets.

Sheep Meadow: mid-park, between 66th and 69th Streets.

Strawberry Fields: west side, between 71st and 74th Streets.

Any playground with a picnic table.

Make sure to mark your area by balloons (The Balloon Man is a great resource; Kelly has used him for years, and he will deliver everywhere. Call Harvey at 268-3900), streamers, etc. Bring lots of blankets, paper tablecloths and napkins for ground cover. A folding table for food and cake is a good idea, too.

If you want a more organized party in the park, the Central Park Carousel is a lot of fun for kids ages 2 to 5. Call 396-1010, ext. 14, to book a party there. Parties start at $18.50 per child, and include four carousel rides per child, plus one hour in the picnic area. Carousel staff supplies paper goods, hot dogs or pizza, juice, plus a small party favor and a helium balloon for each child. All you need to bring is the birthday cake. For an additional fee, you can also request a face painter, clown, magician, or costumed characters. Parties are held April through November, seven days a week, weather permitting.

Birthday Cakes

Everybody has a bakery in the neighborhood that makes perfectly fine, even fabulous birthday cakes. Explore your neighborhood, and be sure to ask other moms where they get cakes. Heck, you can probably get a cake from the supermarket complete with your baby's name and ubiquitous frosting flowers. But for your child's first birthday, you may want to go all out. We've listed some makers of outstanding (though sometimes outrageously priced) birthday cakes, and clued you in on which ones will incorporate themes such as Superman, ballerinas, or Peter Rabbit. Don't panic, though. For Angela's first birthday (Kelly's second child), she had an Entenmann's chocolate cake at home with big brother Alexander, and she was perfectly happy! Entenmann's can be quite good when they're fresh, and for $3.99, who's complaining?

Cakes 'N Shapes, LTD.
403 W. 39th Street bet. Ninth
and Tenth Avenues
629-5512

For $110, Edie Connolly can create a unique cake in the character or design of your choice. She can sculpt everything from a ballerina to a teddy bear, Batman, or Superman. Give her a favorite picture, and she will scan it directly onto an edible Edie cake. A simple round cake for twenty-five costs $75. For Rebecca's Cinderella party, she designed a 3-D cake with Cinderella's gown as the cake, and a Barbie doll as Cinderella. Order at least one week in advance. Delivery available.

CBK Cookies of New York*
226 E. 83rd Street bet. Second
and Third Avenues
794-3383

You can order chocolate or vanilla single-sheet or double-layer cakes in various styles, including cakes baked in the shape of a character of your choice. A basic decorated cake that serves approximately twenty people costs $75. These cakes are so special, CBK makes only two a day, so order at least 2 weeks in advance. They make wonderful cupcakes and cookies, too, in every shape and style. Delivery is extra. By appointment only. For years Kelly has used CBK for birthdays, baby showers, and Halloween parties.

Cupcake Cafe*
522 Ninth Avenue at 39th Street
465-1530

Cupcake Cafe is one of our favorites, and Kelly buys many cakes here for her adult friends. And they are delicious! A round cake serving 15 to 25 people with flowers and an inscription costs $55. A theme cake with Big

Bird or Barney, serving 25 people, is $65. Call two to three days in advance to pick up a cake Monday through Saturday; call Thursday for a cake to be ready on Sunday. Delivery is about $25. No credit cards; cash, money order, or company check only.

Dean & Deluca
560 Broadway at Prince Street
226-6800
www.deananddeluca.com

Dean & Deluca's chocolate cake is phenomenal. A layer cake that serves approximately twenty-five people starts at $50. Order 2 days ahead—although some moms have been lucky enough to walk in and find one already made. D&D also carries fantastic cupcakes as well as adorable (and pricey-$10.50 each) large character cookies featuring Pooh Bear and Madeline. Delivery is free in the neighborhood.

Grace's Market Place
1237 Third Avenue at 71st Street
737-0600
www.homedelivery.com

Grace's has a wide selection, including carrot and chocolate mousse cakes; some are beautifully decorated with flowers and scrolls of dark chocolate. A cake serving twelve people costs $25. You can stop by Grace's on the spur of the moment and find a cake, perhaps their delicious $16 American Beauty chocolate cake. Can you tell we like chocolate? This cake is one of our favorite chocolate cakes in New York City. They will customize with three days notice. Delivery is free within eight blocks.

Lafayette Bakery
26 Greenwich Avenue
between Tenth Avenue and Charles Street
242-7580
anycbakery@aol.com

Lafayette Bakery will custom make a cake with a simple design for an extra $5 to $15 over the regular price of $40 for a cake serving twenty-five. Their cakes have fruit, custard, or mousse fillings, and can be topped with whipped cream or a variety of icings. Order a week in advance. No delivery.

Magnolia Bakery
401 Bleecker Street at 11th Street
462-2572

Specializing in old-fashioned, homemade cakes, Magnolia Bakery offers delicious yellow or chocolate half-sheet cakes. A $60 cake serves twenty-five to thirty-five. They won't custom make a cake, but with a day's notice, they will personalize one. The cupcakes here are famous—don't leave without one. No delivery.

My Most Favorite Dessert Company
120 W. 45th Street bet. Sixth Avenue
and Broadway
997-5032/997-5130

Well known for delicious kosher food and desserts, Dessert Company sells a two-layer round cake (chocolate or vanilla) that serves twenty-five people and costs $65 to $75. A beautifully decorated kid's theme cake is about $80. Call three to four days in advance. Delivery is $10.

Soutine*
104 W. 70th Street bet. Columbus
and Amsterdam Avenues
496-1450
www.soutine.com

Pamela buys wonderful cakes at this tiny bake shop. A two-layer round cake serving twenty people costs $40, and a cake with decoration costs an additional $10 to $15. You can customize designs and flavors. Through a computer graphics program, kids can design their own cake online and Soutine will make the cake of your child's dreams. Order one to two days in advance. Delivery costs $5 to $15 in Manhattan. Cupcakes are also available, made to order with sprinkles.

Sylvia Weinstock Cakes
273 Church Street bet. White
and Franklin Streets
925-6698

Known in New York as "the cake lady," Sylvia creates masterpieces that range from castles for birthdays to fantasies for brides. She is known around the world for her wedding cakes. Her concoctions start at about $350 for a cake that will serve thirty-five people. Give at least three weeks notice. Delivery within Manhattan is $50; outside depends on mileage.

Veniero Pasticceria
342 E. 11th Street bet. First
and Second Avenues
674-7264

Famous not just for fantastic cannoli, they also make light and creamy cakes for kids. A round cake that serves up to thirty people costs $40. Bring in a postcard-size picture of anything you want on the cake, and they'll copy it for an additional $20. Order two days in advance. Delivery is $6 in Manhattan.

William Greenberg Desserts
1100 Madison Avenue bet. 82nd
and 83rd Streets
861-1340
1383 Third Avenue bet. 78th and 79th Streets
988-8548

Another baker well known for elaborate designs and decorations, Greenberg's produces a beautiful baby carriage cake for baby showers. They made President Clinton's 50th birthday American flag cake. A two-layer round cake serving twenty-five costs $98.50; decorated cakes run from $225 to $230. Call at least two days in advance; longer for more elaborate creations. Delivery with one day advanced notice.

With many birthday cakes under our belt, we've discovered there is nothing better than an ice-cream cake from Haagen-Dazs or Carvel, especially in the spring and summer months. These cakes are usually two layers of chocolate and vanilla ice cream with cookie crunch and icing on the sides and tops. These bring us back to our own childhood birthdays, and you can never discount nostalgia as a good reason to buy one; your kids will love it as much as you did. If you call in advance, you can choose your child's favorite ice cream flavors.

There are Haagen-Dazs stores throughout the city, so they are ideal places to pick up a quick birthday cake. Cakes range in prices-a cake that serves 20 to 25 people is around $50, depending on the decoration. Here are some Haagen-Dazs locations:

187 Columbus Avenue bet. 68th
and 69th Streets
787-0265
1221 Third Avenue bet. 70th
and 71st Streets
288-7088
300 W. 23rd Street at Eighth Avenue
929-2255
33 Barrow Street bet. Seventh Avenue
and Bleecker 727-2152

There are fewer Carvel locations in the city, but their cakes are good and inexpensive. For approximately 25 people, an ice-cream cake costs around $37.

1631 First Avenue at 85th Street
879-6210
1091 Second Avenue bet. 57th
and 58th Streets
308-4744

And, if you call 422-7835, you can have a Carvel cake delivered to your home. This service is primarily designed for office parties, so only have a limited variety of decorated birthday cakes are available. You can view these cakes at www.carvel.com.

HAIRCUTS

Many New York moms take their babies to their own hair salon, or attempt to give that first trim themselves. But we think you'll want to try one of these shops that specialize in children's haircutting. Little kids are notoriously bad at sitting still, and most of these places offer fun distractions like Barney or Sesame Street videos to watch, and toy cars for your child to sit in. You might even come away with a first haircut diploma, a lock of hair, or a balloon. Bring some toys from home, so your child won't badger you to buy one of the pricey toys for sale in some of these salons.

Astor Place Hair Designers
2 Astor Place bet. 8th Street and Broadway
475-9854

Nothing special here for children: no cars to sit in or balloons, just a cheap haircut, good people watching, and a friendly staff downtown. $11 to 13 for a kid's cut.

Kids Cuts
201 E. 31st Street bet. Second
and Third Avenues · 684-5252

This store provides a great experience for your child's first haircut. While the haircutter snips away, your child can watch movies and sit in a miniature car. After the cut, you receive a certificate with a lock of your child's hair for your album, as well as a pinwheel for the little one. Haircuts here cost $21.95. Kids Cuts also has a boutique that sells toys for both entertainment and educational purposes. This boutique tends to be pricey, so the pinwheel may have to suffice as a post-cut treat.

Cozy's Cuts for Kids*
1125 Madison Avenue at 84th Street
744-1716
448 Amsterdam Avenue at 81st Street
579-2600

Cozy's Cuts is a fun hair salon with chairs fashioned to look like cars and trucks. There's a television in front of every station, and a video and video game library. All cuts are $24 and include a diploma for the first cut, plus a balloon, a lollipop, and a free gift. You also have the option of buying a Polaroid of your child and his or her new haircut for $5. Cozy's also has a boutique, with a wonderful array of toys and party favors. Appointments are recommended for haircuts, but you can walk in for a bang trim. Kelly and Pamela have used Cozy's salons for years, with good results. Cozy is a mother of two, and is often at one of the stores.

Fun Cuts
1567 York Avenue at 83rd Street
288-0602

Small, colorful, and charming. Each kiddie chair has its own video monitor to keep your child occupied. After first haircuts, you'll get a photograph and a lock of your baby's hair. Cuts are $20. Appointments are recommended, though walk-ins are welcome.

Michael's Children Hair Cutting Salon*
1263 Madison Avenue bet. 90th
and 91st Streets · 289-9612

Many of our friends had their first haircuts at Michael's—that's how long Michael's has been around. There are toy car and pony seats, and diplomas are given for the first haircut. Cuts are $25. No appointments are taken, so avoid the busy after-school hours. Michael's is very popular with the Carnegie Hill crowd.

Paul Molé Haircutters
1031 Lexington Avenue at 74th Street
988-9176

Paul Molé has been around "forever" but has kept up with the times. Your child can watch a video of his choice, eat a lollipop and go home with a toy. Children sit in an old-fashioned kid-sized barbershop chair, and will receive a special certificate for their first haircut. Cuts are $25.

SuperCuts
For branches in your area,
call (800) SUPERCUT

Here are some of their locations:
440 Third Avenue at 32nd Street 447-0070
1149 Second Avenue at 60th Street
688-8883
2481 Broadway at 92nd 501-8200
69 University Place at 10th Street 228-2545
378 Sixth Avenue at Waverly 477-7900

All the salons in this chain cut infants' and toddlers' hair, and award a diploma for the first haircut. Salons are clean and designed to provide quick, easy-in/easy-out service. Haircuts for toddlers cost around $15. Appointments aren't required but, if you wish, you can make one with your favorite stylist.

The Tortoise and the Hare

1470 York Avenue at 78th Street
472-3399

Built by Broadway set designers, The Tortoise and the Hare offers lots of brightly colored diversions, including a gigantic pocket watch on the wall with a tortoise and a hare as hands. Each station is equipped with a television and VCR, and Sony Play Station or Nintendo 64. A child's haircut is $22. Appointments are recommended.

SHOES

Buying your child's first walking shoes is an exciting and important task. Because your one- or two-year-old can't tell you whether the shoes are comfortable, watch carefully as she is being fitted. If it seems difficult to get the shoes on and off, they are probably too small. Shoes should generally last at least two months: if they seem small three weeks after you bought them, go back and have them checked.

The salesperson at the shoe store should measure your child's foot while he is standing toes uncurled. Ask about the width of your child's foot and don't buy a shoe that narrows greatly at the toes. Also, look for a soft, flexible sole. A soft sole is necessary for the first year. After that, when your child is really walking and running, you can buy any shoe your heart desires, except slip-on penny loafers. Your youngster won't develop the gripping action that a slip-on shoe requires until he is four or five.

East Side Kids Inc.*

1298 Madison Avenue at 92nd Street
360-5000

East Side Kids has a wide selection of American and European shoes for first walkers. They also carry such popular brand name sneakers as Nike, Reebok, and Keds. Other excellent brands include Sonnet (English), Elefanten (German), and Aster (French). The salespeople are some of the best in the city. Leon is Kelly's favorite! Service is on a first-come, first-serve basis, but you can call ahead and have your name put on a waiting list. Free popcorn helps pass the time if there is a wait. They also offer free local delivery.

Great Feet*

1241 Lexington Avenue at 84th Street
249-0551 · www.striderite.com

This big, bright store has areas carved out for different age groups. It carries brands like

Stride Rite, Nike, Reebok, LA Gear, Elefanten, and a wide variety of styles. Prices are among the best around, and the staff are generally quite knowledgeable about little feet. This store gets a star because they stand behind what they sell, exchange mistakes readily, and have great sales!

Harry's Shoes
2299 Broadway at 83rd Street
874-2035
www.harrys-shoes.com

An Upper West Side fixture, Harry's carries a wide selection of American and European brands, including Stride Rite, Elefanten, Jumping Jacks, Shoo Be Doo, Nike, Reebok, New Balance, and Enzo. This place can get very crowded, especially on the weekends and after school.

Ibiza Kidz
42 University Place at 9th Street
505-9907

This small downtown store is part shoe store, part toy store, and part clothing store. It carries a large line of shoes with brands such as Aster, Baby Botte, Elefanten, Mod 8, Superga, and Venettini. In the toy section you can find educational toys, Gund and Russ plush toys, and much more. This comfortable neighborhood store has great service and a very loyal customer following. There are good seasonal sales at the end of summer and winter.

Lester's
1522 Second Avenue at 80th Street
734-9292

This Manhattan branch of the Brooklyn chain has an impressive shoe department tucked behind the clothing. Lester's is a discount store carrying a good selection of European and American brands; there's a wide variety of styles that you wouldn't expect a discounter to stock, and friendly service, too!

Little Eric*
1131 Third Avenue at 76th Street
288-8987
1118 Madison Avenue at 83rd Street
717-1513

A wide selection of shoes for children ages six months to seven years. Brands include Nike, Keds, Converse, and Kangaroos, with styles from sneakers to high-end imported designer shoes. The Little Eric store brand makes up the majority of their stock and is excellent and very fashionable. This is a child-friendly store, with plenty of space, and toys to keep children busy as they are fitted. They have a loyal following, but a limited selection of shoes for wide feet.

Shoofly
465 Amsterdam Avenue at 82nd Street
580-4390
42 Hudson Street at Duane Street
406-3270
www.shooflynyc.com

This is one of the most stylish kiddie shoe stores in the city, carrying all the high-end brands for boys and girls such as Aster's, Baby Botte, and Deoso. There's also an excellent selection of purses, hats, barrettes, and other accessories.

They have extra special shoes for girls, and this was Rebecca's favorite place to shop when she was 3 and 4 years old. Try to shop during the week; weekends here are quite busy.

Tip Top Kids*
149 W. 72nd Street
874-1004
www.tiptopshoes.com

This store is nicely laid out, with plenty of space for walking around and trying on shoes. The staff is friendly and helpful, and kids are kept occupied by a supply of toys and movies. Tip Top has shoes for every occasion, with prices ranging from $20 to $80. Popular brands include Stride Rite, Monroe Kids, Nike, and New Balance. This is a welcome addition to the neighborhood, which truly lacked a "basic" shoe store for kids!

PHOTOGRAPHS

It doesn't take long for your drawers to become stuffed with photos taken of your adorable baby by you and your relatives. But there's a reason you've left them in the drawer. When you want a picture to put in that beautiful silver frame you got as a baby gift, it's time to go to a professional. A real photographer can work in your home, the park, or her studio, and can include parents or grandparents in the shots, as well as props such as stuffed animals, antique toys, costumes, and more.

If you don't know a photographer, here are some places to start. These are fairly traditional professionals who are experienced in photographing children (it's an art, truly). Ask to see their portfolios, and if you don't see the kind of work you want, ask your friends for some recommendations. Also, look for photo credits in parenting magazines. There's a good chance the photographers live in New York.

A Child's Portrait
Principal Photographer: Nancy Ribeck
476 Broome Street, Suite 6A, bet. Wooster and Greene Streets
534-3433

Nancy Ribeck's studio photography is often classically lit, but casually designed. This combination gives her portraits the beauty of traditional portraiture mixed with a contemporary look. A basic sitting fee is $395 and includes an assistant's fee and three rolls of two and a quarter film. Each additional roll costs $45. Photos are taken at the studio at 476 Broome Street, or at a location of your choice for an extra $100. Sessions last two or three hours. Print photos are an additional fee.

Barry Burns
311 W. 43rd Street bet. Eighth and Ninth Avenues
713-0100
www.barryburns.com

Barry Burns captures the spontaneity of the moment. He takes 70 pictures of your child, and you receive three 8 x 10" prints. His shoots run from $400 to $600. Family portraits can also be made in color or black-and-white film. Most work is done in his studio in the heart of the theater district, but an outside location is possible for a negotiable additional fee.

Jami Beere Photography

(646) 505-5836

www.jamibeere.com

Jami is a talented photographer who is well-known for her exquisite children's portraits. She is expensive, but many parents believe she's worth it because of the beautiful work she does. Her sitting fee is $975. Once the client chooses the image she wants, Jami hand prints it. Prices vary with size of the print.

Kate Burton Photography

316 E. 84th Street

717-9958

www.kateburton.com

Kate Burton has been photographing children for over eight years in New York City. Her work has been featured in the *New York Times* and *Time Out New York*, and is frequently displayed in children's stores such as Shoofly, Little Eric, and Bu & the Duck. Kate Burton shoots in her own full-service studio, but will also go on location to the park or your home. Studio and local park sitting packages start at $350; in-home sessions begin at $550. A number of Pamela's friends have used Kate, and all of them attest that Kate does beautiful work and is a pleasure to work with.

Creative Photoworks

629-9028

www.heleneglanzberg.com

Photographer Helene Glanzberg is friendly, relaxed, and very patient. She puts no limit on how many shots she takes during the session because children are so unpredictable. With an unlimited amount of film, satisfaction is guaranteed. Helene's preferred method of working is at your home or favorite location, but studio services are available. Basic photo shoots start at $250 for black-and-white or color film and proofs. Prints run anywhere from $15 to $25 each.

Nina Drapacz

500 E. 85th Street at York Avenue

772-7814

Nina Drapacz apprenticed with Richard Avedon and specializes in hand-colored black-and-white photos. She offers a black-and-white or color package of approximately 36 exposures for $525. The enlargements include one 11 x 14", three 8 x 10", two 5 x 7", and a set of contact sheets. Additional prints are available. She does fabulous work and is extremely accommodating and patient. Pamela's friend Marty used her twice for family photos. Nina will shoot outdoors for no extra charge.

Fromex

182 E. 86th Street bet. Third
and Lexington Avenues

369-4821

Tucked in the back of this average-looking "one hour" photo place is a photo studio with a photographer on staff. Fromex offers many packages that range in price from $49.95 to $249.95. A standard package is $100 and includes a sitting fee, one set of proofs, and one 8 x 10". It's best to call ahead for an appointment, but walk-ins are possible. We both have had good results with Fromex.

Jennifer Lee*

40 W. 72nd Street, Suite 53,
bet. Central Park West and Columbus Avenue
799-1501

Jennifer Lee has been photographing kids portraits for four years. She enjoys shooting on location in people's own homes, where kids are most comfortable. A new mom herself, Jennifer is adept at capturing the best moments with your new baby. Her prices start at $200 for a sitting, and she will keep shooting until she believes she has numerous good shots in a variety of poses. Jennifer will also shoot your child's birthday party—Kelly had her photograph Angela's second birthday. She charges approximately $100 an hour; call for prices.

Karen Michele

721 Fifth Avenue at 56th Street
355-7576 · www.karenmichele.com

Karen Michele will design a backdrop for your photo shoot using colorful balloons or anything else you want. She operates from a full retouching production facility, where she personally works with on-film retouching for each portrait. Her photos can be seen in the children's section of Barnes & Noble. There is a shooting fee of $250; a 5 x 7" print costs $125; an 8 x 10" print costs $150; duplicates are fifty percent off. Parents make a selection from approximately thirty proofs. By appointment only.

Manger-Weil Photography*

1556 York Avenue at 82nd Street
717-6203
www.nybabyphoto.com

Manger-Weil Photography captures children's natural expressions by making sittings as much fun as possible. They shoot in your home or at an outdoor location. Manger-Weil has twenty years of experience in photographing children. They charge $350, which includes the sitting fee and thirty-six 4 x 6" prints. Harvey is a dream to work with. You can view Harvey's portfolio on the Web site. Call well in advance, because Harvey is extremely busy.

Sarah Merians Photography & Company

104 Fifth Avenue, 4th floor, at 16th Street
633-0502
www.sarahmerians.com

Sarah Merians Photography has been photographing children and families for fifteen years. Sarah Merians employs thirteen child-experienced photographers, so the company can easily accommodate your family's schedule. The starting price for an in-studio photo shoot is approximately $275 to $300, which includes two rolls of film-color and/or black-and-white. Sarah Merians will also shoot on-location. Prices vary according to the locale you choose. Pamela used them to photograph her wedding, with wonderful results.

Nancy Pindrus Photography

21 W. 68th Street bet. Central Park West and Columbus Avenue
799-8167

Nancy is both patient and accommodating. Her basic price is $275 for black-and-white contact sheets or $325 for color contact sheets, with an additional charge for the prints selected. Prints cost $32.50 for black-and-white photos up to 8 x 10", with duplicates for $15 each. Color photos are $37.50 with duplicates for $25 each (any size up to 8 x 10"). She will work in her studio or on location in Central Park. Other locations are negotiable.

Gail Sherman
88 Central Park West at 69th Street
877-7210

Gail Sherman's work is dramatic. Her photographs are printed in black-and-white, then hand-colored with oil paints. Her photographs are works of art, not just "pictures." Gail Sherman has a $500 minimum for sitting. The sitting and processing fee is $300, and the price per hand-colored portrait is $500. If you want only black and white prints, the cost is $100 per print.

A WORD ON PRESCHOOLS

As you begin to check out preschools—sometime between your child's first and second birthday—you will probably be subject to intermittent panic attacks. You'll hear rumors that this or that school is "hot" this year. You'll be baffled by the complexity of the admissions process. You'll feel as though you're trying to get an eighteen-year-old into Harvard, not a two-year-old into a sweet little place where she'll play and eat crackers and juice. Try to relax. Things will work out.

Here are some basic facts to keep in mind as you and your child march on toward preschool:

Many children begin preschool at age three or three and one-half years old; others begin as early as two years and four months old. Schools decide on cutoff ages for admission and often change these arbitrarily—a one-year-old born before March 15 can apply for admission for the following September; the next year, perhaps, a child born before March 31 can apply. Schools hold tight to their birth date policies, and there are few exceptions.

※ There are many excellent preschools in New York. Pick up a copy of the *Manhattan Directory of Private Nursery Schools* by Linda Faulhaber. This book describes all the private preschools in New York by neighborhood, with pertinent information from phone numbers to cutoff dates. Or look through the *New York Independent Schools Directory*, published cooperatively by the Parents League and the Independent Schools Admission Association of Greater New York (available through the Parents League). But remember, there are excellent schools that are not members of the Parents League, and are therefore not listed in the League guidebook.

※ As you begin your search, look for a school in your neighborhood if possible. Try to keep your travel distance to about ten blocks. Otherwise, you'll spend all your time getting there, when the school time itself is only two or three hours a day twice a week for children under three. Three-year-olds may go every day, and they'd rather spend their time at school than traveling to it.

※ Talk to friends about their experiences with preschools. Make arrangements to visit the schools you're interested in; tours usually take place from October through January. You must call *the day after* Labor Day to make an appointment for a tour and/or request an application. Some schools will not schedule a tour until they receive a completed application; others supply applications only after you have toured the school.

✻ Apply promptly. Schools have been known to stop sending applications by the second week of September, when they have already received enough applicants to fill their classes three times over. Apply to four or five schools. If you have a first choice, indicate it in a letter to the director of admissions of that particular school. It also helps greatly if you know families that attend the school you're most interested in. If possible, have them write or call for you.

Your child will almost surely find a place in a preschool you like, and you will almost surely wonder a year from now what all the fuss was about.

Note: Each spring the 92nd Street Y offers a workshop called "Planning Your Child's Early School Years," conducted by Beth Teitelman and Barbara Katz who run the Parenting Center. The Parents League at 115 E. 82nd Street (737-7385) runs one-on-one advisory sessions for school and summer programs; they will give you the names and phone numbers of parents at various preschools who have agreed to talk to interested prospective parents. You can also find this and other information at there Web site: www.parentsleague.org.

There are a few professionals who specialize in helping parents through the nursery school and (in some cases) the ongoing school process. They will meet with families to discuss their needs and will try to steer them towards schools that will be a good fit for them. Of course, there are no guarantees for admission. Two people we recommend are:

Nina Bauer, M.A.
Ivy Wise Kids
262-1200

Joan Miller Advisory Service
4 E. 88th Street
876-6314

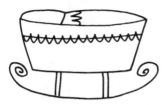

9 · maternity clothes

Whatever clothing your lifestyle demands, you can find it in New York's maternity stores. From Veronique Delachaux for sophisticated French clothing, rental gowns from Mom's Night Out, office wear at Mimi Maternity or the hippest Madison Avenue has to offer at Liz Lange, these stores have everything you need to stay comfortable and look great.

We shopped every maternity store in New York, and tried on dozens of items. We tested oversized and large-cut non-maternity wear by well-known designers such as Joan Vass, Tapemeasure, Eileen Fisher, and Victoria's Secret. We discovered which designers make maternity lines, and which stores carry them.

If you're not much of a shopper, or if you're sticking to a budget, the Belly Basics Pregnancy Survival Kit can be a staple of your wardrobe from day one of your pregnancy. The kit includes boot-cut leggings, a skirt, a long-sleeved tunic, and a baby doll dress, all of which are made of black cotton and lycra. You can mix and match the pieces or wear them with non-maternity clothes. Kits are available at Bloomingdale's and Lord and Taylor for $152; some pieces are sold separately. Pamela bought the leggings when she was pregnant with Benjamin and found them so comfortable she practically lived in them.

This chapter describes the New York maternity scene-its focus, style, quality of merchandise, price range, and level of service. Most of these stores hold their sales in January and July.

SHOPPING TIPS

Before you shop, here's some advice from two women who have learned by trial and error.

Hold off on buying maternity clothes for as long as you can. Remember, nine months is a long time, and you'll need new and different things as you grow bigger.

✳ In the first and second trimester, shop in regular clothing stores for larger sizes and items with elastic waists. The Gap, The Limited, and Victoria's Secret often offer inexpensive, machine-washable items with elastic waists. Buy one or two sizes larger than you usually do.

✳ Don't buy shoes in your first trimester; your feet will probably expand. Kelly had to buy two more pairs of shoes in her eighth month because she had only one pair that fit her.

✳ Buy fabrics you are used to and comfortable with. If you never wear polyester or rayon, there's no need to start now. Stick to cotton or other natural fabrics that breathe, such as heavy-weight cotton blend suits you can wear when you go to a business meeting or out to dinner.

✳ Buy new bras, pantyhose, and maternity panties. You may go up as many as three cup sizes during your pregnancy, and bras with good support are essential. (Can you imagine going from an A to a D? We can.) Maternity pantyhose by Hue and underwear by Japanese Weekend are two of our favorites.

✳ For the last two months, invest in a maternity support belt, sold at every maternity store. The belt is a large, thick band of elastic that closes with Velcro under your belly to help hold it up.

Top Eight Alternatives to Maternity Stores

1. Your husband's shirts and sweaters.
2. Borrow a friend's maternity clothes.
3. Eileen Fisher stores are great.
4. Jumpers and waistless dresses in Victoria's Secret catalogs are perfect, and affordable with clothes at $59 or less.
5. The Pregnancy Survival Kit.
6. Leggings and sweaters.
7. Rent it—check out Mom's Night Out.
8. Secondhand stores.

You will be able to walk more comfortably and for longer periods of time.

✳ A pretty vest is an easy way to dress up an oxford shirt and a skirt or pair of leggings. Kelly loved to wear an oversized black turtleneck with black pants and a bright vest.

✳ Look in your husband's closet. A man's oxford shirt over a long elasticized skirt or leggings provides comfort and a clean, crisp look. Kelly bought some men's sweaters and shirts during her winter pregnancy—now her husband Carlo wears them.

✳ Don't be afraid to wear fitted clothes. As more and more fashion models become pregnant, it's become the trend to wear form-fitting tops and dresses! Feel sexy and be pregnant at the same time. Liz Lange Maternity specializes in that sophisticated pregnancy look.

THE STORES

A Pea in the Pod*
625 Madison Avenue bet. 58th
and 59th Streets
826-6468
www.apeainthepod.com
Return Policy: Exchange and store credit only.

This is a top-of-the line maternity store. It carries its own exclusive line and also commissions suits, dresses, and weekend wear by Carole Little, Joan Vass, David Dart, Shelli Segal, ABS, Lou Nardi, and Adrienne Vittadini. Amenities abound-big bathrooms, extra-large dressing rooms with space to sit down, bottled water, toys for kids, and magazines to occupy husbands and friends. The sales people are extremely helpful and are trained to fit you with the maternity and nursing bras you'll need. Prices run in the $150 to $200 range for most designer pieces. Denim jeans are $58; leggings $78; and bras range from $18 to $50.

Pumpkin Maternity
407 Broome Street
334-1809

Not just a Web site anymore! This shop has many new options, including stretch tops, stretch faux leather pants. Everything is hip and comfortable. They also carry underwear, stockings, Bjorn carriers, and diaper bags.

A Second Chance
1109 Lexington Avenue bet. 77th
and 78th Streets, 2nd floor
744-6041
Return Policy: All sales are final.

A Second Chance offers previously owned clothing for resale. Prices are about one quarter of the cost of a new item, and most of the pieces are in good shape. Although maternity wear is only a small segment of the inventory, the store stocks many basics you might be looking for. A Second Chance is hit or miss, so you'll probably have to go more than once.

Barney's New York Maternity Department
660 Madison Avenue at 61st Street, 6th floor
826-8900
www.barneys.com
Return Policy: Refund with receipt.

A recently opened department of Barney's, focusing on the basics for the quintessential Barney's customer. Barney's has their own maternity label, Procreation. It is a great line with tons of modern, luxurious basics, like cashmere sweaters, capri pants, knit dresses, and cotton button-down shirts-all in a variety of colors. For Barney's, the Procreation line is moderately priced, ranging from $120 to $250 per item. Barney's also carries L'Atessa, a sexy, daring brand with a fun selection of slim-fitting tops, bikinis, leather pants-even vintage Levi's with elasticized tummy panels sewn in. A third brand, Mamma Luna, is a bit dressier, made up mostly of brightly colored raw silk jackets, dresses, skirts, and pants.

Belly Basics
(800) 4-9-MONTHS
www.nystyle.com/bellybasics.com

Along with the Pregnancy Survival Kit, Belly Basics offers other stylish and comfortable maternity items. Everything from twin sets in bright colors to swimwear and Belly Basics' own diaper bag (in basic black, of course), can be ordered directly from the company. Belly Basics is also sold at Bloomingdale's and Lord & Taylor.

Eileen Fisher
521 Madison Avenue bet. 53rd
and 54th Streets
759-9888
1039 Madison Avenue bet. 79th
and 80th Streets
879-7799
341 Columbus Avenue at 76th Street
362-3000
103 Fifth Avenue bet. 17th and 18th Streets
924-4777
314 E. Ninth Street bet. First
and Second Avenues
(Outlet Store) 529-5715
395 W. Broadway bet. Spring
and Broome Streets
431-4567
www.eileenfisher.com
Return Policy: Money is refunded within two weeks of purchase with a receipt; after two weeks a store credit is issued.

Eileen Fisher sells a range of wonderful full-cut separates, including elasticized pants with full legs, loose tunic-type sweaters, roomy skirts, vests, and empire-waist dresses ($100 to $200). Most of it is machine washable. This is not a maternity store, but the clothing is perfect for your first or second trimester.

Liz Lange Maternity*
958 Madison Avenue bet. 75th
and 76th Streets
879-2191
www.lizlange.com
Return Policy: Money is refunded for unworn items within two weeks of purchase.

Liz Lange has taken the maternity business by storm. Chic, trim, and sophisticated, her sweater sets and Pucci-style prints are the rage for hip, well-to-do moms. Most of Liz's separates mix and match very well, allowing both the working and non-working mom to achieve varied looks with just a few pieces. Prices start at $75 for the basic white stretch cotton T-shirt, and go to $375 for a blazer. Our friends rave about the stretch pants. At Liz's sleek, modern Madison Avenue shop, you can find diaper bags, shoes, purses, bathing suits, and hand-knit baby blankets. We love Liz's clothes—the perfect gift for the expecting mom-to-be.

Madison Avenue Maternity and Baby
1043 Madison Avenue bet. 79th
and 80th Streets, 2nd floor
988-8686
www.madisonavenuematernity.com
Return Policy: Store credit only.

Madison Avenue Maternity imports most of its luxurious and stylish clothes—in beautiful cottons, wools, chenilles-from France and Italy. There are outfits for casual daytime wear ($100 and up), as well as dresses and suits appropriate for corporate life or black-tie affairs ($400 to $1,000). This store sells swimwear, underwear, and pantyhose, as well as lovely baby clothing.

Maternity Works Outlet
16 W. 57th Street bet. Fifth and Sixth Avenues
399-9840
www.maternitymall.com
Return Policy: Store credit only.

This third floor store is a clearinghouse for Mimi Maternity, Maternité by Mother's Work, and A Pea in the Pod. It features sale, off-season, and discontinued items all year round. If you don't mind sewing on a few buttons, there's also an "as is" and "sample" section with some real bargains—you just may find a $200 dress for $20. Check out Maternity Works Outlet if you're a midtown working-mom-to-be. You'll find everything you need.

Mimi Maternity*
1021 Third Avenue bet. 60th and 61st Streets
832-2667
1125 Madison Avenue at 84th Street
737-3784
2005 Broadway bet. 68th and 69th Streets
721-1999
2 World Financial Center,
225 Liberty Street, 2nd floor

945-6424
www.mimimaternity.com
Return Policy: Store credit only.

These comfortable stores carry a large and fashionable assortment of career suits, daytime and evening dresses, and casual clothing by Mimi, Mother's Work, BCBG, Paris Blues, and other labels. Most of them are designed exclusively for Mimi Maternity. Average prices: dresses, $150; a plain, elastic waist black skirt, $80; suits, $200 and up. Mimi's stylish black stretch pants with either bead or embroidered trim ($108), remain a bestseller. The Mimi Essentials line is a recent addition, offering inexpensive active wear like cotton tanks, T-shirts, shorts, and jeans for prices ranging from $18 to $54. You'll also find an impressive selection of lingerie and sleepwear, including top brand name bras and panties.

Mom's Night Out*
147 E. 72nd Street, Apt. 2F,
bet. Lexington and Third Avenues
744-6667
www.momsnightout.com
Return Policy: All the clothing is for rent and must be returned. Some accessories may be purchased.

Here's the place to rent formal evening-wear-short and long dresses, pant suits and jackets—for one night or for a long weekend. Owner Patricia Shiland, a former ready-to-wear designer who adapts regular women's formal styles to maternity wear, designs many of the dresses. Prices range from $125 to $225, and all the outfits are dry-cleaned before and after rental. Accessories such as pearl chokers or maternity pantyhose are available. They also do some made-to-orders. Friends of ours have used Mom's Night Out with great success.

Motherhood Maternity

The Manhattan Mall
32nd Street bet. Sixth and Seventh Avenues
564-8170
1449 Third Avenue bet. 82nd and 83rd Streets
734-5984
641 Avenue of the Americas at 20th Street
741-3488
Catalog: (800) 4MOM2BE
www.motherhood.com
Return Policy: Store credit only.

Motherhood Maternity has recently changed their line and reduced their prices, and now carries trendy, inexpensive maternity clothes, many of which are 100 percent rayon. Most suits and dresses cost less than $80. Jeans range from $15 to $35; black leggings are $13 and up; and a three-piece navy suit was $44 when we visited the store. The 32nd Street store is small, but there are three large, well-lit dressing rooms with good mirrors. The sales staff is friendly and helpful.

Veronique Delachaux

1321 Madison Avenue at 93rd Street
831-7800
www.veroniqued.com
Return Policy: Store credit only.

Veronique Delachaux carries its own chic line of imported French-designed maternity wear. These clothes give pregnant women a tailored look, focusing on casual business attire: pants, blazers, and tops, with some special-occasion items. The clothing is French-cut and may not be suitable for tall or larger-sized women. The sales staff is knowledgeable and helpful. Prices are steep; a suit usually costs between $400 and $500, and a pair of jeans can be $140.

The Dan Howard Maternity Outlet

Route 4 West in Paramus, New Jersey,
as well as other stores in Southern
New Jersey and Long Island.
201-843-4980
www.imaternity.com
Return Policy: 10 day exchange policy,
no cash refunds.

Dan Howard has recently updated their clothing line. Their designers have expanded the career line to accommodate fashionable moms-to-be. This store is reasonably priced; an unlined jacket runs between $48 and $58, while a lined jacket costs $88. The Dan Howard clothing line is known for its quality, and the store is recognized for its customer service, making it worth the trip to New Jersey.

10 · baby furniture & accessories

Walk into any baby furniture store in this city and you'll face a sea of cribs, changing tables, and strollers. A year from now you'll be an expert on all of these items—but, for new moms, some advice is in order. This chapter tells you what you need and why you need it.

While cost and style will influence your choice of your baby's new stroller, crib, or changing table, New York mothers-to-be must also consider space. Is your apartment a roomy two-bedroom plus dining room, or is it basically a large studio? Portability will also be a consideration. Do you have any idea how hard it is to maneuver a super-deluxe stroller in and out of a city bus or taxi?

Don't run out and buy everything at once. You'll need the crib and stroller immediately, but wait until after the baby is born for the rest. You may receive useful gifts. Also, try to borrow some things, such as bouncy seats and swings. When you are ready to shop, read through our listings. Baby "superstores" carry almost everything you will need; the information here will give you an idea of what you want *before* you go shopping.

Think about purchasing the *Consumer Reports Guide to Baby Products* as well. This guide lists basic products by manufacturer and notes the pros and cons of each. While the information can sometimes seem outdated, you will be able to see pictures of some of the products you're interested in.

If you're of a mind and pocketbook to go all out and fix up a splendid room for your little one, New York has decorators and design consultants at your service. Several interior designers who specialize in children's rooms are listed below. They can help with choosing paint colors, wallpaper, and furniture and can also contribute great space-saving ideas for city apartments. While you're planning the decor, don't forget to make sure everything is baby-safe. Check here for tips and resources.

A few last bits of advice, however. Order your furniture at least twelve weeks before your due date. Kelly ordered her crib well in advance, and Alexander still arrived first. Also, many items can be called in and ordered by phone or through the Internet. It saves time and anything that saves time helps—especially if this is your second or third child. Finally, if you are a second-time parent, be aware that many car seats and toys have been recalled in the past four years. Please call the Consumer Products Safety Commission (800-638-2772) to see if your old infant car seat is still okay, *before* you use it.

Bassinets

A bassinet is a lovely basket for a newborn to sleep in. It is usually used for about three months. It can be handy if you want your baby to sleep in your bedroom, or if a full-size crib seems too big for that tiny infant. There are a lot of styles-from bassinets with wheels, to those that rock, to those that lift off the stand-and some come with full bedding ensembles, including linens, coverlets, and fitted sheets. Prices generally range from $50 to $130, though you can pay up to $700 for a full, top of the line bassinet set from Monica Noel (see their listing under "Interior Design and Decoration"). Our favorite is the Kids Line

bassinet, featuring carry straps on the detachable basket for portability, and full bedding. The unit collapses for easy storage or travel and the bassinet linens (available in a variety of colors and patterns) are removable for washing.

Here are the most popular brands of bassinets in New York:

Badger
Kids Line*
Lee Hy
Century
Graco

Cribs

There are so many choices of styles, colors, and finishes, it can be overwhelming. And, since the first edition of *City Baby*, new crib manufacturers have entered the marketplace—most of them high-end, offering designs, styles, and colors that reflect trends in the adult market. You can find cribs in sleighbed styles and distressed wood finishes, in traditional styles or sleek, modern designs, but in almost all cases, the choices you're making are purely aesthetic. Don't worry, however-there's no need to be concerned about safety issues. All cribs sold today are certified by the Juvenile Products Manufacturers Association (JPMA), which develops standards for many baby products, including strollers/carriages, highchairs, and playpens. JPMA safety specifications require that the space between crib bars is no more than two and three-eighths inches apart, all crib mattresses fit snugly, and all cribs have firmly locking dropsides and childproof lock-release mechanisms.

Here are the questions to ask when you shop for a crib:

Do both sides, or just one drop? One drop-side provides more stability and is easier to operate while holding a baby in the other arm.

✳ **Can you raise or lower the crib's sides with one hand while holding the baby, or do you need both hands? Some American cribs have kickstands under the side rails, making them easier to raise and lower. More and more American companies (and most European companies) use an easy, leg-operated side-track mechanism.**

✳ **Is the crib stable when you shake it? A loose crib frame, or the sound of metal knocking against metal might indicate faulty construction or assembly.**

✳ **Does the crib include stabilizer bars, metal rods fastened to the endboards and located underneath the crib? These bars provide additional stabilization and protection for baby.**

✳ **Do the wheels have locks to prevent the crib from "walking"?**

✳ **Can the crib be converted into a youth bed (i.e., is one side completely removable)?**

The crib you bring home should have a mattress that fits snugly (a gap of no more than one and one-half inches between the mattress and the crib's sides and ends). Bumpers should be securely tied on with at least six ties or snaps. Keep the crib clear of any items—mobiles, clothing, and toys—that have strings longer than seven inches. Don't set up the crib near any potential hazards in the room, such as a heater, window, or cords from blinds.

Below are the crib manufacturers whose products are widely available in the New York area. Most of these lines are well known and established in the baby market, while others, like Mibb and Million Dollar Baby, are only a few years old. Some lines, like Legacy and Renaissance, are new, exclusive divisions of established lines (Child Craft and Simmons, respectively). The choice comes down to what you like and what you can afford. Shop around: prices range from less than $200 for a Cosco to more than $900 for a Bellini. (At Little Stars, we saw a line of sleek metal cribs from Bratt Decor that started at $1,000!) Ask whether the store delivers and what they charge, and confirm they will assemble the crib in your home. They should.

Bassett
Bellini
Bonavita
Child Craft*
Cosco
Delta
Legacy
Mibb
Million Dollar Baby
Morigeau*
Pali
Ragazzi
Renaissance
Simmons*

Ten Tips for a Baby's Room

1. Good overhead lighting is key for convenience and safety.

2. A humidifier can be important in overheated New York apartments.

3. Have as many dressers, drawers, or shelves as possible—you'll need them.

4. Design the closet in the baby's room to allow for more toy than clothing space; baby clothes are tiny.

5. Baby proof the room (see page 179).

6. Have some toys placed within your baby's reach.

7. A glider or rocker can save the day (or night).

8. Curtains or shades help baby sleep.

9. If possible, leave a play space in the middle of the room.

10. Keep it simple—a busy or overdecorated room gets old quickly.

Changing Tables

Today's most popular changing tables are dressers with changing kits on top, built to grow with your child. The top of the dresser becomes a changing area when you place the changing kit, fitted with a pad, on top of the dresser. Remove the kit once you're beyond the diaper stage, and you have a standard chest of drawers that's great for a bigger kid's room. De Arthur, Morigeau, Bellini, Child Craft and several new, upscale companies carry this type of table. Prices start at about $200.

Conventional changing tables have a little pad with a small guardrail that goes all the way around the top (picture a rectangle) so your baby can't roll off. There are shelves underneath for storing diapers and wipes. However, you should never leave a baby unattended, no matter how secure your baby might seem. Popular brands for these tables include Simmons and Child Craft, and prices start at about $170.

Most crib manufacturers also carry coordinating changing tables as part of nursery suites that also include chests and cribs. These fancier tables generally cost between $100 and $200.

Gliders

A glider or rocking chair is optional, but if you have the space and the money, you may find having one helpful when you're feeding your baby or trying to get him to sleep. Dutalier gliders retail for about $500, and are practical for New York apartments. The popular sleigh glider is very compact. They come in your choice of white or wood finishes, with different fabric patterns for the cushions. Matching ottomans are also available. Albee's, Cradle and All, and other baby superstores will custom-make a glider cover to match your decor. But beware: Alexander got trained to fall asleep while being rocked, and, as he got older, expected to be rocked whenever he woke in the middle of the night. Angela did not have a glider in her room for this very reason, and was a better sleeper from day one.

Carriages/Strollers

Newborns and toddlers alike spend many hours in the stroller going to the park, the supermarket, or window-shopping along the avenues. New York is a walking town, and your stroller is the equivalent of a suburban mini-van. Whether you choose a carriage (a bassinet-like construction on wheels) or a stroller (easily collapsible) depends on your personal needs. While suburban mothers and fathers may be content with an inexpensive umbrella stroller that spends most of its time in the trunk of a car, city parents know a sturdy carriage is a must-have for babies and toddlers, especially since we use it to carry the groceries home, too.

All strollers sold today are safe (the JPMA sees to that), but not every type may be right for you. Consider what time of year your baby is due before you purchase your carriage or stroller. For winter babies, a carriage with a boot (an enclosed end) might be the best bet to keep your infant warm. For summer babies, look for a carriage with good ventilation and a sunshade. Also consider where you live. If your building has a doorman, you can usually get some help carrying a heavier stroller up the stairs and inside. If you're in a walk-up or non-doorman building, look for one that's light and portable, and practice folding it to get it down to a quick routine; you're going to be wrestling that stroller in and out of buses and cabs for a good couple of years.

Other desirable features include a stroller seat that reclines (a must for newborn to three-month-olds), plenty of storage space underneath, brakes on all four wheels, and a handle that reverses to allow the baby to face you or to face out. The latest innovation is the popular stroller/car seat combination. This is an infant car seat that straps and snaps into a stroller base. New moms swear by this for taxi travel and city walking. Popular models include the Snap N' Go by Baby Trend, Century 4-in-1 Plus by Century, the Circus and Sterling LiteRiders by Graco, the Evenflo Trendsetter by Evenflo, and the Kolcraft Secura Travel System by Kolcraft. The Snap N' Go is by far the most popular model, with prices ranging from $100 to $180. Practically all of the moms at Pamela's West Side New Mother's Luncheon swear by it to get them around the city safely.

For umbrella strollers, the English-made Maclarens consistently have the lowest rate of returns or repairs of umbrella strollers and have withstood the test of time for parents who re-use them with their second child. Pamela has had her Maclaren for five years now, without a single repair! They retail for $170 to $300, depending on the model. For a full carriage/stroller, it is generally agreed that the Peg Perego strollers are the best of the lot. We both used the Milano ($360) and loved it. These Italian-made strollers are so popular in New York, the playgrounds look like Peg Perego parking lots! They are sturdy, attractive, stand folded upright for storage, and have a multitude of features that make life easy for mom and baby (reversible handle, large removable storage basket, full boot, and large canopy).

Jogging strollers are also very popular with parents who exercise with their babies. Their cost is between $100 and $400, depending on wheel size—the bigger the wheels, the more smoothly they roll. A marathon runner we know used one of these to run with his daughter for years. For parents of twins or two small children, side-by-side or tandem strollers might be good options. Side-by-sides are great for twins or children close to the same weight, while tandem strollers are great for kids of different sizes—with larger kids in front, and smaller in back. These two-seaters sell for an average price of $125.

When preparing to buy, tell the store clerk how you plan to use the carriage, and ask for a recommendation. Take the carriage for a "test drive" in the store to see whether it feels comfortable for you and your husband; check the height of the handles or bar, and make sure neither of you has to hunch over to reach it comfortably.

Here is a list of popular brands sold in New York:

Aprica
Baby Trend
Century

Chicco
Combi*
Emmaljunga
Evenflo
Graco
Inglesina
Kolcraft
Maclaren*
Peg Perego*

Car Seats

Even if you don't have a car, you must have a car seat. State law dictates that your newborn must leave the hospital in one, and while you could borrow a seat from a friend, purchasing your own will be a practical investment.

Babies must always ride in a car seat whenever in an automobile by law. City taxis must come equipped with rear seat belts to attach over the car seat, so double check before you get into a cab. If you have any questions, call the New York Coalition for Transportation Safety at 516-829-0099. That said, it's very difficult to carry both a car seat and a stroller around with you. Hence, the new stroller/car seat combos, with the removable infant car seats that strap and snap into a base is a great alternative. Prices range from $100 to $180. Some city parents just use a baby carrier for infants, and hold toddlers on their laps.

The more ungainly convertible seats can be used from birth through the toddler years and have a reclining mechanism so that they face rearward for infants and forward for toddlers and young children. With more features and an advanced five-point tethering system, the Britax Roundabout ($200) is by far the most popular model on the market right now. Kelly's using it now, too. Other best-selling brands in Manhattan include Century and Evenflo. As of September 1999, all forward facing car seats had to be shipped with tether straps for extra protection. (They've been doing this in Europe for years.)

Three designs of restraining straps or harnesses are available in car seats: the five-point harness, the T-shield, and the bar shield. Most experts agree that the five-point harness is the safest, but all three are sound options. The five-point harness is also the most time-consuming to put on and off, which can be annoying to impatient toddlers. All of this will make sense once you see them in the stores.

Though convertible seats can be used from birth, experts advise you to buy an infant carrier car seat for babies from birth up to twenty pounds (these range in price from $40 to $80), and the convertible car seat when the child weighs more. Infant car seats are smaller, recline better, often come with a sunshade, and are more heavily padded than the convertible. They're portable and can easily be carried in and out of the car without disturbing a sleeping baby. Remember that these seats must be rear-facing in your vehicle; toddler seats forward-facing.

Booster seats and high-back boosters are designed for kids over 40 pounds—too big for convertible seats, but still too small for regular seatbelts. They have a raised, rigid base that allows children to use adult belts. Prices range from $25 to $150.

Baby Swings

A swing might be your lifesaver during your baby's first few months— or maybe not. This is something your child either loves or hates. (Rebecca hated it, but Alexander loved it and never made a peep when he was in it.) We recommend you borrow one from a friend or relative before making the investment.

The Graco Swyngomatic is the only widely available swing. It's great. There are two models on the market—with and without the overhead bar. The benefit of the Graco Advantage is that without the bar, you can't bump your baby's head on it. Graco Advantage retails for $120; the original Graco can be found for $79 to $109. Fisher Price and Regalo also make baby swings ranging from $40 to $100.

Bouncy Seats

The bouncy seat is another potential lifesaver; in fact, we know women who would not have been able to shower for six months had they not made this investment. It's portable; you can move it from the living room to the kitchen to the bathroom so you can always see your baby and he can always see you. Plus, the newest bouncy seats are more plush than ever, and have a vibrating feature that can lull a fussy baby right to sleep. (Another new innovation we don't know how we lived without!) The bouncy seat is great for feeding your baby when he's starting to eat solid food but is still too small for a highchair. Combi's "Activity Rocker" is the one most people get ($69); it's well made, it vibrates—and it's fancier than other brands. The European style of rocker-bouncers is very popular as well, such as the one from Chicco. Prices range from $30 for a Kids II seat, and $64 for a Chicco. Here's a list of the bouncy seats available in New York:

Chicco
Combi*
Evenflo
Kids II
Summer

Highchairs

When you are buying a highchair, it is advisable to:

1. Buy a chair with a wide base to limit the chances of the chair tipping over.

2. Find a chair with an easy, one-hand tray release mechanism, which makes it easier to take your baby in and out.

3. Look for a wrap-around tray—easier to eat from and keep clean.

4. Find a chair with a detachable seat cushion. These chairs become dirty easily and you will want it to last more than a year.

Most highchair accidents occur (usually with children under one year) when a child has not been strapped in properly and tumbles out. Don't rely on the chair's tray to keep your baby enclosed; use the safety belt and never leave your baby unattended.

Before buying a highchair, decide if you want wood or metal and vinyl. Wooden highchairs are beautiful, but they don't collapse—so they are not ideal for those with limited apartment space. Also they require the use of both hands to take the tray off. Some models require you to flip the tray over the baby's head. If you're not careful, this can be a dangerous maneuver.

Right now, the most popular and functional highchairs are metal and vinyl. They have one-handed tray release mechanisms, reclining and height features. They are easy to clean seats, and have comfy cushioning.

By far, the most popular highchair on the market is the Peg Perego Prima Pappa—with seven height adjustments and four recline positions, a thickly padded seat, a wrap-around tray, and a wide wheeled base, this highchair is ideal. This is also the most expensive model, at $170. Highchair prices start at $90 for a Million Dollar Baby.

First Years' Reclining Three Stage Feeding Seat is a great alternative to a highchair because like a booster seat, it straps onto a regular chair (at $30, it's also an inexpensive alternative). This seat has 3 recline positions for each stage of early childhood: newborn, infant, and toddler. To adjust, you simply press two buttons and slide the seat. This product is ideal for traveling, as well as smaller apartments where space is limited. It retails for approximately $30.

Finally, we must repeat: Never leave your baby unattended in a highchair, even for a few seconds!

Here are some of the best and most popular brands:

Peg Perego
Chicco
First Years
Rochelle
Million Dollar Baby

Booster Seats/Hook-On Seats

You may want to buy a portable chair to use when you take your baby or toddler to a restaurant or other place where no highchair is available.

Hook-on seats have a short life. (Rebecca couldn't sit comfortably in one after she was nine months old.) Also, if the seat is hooked incorrectly onto the table, or if the child can detach the seat from under the table with his foot, these seats can cause accidents. If you do use a hook-on seat, *always place a chair under it*. Manufacturers include Graco, Chicco, and Baby Trend, but *Consumer Reports* does not recommend using hook-on seats at all; the hazards are just too serious.

We have found booster seats to be safer and more practical than hook-ons. They can be used for children up to preschool age, and our favorite, the Safety 1st ($30), can be easily folded. Put this on a chair in your kitchen and you may be able to live without an expensive highchair! Other popular brands include Cosco, First Years, and Kids II, with prices ranging between $12 and $25.

Playpens/Portable Cribs

Playpens are a great place to park your baby when you need five minutes to yourself to shower, answer the door, talk on the phone, or make dinner. Some babies might amuse themselves in the playpen for up to thirty minutes at a time, but not all children like them. Kelly used a playpen for months with Alexander and yet Angela wouldn't stay ten minutes without screaming her head off. Playpens are also big and difficult to store and transport, so you might want to go for the portable crib instead. It can function as a playpen, but it's smaller and can easily be put away. Portable cribs have a thin mattress and sheets, so they can be used as a crib when you're traveling. Many of the playpens and cribs are fundamentally the same, but each brand offers different additional features. When shopping for a playpen, be sure to compare and contrast different brands to find the best features for your specific needs. Prices range between $80 for the Graco Pack 'N Play, to $175 for Arm's Reach Concepts' dual playpen/bassinet. Popular brands include:

Arms Reach Concepts
Century*
Fisher Price
Graco Pack 'N Play*
Regalo

Bathtubs/Bath Seats

At first, bathe your tiny baby in the kitchen or bathroom sink. When he's a little bigger and you'd prefer to use the bathtub, you may want to buy a special baby tub that fits into the big tub. Most baby tubs are similar; they come either with or without a sponge insert. The sponge tends to get a mildew odor, is hard to wring out, and takes days to dry—so we opt for without. The Cuddletub by Graco ($25) is a great bathtub that is carried by many stores. It has an adjustable foam cushion with mesh underneath for newborns to rest on. It can be removed once your baby can sit up on his own. The best-selling Evenflo Two-Year tub ($22) is the sturdiest of tubs and can be used for a child up to two years old. It has an insert for infants up to three months old, which can be easily removed as the child grows.

When your baby is old enough to sit up on his own, he's ready for a bath seat. The Safety 1st bath seat ($17) is a ring that attaches to your bathtub with suction cups. It is roomy enough to hold a two-year-old. We have both been happy with Safety 1st. Once she can sit up on her own, your baby will also enjoy the inflatable Kel-Gar Snug-Tub ($18). It looks like a mini pool and is lots of fun for older babies (over six months).

Baby Carriers

You see these pouch-like, soft cloth carriers strapped onto the fronts of mothers and fathers everywhere. They're often called "snuglis" for the company that invented them. While the actual Snuglis are attractive and functional, Baby Bjorn has surpassed them in quality and price. Pamela's Snugli went virtually unused for Rebecca, but a friend gave her a Baby Bjorn when Benjamin was born, and she used it every day.

This is another item that you'll use for only a short time. Kelly purchased one and then had a nine-and-one-half pound baby, who quickly became too heavy to carry strapped onto her shoulders. Try to borrow one from a friend and test it with your baby before purchasing to see if you're comfortable with it. Baby carriers are popular with second or third time moms who might have a stroller to push or other hands to hold.

Prices range from $25 for a Snugli, to $79 for the best-selling Baby Bjorn. Nojo makes a popular Baby Sling (about $40), which allows you to hold your baby horizontally as well as vertically (allowing baby to sleep more comfortably). This product is wonderful for breastfeeding because you simply pull the fabric up over baby's head and you are guarded from exposure.

Backpacks

Women who use backpacks swear by them for comfort and convenience. Your baby is ready for a backpack once she can sit up on her own. Borrow one from a friend, and try it out with your baby on board before you decide to purchase your own.

The most popular brand is the Kelty backpack, which is strong and durable. Kelty is well known for its outdoor equipment and this product is just as heavy-duty. It costs slightly more than the other brands (about $100), but will last forever.

Gerry and Tough Travelers also make dependable backpacks, starting at about $70.

Baby Monitors

Here's how to be in one room and hear your baby crying in another. These gadgets give you lots of options. Some monitors are battery-operated and can be carried throughout the apartment. It is difficult to say which brand is the most functional because of varying frequencies in different areas. The most secure method in buying the right monitor is to ask other parents in your neighborhood or building which monitors work best for them. Many New York buildings pick up "noise" from other apartments. You may hear another baby crying and think it's your own. Here are the most recent and popular additions to the monitor category:

900 Megahertz (MHz) monitors: These offer greater range and clarity than earlier models, and they are offered by several companies including First Years Crisp 'N Clear ($50), and Safety 1st's Sensitive Sound ($50) or Grow with Me ($65).

Monitors with two receivers: These are great and functional for larger living spaces because you can leave monitors in separate rooms. Graco makes the most popular model ($50).

Rechargeable Monitors: Available from The First Years for $80, these work much like your portable or cellular phone, except it is a direct line to your little darling.

Safety 1st has Angel Care which is a sound and movement monitor created to guard against SIDS. It is an ultra-sensitive sensor pad that is placed under the baby's mattress. If the pad does not sense motion, including heartbeat and breath for twenty seconds an alarm sounds to alert you. It costs about $100. Beware: this can drive you crazy and keep you up at night, even when your baby is asleep.

Safety 1st has also created a Child View Monitor which has 2.4 Gigahertz (GHz) for clarity and additional privacy. It has a camera for sound and image as well as a little television monitor for $150.

You may have to try a few different monitors out before you settle on one—sometimes you pick up your neighbors' conversations instead of the baby's cries.

Diaper Bags

Diaper bags come in two basic styles: over-the-shoulder, which zips or snaps closed, and the increasingly popular knapsack with a drawstring opening.

You won't believe how much stuff you have to carry for your baby. Find a roomy bag with lot of pockets (for bottles, wipes and the like) and a plastic lining. A changing pad is another great feature. The superstores have terrific selections. Babies Alley makes a popular Chanel look-alike, in quilted black with gold chain straps. Peg Perego has patterns that match their carriages. Pierre Deux's pretty (and functional) bag comes in a variety of colors, and Baby Mania offers a funky, fake fur bag for $129.95. Chic designers like Kenneth

Cole, Donna Karan, and Kate Spade have also gotten into the act with stylish, subdued bags (mostly in basic black, of course), available at Bellini and other upscale stores. Prices range from $20 for a Babies Alley diaper bag to $200 for a Pierre Deux. Baby Bjorn and Evenflo make popular knapsacks that don't even look like diaper bags.

THE STORES

Our baby superstores are not necessarily large in size, but we consider them super because they provide one-stop shopping. Here you can buy all the furniture you need (crib, changing table, dresser), as well as sheets, towels, diapers, nipples, bottles, layettes or clothing for newborns, strollers/carriages, highchairs, playpens, baby carriers/ knapsacks, and much, much more. You get the idea. We like them because they make your life easy. Most sell toys, too, but be aware that the selection is limited and the prices are often higher than at Toys "R" Us or other toy stores.

Some stores are ritzier than others, some more value oriented. The proximity of the store to your home should help you decide where to shop. Many expectant moms in New York visit too many stores in their quest for the perfect crib, sheets, and towels. You don't have to! Find a place that's convenient, and use it for all your needs. Patronize one store consistently, so the staff gets to know you and will go that extra mile when necessary. Also, buy in bulk. Many stores never "officially" discount, but may give you a better price if you are placing a large order. Don't be afraid to ask. And there's no harm in asking if they'll match a better price that you have seen somewhere else.

Also check out the store's delivery policy. Policies vary widely.

Superstores

Albee's*
715 Amsterdam Avenue at 95th Street
662-8902
www.babyexpressstores.com
Return Policy: Refunds with receipt.

Albee's is not glamorous—fluorescent lighting, no carpeting, and lots of chaos give you an idea of the atmosphere—but we love it. Carla and Michael, the owners, are friendly, knowledgeable, and down-to-earth, and the store is packed full of just about everything your baby could ever need. We also appreciate their honesty. Pamela was talked out of purchasing a slew of newborn sleepers that Carla said the baby would outgrow in a month. (And, she was right!) Prices here are the best in the city on many items including highchairs, playpens, and strollers. Yet it's not for the faint of heart. Albee's is always busy and so fully stocked that you have to navigate carefully. They carry Simmons, Child Craft, and Morigeau cribs, as well as some Ragazzi and Lexington brands and all the carriage/stroller brands. What they don't have in stock, they can order for you. Albee's also sells clothing, bedding, nipples, bottles, bottle racks, carriage accessories, tapes, videos, books, bibs, cloth diapers, and diaper bags, but not formula.

There is a baby registry-great for people looking to purchase gifts for a new mom.

Baby Depot
707 Sixth Avenue at 23rd Street
229-1300
www.coat.com
Return Policy: Store credit only.

Baby Depot is part of Burlington Coat Factory, a huge store at 23rd Street and Sixth Avenue. This neat and brightly lit department carries everything you'll want, including cribs, highchairs, strollers, clothes, and accessories. The prices are very good. Baby Depot carries a large selection of Simmons and Child Craft cribs. Their stroller selection includes Peg Perego, Aprica, Graco, Combi, Kolcraft, and Maclaren. There is a nice selection of books and videos for babies and toddlers as well as all the nipples and bottles, bibs, cups, and spoons you could ask for. Their layette and clothing selection is great, (they carry maternity clothing, too), and they have good prices on Carter's. The store manager, David Perry, a father himself, is extremely knowledgeable and eager to help. But, it's best to know what you're looking for when shopping at Baby Depot, because the service can be hit or miss. Still, it's worth the trip—the prices are some of the best in town.

Ben's for Kids*
1380 Third Avenue bet. 78th and 79th Streets
794-2330
Return Policy: Refund with receipt, otherwise store credit. Merchandise must be in salable condition and in the original boxes.

This pretty and comforting store is an Upper East Side fixture. Don and Madeline Wein and their helpful staff work hard to keep it top-notch. Ben's for Kids has a modest selection of cribs, a larger selection of strollers and highchairs, and all the accessories you could ever want. When Kelly went in looking for a bottle sterilizer after Alexander was born, Don convinced her she didn't really need one. He was right. Ben's sells cribs by Child Craft, Legacy, Ragazzi, and Simmons. The strollers/carriages include Baby Trend, Combi, Evenflo, Inglesina, Kolcraft, Maclaren, and Peg Perego. Shop here for kiddie clothing too, up to age 24 months. Ben's for Kids delivers five days a week. Delivery is free in New York; they ship UPS outside the city. Upper East Siders love Ben's for its quality, service, and selection.

Planet Kids
247 E. 86th Street bet. Second
and Third Avenues
426-2040
www.planetkidsofny.baweb.com
Return Policy: Return within 7 days, exchange within 12. After 12 days, store credit only.

Opened in July 1999 by the owner of Regine Kids, Shlomo Moskatel, this bright, spacious store contains everything your child needs. There are three stories filled with clothes, cribs, changing tables, car seats, strollers, huge, colorful displays of toys and accessories. Cribs include those from Ragazzi,

Bonavita, C & T, Status, and Child Craft. Strollers include Graco, Maclaren, Peg Perego, Kolcraft, Aprica, Combi, Baby Trend, and Century. Planet Kids also sells Dutailier gliders ($300-490). Children's clothing is by Oshkosh B'Gosh, Le Top, Carter's, and Gerber (up to toddler sizes), and there is a full layette department as well.

Regine Kids

2688 Broadway bet. 102nd and 103rd Streets
864-8705
Return Policy: Return within 7 days, exchange within 12. After 12 days, store credit only.

Uptown moms swear by Regine Kids as the only place in their neighborhood to pick up baby supplies and quality clothing. Regine Kids carries the same wide selection of children's products and accessories as Planet Kids (the stores have the same owner), but has a larger selection of children's clothing, and no cribs. Parents can order cribs, or go to the Planet Kids location. Clothing ranges from newborn sizes to age 16, and brands includes Flapdoodles, Oshkosh and Levi's. A full line of school uniforms is also available.

Schneider's

20 Avenue A at E. 2nd Street
228-3540
Return Policy: No refund. Store credit or exchange with receipt on new merchandise in original package, within 20 days.

Schneider's is a neighborhood store that's been serving the downtown crowd for over fifty years. They carry brands such as Pali, Legacy, Vermont Precision, Maclaren, Perego, Combi, Baby Bjorn, Century, Evenflo, and Tough Traveler. This well-stocked store carries a full line of accessories, but no clothing.

Toys "R" Us

2430 Union Square East at 16th Street
674-8697
1514 Broadway at W. 44th Street
(646) 366-8858 www.toysrus.com
Return Policy: Refund with receipt, otherwise store credit only.

We love Toys "R" Us. They sell furniture and accessories at the best prices in town. You'll find cribs for under $200, strollers, highchairs, playpens, bottles, bibs, and waterproof bed pads, as well as diapers and formula (available by the case). While Toys "R" Us favors the mass-market labels, you can find some of the better brands such as Peg Perego and Graco, plus Cosco, Evenflo, Kolcraft, Aprica, and Fisher-Price. Weekdays and evenings are your best bet for shopping; these stores are mobbed on the weekends. Delivery service is available; prices depend on the size of the items to be shipped.

Specialty Stores

ABC Carpet & Home

888 Broadway at 19th Street
473-3000
www.abchome.com
Return Policy: Refund with receipt, otherwise store credit only.

Style-conscious parents need not worry about outfitting their little one's room. ABC Carpet and Home stocks a small but carefully chosen selection of nursery furnishings in keeping with its antique and country chic theme. The look here is sophisticated rustic, evoking the nineteenth century. You'll find everything from Victorian-inspired cast iron cribs and cradles to fashionably distressed decorative accessories. In addition to home furnishings, there is an impressive selection of high quality baby and toddler clothing, a huge range of plush and classic toys, and children's books and stationery. This is an excellent spot to pick up gifts.

Bellini

1305 Second Avenue bet. 68th
and 69th Streets
517-9233
www.bellini.com
Return Policy: Store credit.

Customers who shop here rave about the top-of-the-line furniture and service at this Tiffany's of baby stores. The store is beautiful, with bright, muraled walls and the longest list of baby necessities we've ever seen! The staff will spend hours helping you select the perfect crib, (this is the only place in town to find a Bellini crib), and coordinating furniture, bedding, and accessories. They custom-make bedding sets and have a library of fabrics you can choose from. Special knit items like sweaters and christening outfits are exquisite. Kelly got a wonderfully trimmed receiving blanket from Bellini with a matching diaper and bib. Delivery is a flat rate of $65; smaller items are shipped UPS. They say they will match prices if they can verify what another store charges.

Buy Buy Baby

Opening Fall 2002
270 Seventh Avenue (24th St.)
www.buybuybaby.com
See description p. 176

Chelsea's Kids Quarter

33 W. 17th Street bet. Fifth and Sixth Avenues
627-5524
Return Policy: Store credit only.

When a child has outgrown his crib, it is time to venture into the world of children's beds, and this store provides the next step. Chelsea Kids supplies you with all you will need to furnish a child's room—tables and chairs, beautiful toy chests, plush toys, bedding, and lighting. We saw a gorgeous red toy chest for $299. All of the furniture is made of solid wood and will heartily withstand the tests of time and usage. A basic wood bed costs about $400, and there are many add-ons to choose from, such as storage drawers, a trundle bed, a bunk bed, or bookcases, as well as a large variety of wood finishes. This store will also do interior design, helping you to choose fabrics and wallpaper, and do general color coordination.

Cradle & All

1384 Lexington Avenue
996-9990
www.cradleandallnyc.com
Return Policy: Store credit only.

This upscale juvenile furniture, accessory, and clothing store sells American and Italian made wood furniture by De Arthur, J. R. Conte, Vermont Tubbs, and Vermont Precision. Between the friendly staff and the welcoming layout (carpeting, walls painted like the sky, soft music), customers feel right at home. Cradle & All offers a wide range of furniture and accessories, as well as some baby clothes and a full line of custom bedding, with brands such as Amy Coe, Liz Wain, Blauen, and Shabby Chic. They also carry a selection of wrought iron cribs, all of which are standard size and have drop side mechanisms, by Benecia. Most of the cribs sold at Cradle & All convert to youth beds.

Just for Tykes

83 Mercer Street bet. Spring
and Broome Streets
274-9121
Return Policy: Store credit only
with receipt within 10 days.

Just for Tykes is a high-end hybrid of a superstore and specialty store. While they don't stock nipples and diapers, they offer high-end baby furniture and baby bedding. Brands include Liz Wain, Sleeping Partners, Designer's Guild, and Bellisimo. They stock car seats (Britax and Century), strollers, toys, swings, and more. They also have infant and toddler clothing by such designers as Portofino, Petit Boy, Deux Par Deux, and more. Just for Tykes was opened very recently by Erika O'Brien, a downtown mom frustrated by the lack of high quality merchandise in her neighborhood.

Karin Alexis Sentry

490 Amsterdam Avenue bet. 83rd
and 84th Streets
769-9550
www.karinalexis.com
Return Policy: Store credit or exchange.

An eclectic shop replacing a furniture store reflects the Upper West Side's practical, yet funky sensibility. Karin is the owner and operator of this shop specializing in clothing, accessories, and gifts for children newborn and up. She designs many of the items in her store, and they are usually boldly patterned and brightly colored.

This is also a great spot for baby gifts and accessories.

Kid's Supply Co.

1325 Madison Avenue bet. 93rd
and 94th Streets
426-1200
www.kidssupplyco.com
Return Policy: Quite restrictive,
call store for details.

Kid's Supply Co. is a small, high-end store brimming with an eclectic mix of timeless, sophisticated furniture, and unusual accessories. Befitting its tony neighborhood, Kid's Supply is quite pricey, and designs and manufactures their own line of fine quality goods. The staff will work closely with you to create the room of your dreams. Beds convert from bunk beds to twins, and they come as day beds and trundle beds. They can be custom finished, too. Cribs and changing tables, which convert into dressers, are available as well. Linens can be customized and Kid's Supply Co., and they have an especially wide selection of boy's bedding. Kid's Supply Co. also has a larger store with beautiful displays in Greenwich, Connecticut (203-422-2932), one hour outside of New York City.

Little Folk Art

159 Duane Street bet. Hudson Street
and W. Broadway
267-1500
Return Policy: Store credit only.

This beautiful Tribeca store is spacious, clean, and bright, and displays exquisite solid wood pieces such as cribs, rocking chairs, bureaus and desks. Most items in the store are fashionably distressed with an heirloom quality about them. Little Folk Art carries toys, books, and stuffed animals as well. Susan, the store's owner, provides a full interior decorating service, and will come to your home to take pictures and measurements, and help you choose everything from colors to fabric, rugs, and curtains. The rooms are classic, making them a one-time investment.

Pamela Scurry's Wicker Garden

1327 Madison Avenue bet. 93rd
and 94th Streets
410-7001
Return Policy: Store credit only.

This top-of-the-line boutique is exquisite, and the baby furniture, much of which is hand-painted, is some of the loveliest (and most expensive) in town. You'll find finishing touches, such as coordinating wastepaper baskets, diaper pails, chests, and changing tables to match a crib. They have books of linens to choose from, will custom-make anything, and carry top brands such as Blauen. The main floor has a full layette selection; most of the clothing is imported from France and Italy, all with the Wicker Garden label. This is the place for beautiful children's clothes and hand-painted furniture when you choose to go first class.

The Upper Breast Side

220 West 71st Street Suite 1
New York, NY 10023
873-2653
www.upperbreastside.com
Return Policy: Exchange only within two weeks of purchase.

This new boutique for breastfeeding moms is all the rage with Upper West Side moms. This is a one-of-a-kind place offering every accoutrement for breastfeeding. Bras, breast pumps, nursing pillows, and more. The owner is extremely knowledgeable, and committed to finding the best products for nursing. She also carries some baby accessories.

Superstores Outside of New York City

The Baby and Toy Superstore*
11 Forest Street, Stamford, CT 06901
203-327-1333
www.babyandtoy.com
Return Policy: Refund within fifteen days with receipt and original packaging, otherwise store credit only.

The store is clean, bright, and big, and offers all the best brands at some of the best prices around. Roz, Harvey, and Seth, the owners, work closely with customers and know their merchandise. They offer every Pali and Ragazzi crib and set of furniture, and carry items that aren't available anywhere else in the New York area. Other brands include Legacy, AP Industries, Morigeau, Moosehead, and Michael's Wicker. They sell ready-made linens, but will custom-make beautiful crib sets as well. New York residents pay no sales tax, but delivery is $85 and up (assembly is included). Kelly loves Baby and Toy Superstore and uses them to this day.

Buy Buy Baby
1019 Central Park Avenue
Scarsdale, NY 10583
914-725-9220
350 Route 110
Huntington Station, New York
631-425-0404
240 Route 17 North
Paramus, New Jersey 07652
201-599-1900
www.buybuybaby.com
Return Policy: Refund within 30 days if the item is unused; after 30 days, store credit only.

This store is huge (40,000 square feet and over 20,000 products), and known for its top-notch personalized service and guaranteed low prices. Product brands include Peg Perego, Maclaren, Graco, Century, Britax, Cosco, Evenflo, Simmons, Child Craft, Dutalier, and more. Clothing is available from Baby Lulu, Carter's, Little Me, Calvin Klein, Nautica, Baby Dior, and Flapdoodles, among others. Aside from offering just about anything a parent could want, Buy Buy Baby also has three artists on staff to customize furniture; an electronic baby registry; nursing rooms; and free gift wrap. Delivery to Manhattan is $80, plus an extra $25 for assembly, and smaller items can be shipped through UPS. This store tends to get very crowded, especially during the weekends—so go early or check out the Web site instead.

Darling's
169 South Central Avenue
Hartsdale, NY 10530
914-993-0800
5 Perlman Drive, Pascack Plaza
Spring Valley, NY 10977
914-352-5600
Return Policy: Refund with receipt within fourteen days, otherwise store credit only.

Our friends in Westchester recommend this store, which has infant and baby clothing, furniture, strollers, car seats, playpens, and more at discounted prices. Darling's carries cribs by

Simmons, Child Craft, Morigeau, Ragazzi, Pali, Tracer, and more. They also have a large stroller selection, including Peg Perego, Maclaren, Graco, and Aprica. Darling's has a full layette department, clothing for children up to two years, and a baby registry. They will special order furniture and accessories they don't stock.

INTERIOR DESIGN AND DECORATION

Ready to get creative? The following New York stores sell children's wallpaper and accessories to help you pull together your baby's room. Many have in-store consultants with experience or degrees in interior design. We have also listed a few interior designers and consultants who specialize in children's rooms. We have seen their work, and it is truly special.

Charm and Whimsy
Esther Sadowsky, Allied A.S.I.D
114 E. 32nd Street
683-7609

Esther has found her niche designing nurseries and children's rooms. From a small room to a suite of rooms, she will create a fun, delightful space for your child to grow up in. She can design furniture, select fabrics and carpeting, and hand-paint your chairs and benches. She can even paint a mural on your child's ceiling; the cost is $500 for a mural with a simple image. Custom, hand-painted furniture, murals, and finishes are all specialties of Charm & Whimsy. Esther designs rooms for the parents, too.

Funtastic Interiors, Inc.
Kimberley Fiterman, A.S.I.D.
60 W. 12th Street
633-0660

A mother of two, Kimberley has a library of resources and is a specialist in designing unique yet functional nurseries, children's bedrooms, and playrooms. She'll even design all the furniture that makes these rooms cozy and safe. Her work has been featured in the *New York Times* and *New York* magazine. Her rate is $125 an hour or thirty percent of an established budget.

Gracious Home
1217/1220 Third Avenue at 70th Street
517-6300
1992 Broadway at 67th Street
231-7800

Gracious Home sells beautiful coordinated borders, wallpaper, and paint. They have a children's section offering beautiful bumper sets and bedding. They carry area rugs, wastepaper baskets, lamps, and bathroom accessories. Gracious Home will make up any window treatment you desire, or coordinate an entire room. The entire selection is quite beautiful.

Janovic Plaza*
Many locations throughout Manhattan
772-1400

Janovic Plaza offers a wide selection of wallpaper, borders, paints, and window treatments, and designers there will help plan your room and coordinate everything. There's a broad selection of reasonably priced fabrics suitable for a child's room. Ask about Janovic's classes on painting and wallpapering. Pamela has used the Janovic Plaza store on W. 72nd Street for borders and window treatments, with happy results.

Kids Digs

Carol Maryan Architects
212 W. 79th Street, suite 1C
787-7800

Owner Carol Maryan is an architect and designer who specializes in child-oriented spaces. Her room designs can be adapted to your child's needs as the years go by. A consultation, which is a problem-solving session and includes a sketch of the proposed room, is usually about $350, but price depends on job size and scope. Carol will complete a design project at an hourly rate of around $90 (again, depending on the job).

Laura Ashley Home

398 Columbus Avenue at 79th Street
496-5110
Return Policy: 90 days with receipt or tags attached.

In their Mother and Child collection, Laura Ashley offers complete bedding ensembles to match window treatments, lampshades, and diaper stackers. Check out their Gingham and Hey Diddle Diddle collections. Laura Ashley has one of the best border selections around;

everything is pre-made and ready to go. You can find custom-made bedding and window treatments available at reduced prices several times a year.

Laura Beth's Baby Collection

300 E. 75th Street, Suite 24E
717-2559

Laura Beth, a former buyer in the famed Baby Department at Barney's New York, meets one-on-one with stylish Moms-to-be to help them pick out linens and accessories for the wee one's room. She offers one-stop personal shopping for crib linens, custom bedding, and a variety of accessories for the nursery, including mobiles, frames, bookends, and more. Laura has great taste, and carries only the finest collections the baby market has to offer at prices better than retail. By appointment only.

Nursery Lines Ltd.

1034 Lexington Avenue at 74th Street
396-4445
www.nurserylines.com
Return Policy: Store credit only.

This small yet intimate store focuses on creating classic and traditional rooms for your child. It provides full interior design services-everything from cushions to window treatments. Store owner Pearl Thompson uses mostly English fabrics like Bennison, Osbourne and Little, and high-caliber Italian and French brands such as Minnie, Molli, and Claudia Monet. This store does not cater to those looking for theme-rooms featuring characters like Winnie the Pooh or Pokemón; they pride themselves in creating rooms that last throughout the teenage years. This store also carries gifts, clothing, and accessories for children ages newborn to 4.

Plain Jane

525 Amsterdam Avenue at 85th Street
595-6916
www.plainjanekids.com
Return Policy: Store credit only.

If you want to put together a 40s/50s retro look, this eclectic store sells decorative accessories, furniture, and bedding for the home, especially for a baby's room (which, of course, is exactly what you're looking for). They do a wonderful job with custom bedding and furniture, and have a knack for arranging items in displays that will give you lots of ideas.

SmartStart

Susan Weinberg
334 W. 86th Street, Suite 6C
580-7365

Susan, an interior designer, starts with a consultation to focus on your needs and to analyze the space. She shops for you, starting from a list of your basic needs, then helps you select the furniture. A consultation is $150 in the city; $200 outside the city. Her hourly rate is $100; for large projects, her fee is twenty percent of the cost. She can also help order birth announcements.

BABY PROOFING

Little did you know your apartment was a danger zone. Beware if you have—as do most of us—a glass or sharp-edged coffee table, electrical outlets, lamps, lamp cords, drawers, cleaning solutions and cosmetics under sinks/vanities, or anything sitting on a table. Baby proofing your home is one of the most important tasks you'll undertake. By the time your child begins to creep and crawl, all potentially dangerous objects must be covered, secured, removed, or replaced.

Here are three ways to get baby proofing help:

Buy a book or video such as Mr. Baby Proofer, a thirty-minute video that shows parents how to create a safe environment for newborns.

❋ **Ask for advice at any of the baby superstores. A salesperson will talk you through what you need in order to create a safe home.**

❋ **Hire a baby proofing expert. Howard Applebaum of Babyproofers Plus (800-880-2191) will come to your home for a free consultation, determine what you need, prepare an estimate, and install everything. We have both used Howard, who gives seminars on child safety at local hospitals, and we highly recommend him. Another excellent baby proofing company is All Star Baby Safety, Inc. (877-668-7677), run by Tom Treanor, who will come to your home for a free consultation and price estimate for the full service. He will also travel to Long Island and Westchester if you want to baby proof a beach or country house. Tom is a distributor of the magnetic Tot-Lok safety sys-**

tem and a member of the International Association for Child Safety.

Many people baby proof their own apartments. Howard Applebaum suggests the following safety tips:

Poisons or toxic materials (i.e., all cleaners) should not be stored under the sink; place them high up, out of your baby's reach.

* Attach all busy boxes, mirrors, or crib toys on the wall side of the crib, so that your baby cannot use the objects to climb out of the crib. Do not mount a wall hanging above the crib, where your child can pull it down and perhaps dislodge nails.

* Toilet lids should be locked closed.

* Keep all trash containers locked up and out of baby's way.

* Remove tall lamps or coatracks or block them with furniture, so that your baby can't pull them over.

* When cooking, all pot handles should be turned inward so your baby cannot reach them. Use back burners when possible.

* Separate plants and babies. Some plants are poisonous, and a young child may eat the leaves or pull the whole plant on top of himself.

* Hanging cords from answering machines, phones, lamps, and appliances should be out of your baby's reach.

* Do not take pills or medication in front of children; they mimic what they see.

* Remove all soaps, razors, and shampoos from around the edge of the bathtub.

* Do not use tacks or staples to secure electrical cords to walls; they can fall out or be pulled out and swallowed. Use tape.

* Discard plastic dry cleaner bags before entering the house. Babies can suffocate in them or pull off pieces and choke on them.

* Keep emergency phone numbers, including poison control center, near all telephones.

* To prevent carpeting from sliding, use a foam grid padding beneath it.

* Babies like to pull off the tips from doorstops. Place some glue inside the cap, then stick the cap back onto the doorstop.

* Remove magnets from your refrigerator door. If they fall to the floor and break, a child may pick up the pieces and swallow them. Invest in baby magnets or plastic non-breakable ones.

* If you have a fireplace, place a piece of carpet or foam on the whole base so your child won't bang into the brick.

* Get a bathtub spout cover to prevent your child from hitting his head against it.

* If you have a home gym, keep that room closed when you're not in it. Babies can get their fingers stuck in the spokes of exercise bikes, put their fingers in the gears, or pull weights onto themselves.

* Glass panels in coffee tables can break under the weight of a child. Replace with acrylic.

* Mobiles should be removed when a child is five to seven months old. A baby of that age can pull the mobile down, or be injured if the little strings from the mobile can be wrapped around his fingers.

✳ Cords for window blinds should be lifted high and out of reach. Babies can accidentally wrap them around themselves.

✳ Wash out cleaning fluid bottles before putting them in your recycling bin. Just a drop of cleaning fluid can cause serious injury to a baby.

✳ Never leave infants alone in the bathtub. Ignore telephone calls and doorbells. Babies can drown in just an inch of water. Never leave a tub with water standing in it.

✳ Check the underside of upholstered furniture for loose staples or sharp points.

11 · baby & toddler clothing

If you've always thought baby clothing was the cutest thing in the world—well, you are going to love this chapter! New York stores have all the baby clothing you need, want, or have dreamt of. There's tons of adorable stuff to choose from, but don't bring all of it home at once. Babies grow very, very quickly, and the outfit that fit the last time you put it on may not even come close a few weeks later. We'll tell you about some of the best clothing shops in the city to help you save time, energy, and money.

What a difference a second child made in our shopping habits! Wow! The first time around, only the "best"—meaning most expensive—would do for our little ones. From dresses to pajamas we spared no expense. Now, with our second children, Benjamin and Angela, we've opted for a different strategy: Buy on sale! Shop at the Gap, Children's Place, and Old Navy. Pamela swears by Greenstones fifty-percent-off sales in January and June, and Kelly has been known to travel down to Baby Depot for bargain-priced turtlenecks. And, Century 21 can't be beat for socks and underwear.

SHOPPING TIPS

If your shower gifts include too many outfits in three- and six-month sizes, return most of them for a credit, or exchange them for twelve- or eighteen-month sizes. Don't dawdle, either. If you put it off, you'll find the stores won't take them back or they'll have been marked down. Also, wait until all the baby gifts are in—you many not need as much as you think.

Pay attention to a store's return policy. Most of the shops—especially the European-style boutiques, such as Jacadi and Au Chat Botté—are very strict when it comes to returns. Department stores tend to be the most lenient; goods can usually be brought back for cash or credit for up to one year.

❊ Ask about the sales. Small shops often have January and June/July special pricing events; some have quarterly sales. Department stores always seem to have sales. In some shops, you won't be able to use gift certificates on sale items.

❊ If you plan to shop with your little one in tow, use a baby carrier or small stroller. Some of these stores are small, crowded, and you may have to walk up a flight of stairs.

❊ Onesie outfits are practical. You can't have too many of these pullover, short sleeve T-shirts with bottom snaps to layer under winter clothes or to use as-is in hot weather. All the stores carry onesies, in a variety of price ranges. Buy the least expensive ones you can find, and always in 100 percent cotton.

❊ Think cotton. It's cozy, soft, and easily washable. (Your pediatrician will probably tell you to wash your baby's clothes for the first year in the non-detergents Dreft or Ivory Snow, which do not irritate a baby's sensitive skin.)

❊ You'll find it convenient to have many sleeping outfits, but test several before buying a bunch to see which your baby prefers. Pamela bought half a dozen Carter's sleeping gowns with drawstring bottoms, but found that Rebecca was uncomfortable with her feet restricted. She

---

Best Department Stores for Style and Selection

Lord & Taylor

Saks Fifth Avenue

Bloomingdales

Macy's

---

exchanged them for open sleeper bag pajamas, and Rebecca was much happier. (All sleepwear must be 100 percent polyester to be flame retardant.)

❊ Don't buy any infant clothes with strings around or near the neck, which can be dangerous. Most manufacturers have stopped making baby clothes with strings.

❊ Use clothing with snaps around the bottoms, for easy changing.

❊ Give some thought to how and when you'll do laundry. Your baby will go through several outfits a day. If you have a washer and dryer in your apartment, and it's easy to throw in a load at odd moments, a large layette may be unnecessary. If you use a machine in your building's basement or take clothing to a neighborhood laundromat, it may be more convenient and easier on your pocketbook to stock a relatively large supply of clothing. Either way, all clothing should be machine washable.

❊ Buy ahead whenever possible. (Winter coats are

often on sale in January.) Also, try to borrow expensive items, such as snowsuits.

✳ If you receive many gifts in small sizes, always exchange some for larger ones.

✳ Many stores have prepared an essential layette list for you-some of them incredibly long! Take such lists with a grain of salt, keeping in mind your own budget and storage space.

✳ Because hours change frequently, call ahead. Most stores are open 7 days a week, from 10 or 11 A.M. until 6 P.M.

Here's a practical layette:

FOR BABY

6 onesies

2 side-snap or side-tie shirts
(until umbilical cord separates)

6 stretchies or coveralls, which cover
your baby from neck to feet, and have
snaps (these in heavier material are good
for sleeping)

4 sleep gowns or sleeper bags
(Kelly favors the Sleeper Bags—great
in cold weather and with air conditioning)

2 caps

6 pairs of socks

1 snowsuit (for winter babies)

4 receiving blankets (to lay the baby down
on and wrap her up in)

2 heavier blankets (one for stroller,
one for crib) waffle weave.

3 hooded towel/washcloth sets

12 cloth diapers (for burping the baby)

4 bibs

1 outdoor hat (keeps winter babies warm,
protects summer babies from sun)

1 pair cotton mittens (to prevent your
baby from scratching her face)

1 pair outdoor mittens (for winter babies)
baby scissors, nail clipper, non-glass
thermometer, nasal aspirator,
hairbrush/comb
bath tub

FOR CRIB

2 quilted mattress pads

2 waterproof liners

3-4 fitted crib sheets

6 crib bibs (to protect sheets from
baby spit up)

1 bumper pad

THE STORES

From expensive designer boutiques to discount department stores, children's shops dot the retail landscape of New York. We can't even begin to explain the prices at some of these European boutiques found on Madison Avenue. (Neither of us would pay $100 for a child's T-shirt from France, but apparently someone does.) Meanwhile, Sixth Avenue, from 16th to 23rd Streets, is home to terrific bargain shopping: Baby Depot in the Burlington Coat Factory, Old Navy and Daffy's.

Au Chat Botté
1192 Madison Avenue bet. 87th
and 88th Streets
722-6474
Return Policy: Store credit or exchange only.

This French boutique carries beautiful imported baby clothing, cradles, bassinets, furniture, bedding, and accessories. It's for truly special gifts and exquisite nurseries.

Bambini

1367 Third Avenue at 78th Street
717-6742
Return Policy: Store credit within seven days.

The epitome of the Upper East Side shop. Bambini offers fine Italian clothing for children from three months to eight years old. Their selection is formal and pricey; this is a good place to purchase a holiday or special occasion outfit for a boy or girl.

Barney's

660 Madison Avenue at 61st Street
826-8900
Return Policy: Refund with receipt.

The children's department at Barney's is small but well stocked. Just as you'd expect, most of the clothes and accessories—for newborns to children age four—are stylish and expensive. The department also carries pretty linens, shoes, albums, hand-painted pillows, stuffed animals, toys, and Kate Spade diaper bags. *Brands Carried: Grain de Lune, Paul Smith, Maharishi, Bonpoint, Lilly Pulitzer, Burberry's for Kids, Flora & Henry, Metropolitan Prairie, and Barney's private label.*

Prettiest (and priciest!) Layettes in Town

La Layette
Bonpoint
Tartine Et Chocolat
Au Chat Botte

Bloomingdale's*

1000 Third Avenue bet. 59th and 60th Streets
705-2000
www.bloomingdales.com
Return Policy: Lenient.

The sprawling children's department on Bloomingdale's eighth floor has one section for layettes, newborns, and toddlers, then separate sections for girls, boys, and teens. You'll also find accessories, toys, and gifts—and end of season sales. Kelly and Pam have shopped here for years. *Brands Carried: Carter's, Little Me, Baby Dior, Classic Pooh, Miniclasix, Absorba, Ralph Lauren Baby, Esprit, Flapdoodles, Baby B'Gosh, Baby Guess, and their private label, Next Generation.*

Bombalulus

101 W. 10th Street bet. Sixth
and Greenwich Avenues
463-0897
244 W. 72nd Street bet. Broadway
and West End Avenues

501-8248
www.bombalulus.com
Return Policy: Store credit only.

Bombulas is an African word that loosely translates as "a group of artists working together." Most of the clothes are handmade and moderately priced. You'll find hand-painted onesies, T-shirts, shorts, leggings, sweatshirts, and hand-sewn jackets and hats. The store imports colorful clothing, as well as unique toys and collectibles from Bali and Guatemala.

Bonpoint
1269 Madison Avenue at 91st Street
722-7720
811 Madison Avenue at 68th Street
879-0900
Return Policy: Store credit only.
No returns on sale items.

All clothes have the Bonpoint label and are imported from Paris—but so are the prices! Sizes begin at newborn and go up to size sixteen for preteen girls, and size twelve for boys. The store has a wide selection and is easy to shop in. Styles range from casual to dressy, with fabrics from cotton to silk. The atmosphere is formal, but if you (or Grandma) are looking for only the best, their beautifully tailored French clothing is perfect.

Bu & The Duck
106 Franklin Street bet. Church Street
and W. Broadway
431-9226

www.buandtheduck.com
Return policy: Store credit only.

This lovely Tribeca shop carries clothing for newborn to six years old. Susan Lane, the owner, designs and sews most of the clothing herself—beautiful rayon sundresses with lace trim, striped leggings, flowery knit cardigans, and much more. The prices range from moderate to expensive; you can purchase a T-shirt for $30 or a special winter coat for over $200. Along with clothing, Bu offers imported children's shoes as well as a special selection of accessories, toys, and gift items. *Brands Carried: Lalalou, Quincy, Melagrano, Boofoo-woo, Pom D'Api, Naturino, and Magnolia.*

Bunnies
100 Delancey Street bet. Ludlow
and Essex Streets
529-7567
www.bunnies.com
Return Policy: Refund with receipt
within ten days, otherwise store credit only.

Bunnies is a discount children's department store with moderately priced casual play clothes from brands such as Heartstreet and Miss Lana. They also carry baby furniture and equipment.

CALYPSO Bébé
284 Mulberry Street bet. Houston and Prince
Streets
965-8910

CALYPSO Enfant
280 Mulberry Street bet, Houston
and Prince Streets
924-6544

These two boutiques offer fine one-of-a-kind children's clothing from a variety of European, American, and in-house designers. You can find knit booties and hats, cashmere sweaters (even for newborns), silk and corduroy bustles, and adorable dresses—all in a wide array of Calypso colors—as well as great heirloom blankets and wooden toys. On weekends every kid gets a free balloon. Holidays bring in Santa, the Easter Bunny, and the Halloween Witch!

Catimini
1284 Madison Avenue at 91st Street
987-0688
Return Policy: Store credit only.
Sale items cannot be returned.

Catamini's stylish French clothing is bright and colorful and available in sizes ranging from newborn to age twelve. (Catamini's label is carried at Saks Fifth Avenue, Neiman Marcus, and Nordstrom.)

Century 21 Department Store
22 Cortlandt Street bet. Broadway and Church Streets
227-9092
www.c21stores.com
Return Policy: Refund within 30 days with receipt and price tag attached.

Century 21, the discount department store, has a large children's department. It's not difficult to find a bargain, with prices that hover around twenty-five percent below retail. Accessories include diaper bags, cloth diapers and bibs. It's crowded, especially on weekends; it's best to shop here without your baby. *Brands Carried: Carter's, Little Me, Ralph Lauren, Gerber, and Absorba.*

The Children's Place*
Locations throughout Manhattan
529-2201
www.childrensplace.com
Return Policy: No sale is ever final.

This growing chain with shops in Manhattan and many across the tri-state area is a real find, and could well be the next Gap. The store is clean, its return policy is flexible, and the clothing is comfortable, high quality, stylish, and affordable. The collections are basic and come in bright and traditional colors, with some fashion sense. We've seen beautiful fall/winter corduroys in rich, royal colors—deep blue, ruby red, and emerald green—as well as bright, multi-colored summer clothing and bathing suits. You can also find socks, hats, headbands, scrunchies, and adorable sunglasses.

Chock's

74 Orchard Street bet. Grand
and Broome Streets
473-1929
www.chockcatalog.com
Return Policy: Refund with receipt
within thirty days.

Established in 1921 on the Lower East Side, Chock's carries a complete line of infant layette items. They also offer many gift items and wooden toys, including blocks, trains, and cars. *Brands Carried: Carter's, Gerber, Little Me and Colimacone.*

Cremebebe

68 Second Avenue bet. 3rd and 4th Streets
979-6848
Return Policy: Store credit only.

This store is funky and cheerful, with a wide selection of colorful American and Italian clothing in sizes ranging from ages newborn to five years. The owner creates some of the items herself, scanning bright designs of apples, trains, and the Cremebebe logo, onto T-shirts that sell for $8. She also sells her own plastic bibs and hand-knit sweaters. Racks of vintage jeans for kids (around $20 a pair), fancier silk dresses (for about $50) and a selection of toys, stuffed animals, and accessories complete the mix. *Brands Carried: Malina and Shortcake.*

Funkiest Kids' Clothes

Space Kiddets

Z'Baby Company

Peanut Butter and Jane

Daffy's

111 Fifth Avenue at 18th Street
529-4477
335 Madison Avenue at 44th Street
557-4422
125 E. 57th Street at Lexington Avenue
376-4477
1311 Broadway at 34th Street
736-4477
Return Policy: Refund within fourteen days, otherwise store credit only.

Daffy's is a discount store for the whole family. Their children's department is particularly good, and our bargain-hunting friends swear by Daffy's for some of the best deals in town. Like Loehmann's, be prepared to pick through racks and hunt for infant clothes that were misplaced in the toddler section. Pamela picked up Flapdoodle leggings here for $5.99;

Daffy's also stocks Rebecca's favorite brand, Le Tout Petit, which can sometimes be found here in the right size. *Brands Carried: Mini Basix, Absorba, Wee Play, Little Me, Baby Incorporated, and Flapdoodles.*

Baby Gap*
Many locations around New York
and the tri-state area
www.gapkids.com
Return Policy: Lenient.

Who doesn't love the Gap? There are over twenty Baby Gap stores in town, usually within grownup Gap stores. Nothing outrageous here. The Gap's baby clothing is often 100 percent cotton, and in traditional colors and styles. But, the sales are great! Comfortable play clothes hold up well after repeated washings. (Just be prepared to see other babies at the playgroup wearing the exact same outfit.) For extra special events, try Baby Lux located at the Gap at 680 Fifth Avenue at 54th Street (977-7023), where cashmere, silk, linen, and leather are the materials of the day.

Greenstones
442 Columbus Avenue bet. 81st
and 82nd Streets
580-4322
Greenstones, Too
1184 Madison Avenue bet. 86th
and 87th Streets
427-1665
Return Policy: Store credit only.
No returns on sale items.

These family-owned-and-operated stores contain a wide selection of European-imported clothing for boys and girls from newborn to age twelve, with an especially good selection of outerwear. Prices are moderate for sportswear and more expensive for dressier designer items. Watch for their unbeatable fifty percent off sales in January and June. (Rebecca and Benjamin get their winter coats here every year.) *Brands Carried: Catamini, I.K.K.S., Jean Bourget, Miniman, Kenzo, Naf Naf, and Petit Boy.*

Gymboree
1120 Madison Avenue bet. 83rd
and 84th Streets
717-6702
1049 Third Avenue at 62nd Street
688-4044
1332 Third Avenue at 76th Street
517-5548
2015 Broadway bet. 68th and 69th Streets
595-7662
2271 Broadway bet. 81st and 82nd Streets
595-9071
www.gymboree.com
Return Policy: Lenient.

The large, roomy Gymboree stores specialize in play clothes and active wear for boys and girls from newborn to eight years. The moderately priced clothes are 100% cotton and come in brightly colored designs, with new collections arriving every six to eight weeks. Kelly shops the 83rd Street location often, and loves it.

Ibiza Kidz

46 University Place bet. 9th and 10th Streets
533-4614
Return Policy: Exchange or store credit only.

This is *the* shop for cool downtown kids. Located within the Ibiza women's store, it offers a great selection of colorful print clothing for newborn children to size twelve. Ibiza carries the Malina line of beautiful silk suits and jackets, for age newborn to eighteen months, not to mention elaborate tutus with matching wings and wands, funky suitcases, hats and a good selection of shoes. Prices are moderate to expensive. *Brands Carried: Kenzo, I.K.K.S., Petit Boy, Zutano, Pompolina, Malina and Chevignon.*

Jacadi

1281 Madison Avenue at 91st Street
369-1616
787 Madison Avenue at 67th Street
535-3200
www.jacadiusa.com
Return Policy: Store credit only within seven days. No returns on sale items.

The two Jacadi stores in New York (more in outlying suburbs) are independently owned and operated. The merchandise is imported from France and is mostly the Jacadi label. Both dressy and play clothes are available for newborns to twelve-year-olds, as well as towels, nursery furniture (by Pali, Pereculture, and Peg Perego), and wallpaper. Be discriminating about what you buy because returns

are next to impossible. Watch for semiannual sales from December through February and May through August.

Julian & Sara

103 Mercer Street bet. Spring
and Prince Streets
226-1989
Return Policy: Store credit with receipt.
No returns on sale items.

This tiny boutique imports most of its clothing from Europe and features an incredible selection for girls, with everything from party dresses to play clothes in sizes for newborns to twelve-year-olds. There's also shoes and accessories, plus a beautiful line of pajamas by Arthur. *Brands Carried: Jean Bourget, Lili Gaufrette, Petit Bateau, Mona Lisa, Confetti, Petit Boy, Charabia, Kenzo and Arthur.*

Kids Generation USA

875 Sixth Avenue at 31st Street
947-1667
Return Policy: Store credit only.

This well-stocked clothing store carries mostly casual and trendy styles, and a variety of suits, tuxedos, and party dresses for special occasions. Christening gowns range between $50 and $80. Kids Generation stocks many "character" items as well, especially from Disney, as well as a large selection of children's toys and accessories. *Brands Carried: Baby Guess, DKNY, Nautica, Oshkosh B'Gosh, Little Me, and Harley Davidson.*

Kids 'R' Us

1311 Broadway at 34th Street, 3rd floor
643-0714 www.kidsrus.com
Return Policy: Lenient.

This huge discount store located next to the Manhattan Mall has it all for newborns to boy's size twenty and girl's size sixteen. The store is jam-packed with merchandise, but well organized by size and gender. Everything here is discounted—Carter's stretchies were priced at two for $15, the lowest we saw. And, of course, Kids 'R' Us has a nice selection of toys, books, and stuffed animals, as well as socks, barrettes, knapsacks and accessories. *Brands Carried: Carter's, Healthtex, Levi's, Oshkosh B'Gosh, Izod, Nike, Color & Co., Baby Beluga, and Classic Pooh.*

Koh's Kids

311 Greenwich Street bet. Chambers
and Reade Streets
791-6915
Return Policy: Store credit only.

This intimate little store has served the Tribeca area for over ten years. With funky clothing for children ages newborn to seven years old, Koh's Kids clothing goes from dressy to casual. Store owner Grace Koh, is famous for her knit outfits. She handknits sweaters, dresses, blankets, and onesies which run on the expensive side, but are excellent in quality and last for years. Grace stocks sparkly sequined shoes, adorable knit hats, and toys and accessories too. *Brands Carried: Baby Armadillo, Flapdoodles, and Petit Bateau.*

La Layette . . . Et Plus Ltd.*

170 E. 61st Street bet. Third
and Lexington Avenues
688-7072
Return Policy: Store credit only.

This tiny boutique near Bloomingdale's specializes in personalized service (an appointment is recommended) and layettes. Almost everything is made especially for La Layette, and the selection is exquisite. These layettes can be rather expensive, however: from $500 to $5,000, with an average price of $800. Go see their beautiful (many one-of-a-kind) bris and christening outfits and custom clothing for older children (a girl's party dress for $350). Hand-painted cribs ($1,250) are sold with coordinating sheets, bumpers, and pillows. Everything is exquisite!

La Petite Etoile

746 Madison Avenue bet. 64th
and 65th Streets
744-0975
www.lapetitetoile.com
Return Policy: Store credit only.
No returns on sale items.

This European boutique features all the top brand names from Europe, such as Christian Dior and Pinco Pallino. They carry a large, ultra-chic layette selection, with onesies from $15. Sizes range from 0 (preemie baby) to children age fourteen. *Brands Carried: Christian Dior, Pinco Pallino, Pomme Framboise, Petit Faune, Sonia Rykiel, Pappa &*

Ciccia, Florian, and Petit Bateau.

Lester's*

1522 Second Avenue at 80th Street

734-9292

Return Policy: Refund with receipt within seven days, otherwise store credit only.

This discount store has a wide variety of play clothes, accessories, and shoes for newborns to teens. Lester's enjoys putting layettes together, and appointments are preferred. Much of the merchandise is trendy, yet is priced below their competitors, making this a definite find on the Upper East Side. *Brands Carried: Petit Bateau, Little Me, Mini Basix, I.K.K.S, Juicy, Tractor, Mini Man, and Flapdoodles.*

Little Folks

123 E. 23rd Street bet. Park and Lexington Avenues

982-9669

Return Policy: Refund with receipt within seven days, otherwise store credit only.

Little Folks could fit in the superstore category, since it carries cribs, highchairs, and accessories, but we call it a clothing store because the large, selection of discounted merchandise is terrific. Pamela bought Rebecca's snowsuit at Little Folks for $40 less than what she saw in another store. The staff at Little Folks is particularly knowledgeable. *Brands Carried: Brambilla, Carter's, Baby Guess, Weebok, and Sara's Prints.*

Little O

1 Bleecker Street at Bowery Street

673-0858

Best Places for Sale Items Under $10

The Children's Place

Talbot's Kids

Old Navy

Return Policy: Store credit only.

This one-of-a-kind downtown store is the place to find vintage kids' clothes, some never-before-worn items from the seventies and eighties, along with finds from antique fairs and Parisian thrift shops. Most items are priced no higher than $35, and range in size from zero to ten. One can find Smurf T-shirts, Transformer raincoats, onesies with bright floral appliqués, Jordache sneakers, Oshkosh B'Gosh overalls, and Petit Bateau brand clothing. Search for treasures such as a beautiful antique christening gown from the late 1800's—a bit more expensive, but still a bargain. And look out for the $5 sale bins filled with treats like Snoopy or Simpsons T-shirts.

Lord & Taylor

424 Fifth Avenue bet. 38th and 39th Streets

391-3344

www.maycompany.com

Return Policy: Lenient.

Spacious and inviting, the children's department at this grand old department store is filled with a wide variety of quality layette items and clothing. They have recently added a Saturday morning story hour for children, too. There's also a wonderful selection of stuffed animals, diaper bags, knapsacks, bedding sets, and christening outfits. The staff at Lord & Taylor always seems to be exceptionally helpful. *Brands Carried: Nautica, Ralph Lauren, Carter's, Little Me, Absorba, DKNY, and Oshkosh B'Gosh, and Lord & Taylor's private label.*

Macy's

Herald Square, 151 W. 34th Street
bet. Broadway and Seventh Avenue
695-4400
www.macys.com
Return Policy: Lenient.

The largest kids floor in the world sells everything from baby skin cream to Sam & Libby leopard print shoes, and offers a changing room for your baby. Macy's carries a huge variety of clothing for newborns and older children. The prices are generally moderate, and you can always find something on sale. Huge, bright gumball machines, televisions, and sticker and postcard stations help keep kids happy while you shop. *Brands Carried: Oshkosh B'Gosh, Esprit, Disney, Mickey & Co, Sam & Libby, Tommy Hilfiger Kids and Polo Ralph Lauren kids.*

Madison Avenue Maternity & Baby

1043 Madison Avenue bet. 79th
and 80th Streets
988-8686 ·www.madisonavenuematernity.com
Return Policy: Store credit only.

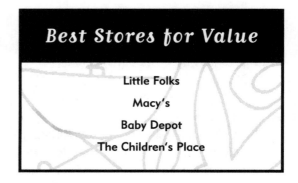

Best Stores for Value

Little Folks

Macy's

Baby Depot

The Children's Place

This is a good place to find unique baby clothing for age newborn to twelve months. The store also has a selection of books, diaper bags, and other accessories. Delivery is available in Manhattan. *Brands Carried: Sottocoperta, Petite Faune, and Petit Bateau.*

Magic Windows*

1186 Madison Avenue bet. 86th
and 87th Streets
289-0028
www.magic-windows.com
Return Policy: Store credit only.
No returns on sale items.

Magic Windows specializes in the unique. Petit Bateau is a large part of their layette business, along with other truly special lines. This is the place to find baby clothes with handmade smocking, Periwinkle cribs, changing tables, and bureaus. You can also find children's clothing up to size sixteen. *Brands Carried: Petit Bateau, Absorba, Baby Steps, Agabang, Florence Eiseman, Sophie Dess, L'Agneau, D'Or, and Anavini.*

New York Exchange for Woman's Work
149 E. 60th Street bet. Lexington
and Third Avenues
753-2330
www.nywomans-exchange.com
Return Policy: Store credit only
within two weeks.

For over 120 years the Exchange has been a treasure trove of beautiful handmade articles-one-of-a-kind baby blankets, dresses with hand smocking, baby booties, onesies, and more. Prices range from moderate to expensive.

Oilily
870 Madison Avenue bet. 70th and 71st Streets
628-0100
www.oililyusa.com
Return Policy: Refund with receipt
within two weeks, otherwise store credit only.

Exclusively carrying their own designs, this Dutch store's trademark is bright colors and eye-catching patterns. Children's sizes start at three months. They sell sportswear, play clothes, and shoes. They also sell women's clothing if you desire that "mother/daughter" matching look. Prices are comparable to other Madison Avenue European clothing stores.

Old Navy Clothing Co.*
610 Sixth Avenue at 18th Street
645-0663
150 W. 34th Street at Seventh Avenue
594-0049
503/511 Broadway bet. Broome
and Spring Streets

226-0838
300 W. 125th Street bet. Eighth
and Frederick Douglass Avenues
531-1544
www.oldnavy.com
Return Policy: Refund with receipt
within thirty days.

The Old Navy Clothing Co. is owned by the Gap and is a lower-priced alternative. These warehouse-like stores are great to visit, even if you don't need kiddie clothes. The Sixth Avenue store and the 34th Street location have their own café (with quite a few strollers parked next to the tables) and lots of candy, gadgets, candles, and lotions, plus basic jeans and other essentials for grownups. At all of the locations, you will find reasonably priced, 100 percent cotton items for newborns to adults. There are adorable overalls for $10, infant dresses for $10 to $16, and onesies in bright colors for $5.50, in addition to sunglasses, socks, hats, bathing suits and whatever else is currently fashionable. Be warned: Old Navy is a mob scene on weekends.

Peanut Butter & Jane*
617 Hudson Street bet. Jane
and W. 12th Streets
620-7952
Return Policy: Store credit only.

This store is filled to the brim with all types of clothing, from everyday to funky or dressy. Prices are reasonable, with T-shirts for $20 and up, dresses for $50 and up, onesies for $15 and up, and rompers from $25 and up. There is a small selection of shoes as well. You can find mint vintage pieces in all sizes, along with unusual gift items like puppets, Curiosity Kits for making anything and everything (from jewelry to exploding volcanoes), and a wide range of developmental toys for newborns and up. This is also the place to find great costumes for holidays and parties. *Brands Carried: Petit Bateau, Flapdoodles, Wizard of Oz,* and *Les Tout Petits.*

Prince & Princess

33 E. 68th Street bet. Madison
and Park Avenues
879-8989
www.princeandprincess.com
Return Policy: Store credit only.

With prices such as $185 for a knit onesie, this European children's boutique is truly for princes and princesses or just the place to find a special holiday suit or dress. They also carry high-end sportswear and accessories such as headbands, bags, and hats. The store carries clothing for newborns to children age fourteen, but will take special orders for women up to age twenty. Be prepared to browse on your own.

Regine Kids

2688 Broadway bet. 102nd and 103rd Streets
864-8705
Return Policy: Refund with receiptwithin
seven days.

Uptown moms swear by Regine Kids as the only place in their neighborhood to pick up baby supplies and quality clothing. The store

carries layette clothing from newborn to sizes fourteen and sixteen. It also sells furniture and accessories for babies. *Brands Carried: Flapdoodles, Oshkosh, Healthtex,* and *Levi's.*

Robin's Nest

1168 Lexington Avenue bet. 80th
and 81st Streets
737-2004
Return Policy: Store credit only.
No returns on sale items.

Robin's Nest is tiny, but well stocked with clothes for newborns to children up to age twelve. Most styles found here are casual. The store also carries accessories such as backpacks, barrettes, bibs, hats, and specialty picture frames, as well as handmade toys and blankets. Prices range from moderate for T-shirts to expensive for a large selection of sweaters. Robin's Nest also sells hand-knit sweaters with pewter buttons and matching hats; these can be special ordered in the customer's choice of colors (the cost is $94). Robin's Nest books private appointments, and will come to your home or hospital to help you with your layette needs. *Brands Carried: Lili Gaufrette, Kenzo, Jean Bourget, I.K.K.S., Pappa & Ciccia, Petit Bateau,* and *Chevignon.*

Saks Fifth Avenue*

611 Fifth Avenue bet. 48th and 49th Streets
753-4000
www.saksfifthavenue.com
Return Policy: Lenient.

This top-notch department store has an

excellent infant and toddler department and carries a variety of brands, including a number of designers not found elsewhere. The department is wonderfully laid out and easy to shop. The sales staff is extremely helpful and courteous. The sales at Saks are terrific—all the best for less. *Brands Carried: Absorba, Petit Bateau, DKNY, Ralph Lauren, Heartstrings, Florence Eiseman, Sylvia White, Baby Lulu, Monkey Wear, Catamini, Simonetta, Joan Calabrese, Zoe* and *Magil.*

Small Change
964 Lexington Avenue bet. 70th
and 71st Streets
772-6455
Return Policy: Exchange and store credit only.

This small store has a diverse selection of European clothing in sizes newborn to sixteen years. The merchandise runs the gamut from the classic to the more avant-garde. Small Change also sells shoes, socks, tights, hair accessories, hats, gloves, and more. *Brands Carried: I.K.K.S., Petit Bateau, Magil, Sophie Dess, Sonia Rykiel, Lili Gaufrette* and *Mini Man.*

Space Kiddets*
46 E. 21st Street bet. Park Avenue South
and Broadway
420-9878
Return Policy: Store credit only.

Most of the clothing here is funky, but moderately priced. Space Kiddets has a little of everything, including toys, table and chair sets, fantasy play clothes, even Elvis memorabilia!

Brands Carried: Maxou, Mouse Feathers, Mini Thallion, and *I.K.K.S.*

Spring Flowers*
1050 Third Avenue at 62nd Street
758-2669
905 Madison Avenue at 72nd Street
717-8182
Return Policy: Store credit only.

Spring Flowers is known for its extensive collection of top-quality French and Italian clothes for children, newborn to ten years. (A Spring Flowers Layette store adjoins the Third Avenue store.) Spring Flowers carries play clothes and an outstanding selection of party and holiday clothes for boys and girls. Dresses are sold with matching hats, tights, purses, and accessories. Boys' navy blazers and flannel pants are beautifully tailored. Spring Flowers also has a wide selection of European shoes, including the Sonnet brand from England— popular first walkers. Prices are high, as you'd expect, and the service is excellent. *Brands Carried: Sophie Dess, Sonia Rykiel, Florian, Petit Bateau, Giesswien, Cacharel, Joan Calabrese, Magil,* and *Pappa & Ciccia.*

Talbot's Kids & Babies*
1523 Second Avenue at 79th Street
570-1630
www.talbots.com
Return Policy: Refund with receipt, otherwise store credit only.

This large, well-lit store sells attractive clothes for boys and girls from newborn to size sixteen. Their high-quality, preppy style of clothing is worth a look. Classic polo shirts and elastic waist khakis are perfect for husky boys. The store concentrates on toddlers and older children; the layette and infant/toddler section is smaller. They have excellent sales, with prices often half the original. This is one of Kelly's favorites.

Tigers, Tutu's & Toes

128 Second Avenue bet. St. Mark's Place
and 7th Street · 228-7990
Return Policy: No refunds; exchange
or store credit only within six months

This East Village newcomer has a jungle theme, with a faux leopard rug, fake trees, and a giant stuffed tiger sitting on the floor. Of course there are tutus—in red, pink, yellow, and orange—as well as shoes both classic and outrageous. You can also find a large selection of casual Zutano clothing—some leopard print items are in keeping with the motif. Everything is well priced. Also, look for stuffed animals, animal knapsacks, puppets, puzzles, crayons, and other jungle-theme toys. *Brands Carried: Elefanten, Skechers, Aster, Venettini, Zutano, I.K.K.S., Rubbies,* and *Petit Bateau.*

Tutti Bambini

1490 First Avenue bet. 77th and 78th Streets
472-4238
Return Policy: Store credit only.
No returns on sale items.

Tutti Bambini is a small boutique that carries a full line of clothing and accessories for newborns to pre-teens. You'll also find some sumptuous (and expensive) Penny Candy sweaters. *Brands Carried: Petit Boy, I.K.K.S., Confetti, Chevignon, Lorilyn, Les Tout Petits, Catamini, Cotton Caboodle, Penny Candy* and *Suss Designs.*

Village Kidz

3 Charles Street bet. Greenwich
and Seventh Avenues
807-8542
Return Policy: Store credit only.

Village Kidz sells stylish and attractive everyday wear and dressy clothes for boys and girls, newborn to age twelve. They stock everyday play clothes, with T-shirts at about $20 and dresses $50 and up. Village Kidz also carries shoes as well as selling stuffed bears from the Muffy Bear Collection. *Brands Carried: Chloe's Closet, Jean Bourget, Cow & Lizard, Shoe Be Doo, Right Step, Baby Botte,* and *Rebels.*

Z'Baby Company*

100 W. 72nd Street at Columbus Avenue
579-BABY
996 Lexington Avenue at 72nd Street
472-BABY
www.zbabycompany.com
Return Policy: Store credit within 10 days of purchase with receipt. No returns on sale items.

At Z'Baby Company, you'll find a particularly good layette department—and the store's buyer and head layette specialist, a mom herself, will work with you to put together the layette of your dreams. Best to make an appointment! Z'Baby carries a wide range of clothing, shoes and accessories from France, Italy, and New York—for boys from newborn to eight and girls to age sixteen. Store services include phone orders, a baby shower registry, personal shopping, and layette by appointment. *Brands Carried: Grain de Lune, Petit Bateau, Bienvenue sur Terre, Kenzo, Petit Industrie, Sonya Rykiel, Charabia, Cacherel, Aster, Pom Dapi, Buckle my Shoe,* and *Primigi.*

Z'Baby Warehouse!
445 W. 50th Street bet. Ninth
and Tenth Avenues
245-BABY
Return Policy: Store credit within five
days of purchase with receipt.

Ever wonder where you can find the best European designer clothing, shoes, and accessories at half-off usual prices? Try Z'Baby Warehouse!, the company's factory outlet store! Here you'll find the best off-season items such as leopard bunting and chenille rompers at thirty to sixty percent off retail prices, as well as current season fashions at significant savings. Petit Bateau shirts and pajamas at the city's best prices are a highlight. Diaper and formula delivery service is also available. Be sure to get on their mailing list—you'll be notified of special sample and warehouse sales that are not to be missed.

Zitomer
969 Madison Avenue bet. 75th
and 76th Streets
737-2037
www.zittles.com
Return Policy: Refund with receipt
within ten days.

With Zitomer's convenient shopping hours and flexible return policy, every neighborhood would be lucky to have a store like this one. This is a mini department store with toys, clothes, chocolates, and lingerie, as well as children's clothing, ranging from newborn to fourteen years. The service is good and the selection is excellent. You can open a charge account here, which comes in handy when filling prescriptions at their full-fledged pharmacy. *Brands Carried: Petit Bateau, Florian, Aletta, Carter's, Sophie Dess, Mini Basix, Mini Man, Joseph Baby,* and *Galipette.*

Trunk Shows and Private Boutiques
This section includes makers of high quality children's clothing that is either not readily available in stores, new to the U.S., or, in the case of Monica Noel and others, sold at trunk shows two to three times a year as well as in stores. At some shows you will have to custom order pieces; others display racks of clothing you can buy that day. Get on these designers' mailing lists to be invited.

Bodyscapes, Inc.
20 W. 22nd Street, Room 502
243-2414

www.bodyscapeskids.com

Henrietta Drewes has been designing clothes for over thirty years and, for the last fifteen, bright, whimsical clothing for children ages six months through eight years. Henrietta has a unique and loyal following of people she's worked with for years; she's dressed many of the daughters of her original clients, and just recently dressed one of their granddaughters! Most of her pieces are reversible and made of 100 percent cotton, corduroy, flannel, or any combination of the above. She has a huge array of prints to choose from. In fact, whatever you could imagine to interest a child, she's got it. You might find a black corduroy pant that reverses into plaid flannel, a colorful farm print, or any number of other fun combinations. Parents are welcome to visit Henrietta's Chelsea loft (be sure to make an appointment) to pick out their own. Prices range from $16 for a bib to $175 for a leather jacket.

Judy's Fancies
689-8663

Judith Correa handsews clothing for newborns to toddlers from the finest fabrics (and creates beautifully tailored christening gowns for $150 and up). Other prices range from $45 for a simple cotton dress to $60 for a velvet outfit. Her clothing is pastel-colored and very European in style. She will custom-make clothes for children of all ages and sizes, and parents are welcome to contribute to the design (or even design the clothing themselves).

Little Follies
P.O. Box 111
Englewood, NJ 07631
(800) 242-7881
212-585-1940

Known for their pretty, classic hand smocked rompers, dresses, and shortalls, Little Follies has recently expanded its line to include pants, shorts, shirts, and hand-knit sweaters. Almost all of the clothing is machine washable, and made of either 100 percent cotton or a cotton/polyester blend. Sizes start at three months and go up to size eight (shortalls stop at five), and prices average between $50 and $75 for cotton outfits, $85 for velvet shortalls, and $110 and up for velvet dresses. Little Follies holds trunk shows at the Mark Hotel (77th St. between Fifth and Madison Avenues) two to three times a year; call their 800 number for catalogs and show dates.

Papo d'Anjo
396-9668 (voice mail)
Praça Luis de Camões n.36 3º Esq.
1200-243 Lisbon Portugal
011 351 21 324-1790
www.papodanjo.com
e-mail: papodanjo@papodanjo.com

Portugal-based designer Catherine Connor travels all over Europe selecting fine, unusual fabrics for this high-end children's clothing line. Her clothes are all handmade, and the style is classic European. Sizes range from ages six months to twelve years; prices start at $39 for an oxford or vyella long-sleeved shirt, and go up to $250 for a traditional wool tweed coat. These clothes are sold in stores such as Saks, Small Change, Magic Windows, and other fine children's clothing boutiques, as well as in twice-yearly trunk shows at various locations in New York. E-mail for trunkshow information.

Resale Shops

On the other end of the scale, here's where you'll find real bargains—the big names, hardly worn, at prices way below those of the boutiques.

Children's Resale
303 E. 81st Street bet. First
and Second Avenues
734-8897
www.resaleclothing.baweb.com
Return Policy: No returns, all sales final.

This shop stocks upscale labels such as Petit Bateau, Bonpoint, and Oilily. They are also strong in their basics in sizes up to six years, although their best selection is for infants and toddlers. Prices range from $5 for a Gap T-shirt to $35 for a Petit Bateau toddler outfit. You can also find a good selection of used strollers, carriages, playpens, cribs, toys, and stuffed animals.

Good-Byes Children's Resale Shop
230 E. 78th Street bet. Second
and Third Avenues
794-2301
Return Policy: No returns, all sales final.

This is one of the nicest of the resale shops. Clothing here ranges from $5 to $75, with the average price of a baby outfit around $15. The store has a play area for kids with coloring books and crayons.

**First & Second Cousin New and
Resale Children's Shop**
142 Seventh Avenue South bet. 10th
and Charles Streets
929-8048
Return Policy: Store credit only.

This shop offers mostly new (and hip) clothing with brands like Flapdoodles and

Mulberry Bush for newborns to size fourteen. They also have fun handmade clothing such as batik and tie-dyed pieces. First and Second Cousin also sells pajamas, and baby carriers made by Baby Bjorn and Sara's Ride. The selection of resale clothing is small, but clean—and prices are about half of what the new merchandise costs.

Jane's Exchange
207 Avenue A bet. 12th and 13th Streets
674-6268
Return Policy: Store credit only.

This Alphabet City consignment shop is brimming with top quality one-of-a-kind clothing and accessories for children ages newborn to ten years, with ages newborn to five being their strong point. Adorable dresses, onesies, and shirts fill the walls. Prices can range anywhere from $3 to $100 for a single outfit, but most are under $20. You'll find everything from simple Gap basics to hip European styles. They also carry children's furniture, accessories, books, games, toys and maternity wear in good condition for $5 to $25 for expecting moms. Most of the items sold here are gently worn, but there are also brand new items. This store carries only in-season clothing, so there are no end of season sales—but with prices like these who needs them?

Second Act
1046 Madison Avenue at 79th Street,
2nd floor
988-2440

Return Policy: No returns, all sales final.

Second Act has been providing clothing to Upper East Side families for over twenty-six years. Savvy shoppers can find clothing here from labels as varied as Sears and Bonpoint. The prices are set according to brand so that you can spend $145 for a Bonpoint outfit, $16.50 for a Gap ensemble, or $3.50 for a onesie. This store carries many European designer dresses and party clothes for girls and boys. All clothing sold here is in excellent condition and sizes range from newborn to pre-teen. Second Act also stocks a small selection of children's books, shoes, and toys.

Malls
Consider the possibility of leaving town from time to time to do your children's clothes shopping—find bargains, skip the sales tax (in New Jersey), or enjoy strolling your baby around an air-conditioned mall on a hot and sticky New York day. Mall shopping makes for a good outing, and the food courts will keep the kids happy. We list malls in the tri-state area that have several children's stores and are within an hour of the city. All driving directions are from New York City.

Many of the mall stores have been described throughout this chapter. Most, if not all, of these malls have large department stores with wonderful children's departments. Make a day of it. Pop into FAO Schwarz, Zany Brainy, or the Disney Store to start the day off right, and then feed the kids an early lunch at the food court. (And while they nap in the stroller, you can shop for yourself!)

NORTHERN NEW JERSEY

Fashion Center

Route 17 and Ridgewood Avenue
Paramus, NJ
201-444-9050

Directions: Take the George Washington Bridge to Route 4 West. Take Route 4 to Route 17N and Ridgewood Avenue.

Stores:

Denny's • Zany Brainy • Jenny John Shoes

Paramus Park Mall

Route 17 North, Paramus, NJ
201-261-8000

Directions: Take the George Washington Bridge to Route 80 West, stay on Route 80 until you reach the Garden State Parkway North (Exit 163). Take the Garden State to Route 17N. Go ½ mile, and you will see two entrances to the mall in the northbound lane.

Stores:

The Children's Place • Gap Kids Gymboree

Garden State Plaza

Route 17 South, Paramus, NJ
201-843-2404

Directions: Take the George Washington Bridge to Route 4 West. Take Route 4 to Route 17 South, go 100 yards past the Route 4 interchange, and make a right into the mall entrance.

Stores:

Baby Place • Bambini Italiani Brooks Brothers • The Children's Place The Disney Store • Finish Line • Gap Kids

Baby Gap • Gymboree • Jacadi JC Penny • Kid Cool • Lord & Taylor Macy's • Motherhood Maternity Mothertime • Mimi Maternity • Neiman Marcus • Nordstrom • Old Navy The Right Start • Talbot's Kids & Babies Warner Bros Studio Store

The Mall at Short Hills

Short Hills, NJ
973-376-7350

Directions: Take the George Washington Bridge to the Garden State Parkway and continue to exit 142-Interstate 78. Then take 78 West to Route 24 West and exit at 7C—JFK Parkway. Follow signs to the Mall at Short Hills. The mall will be on your right-hand side.

Stores:

A Pea in The Pod • Benneton Kids Eileen Fisher • Galo Shoes • Gap Kids Gymboree • La Petite Gaminerie Limited Too • Talbots Kids • Oilily

Riverside Square Mall

Route 4 West, Hackensack, NJ
201-489-2212

Directions: Take the George Washington Bridge to Route 4. The mall is on the right-hand side of the street, past the Hackensack exit.

Stores:

A Pea in the Pod • Benetton Kids Bloomingdale's • Eileen Fisher • Gap Kids • Gymboree • La Petite Gaminerie Saks Fifth Avenue

WESTCHESTER/ROCKLAND

The Westchester

Bloomingdale Road, White Plains, NY
914-683-8600

Directions: Take the Hutchinson River Parkway or I 95 North to 287 West. Take 287 to Westchester Avenue (Exit 8). Make a left onto Bloomingdale Road for parking at The Westchester.

Stores:

A Pea In The Pod • Baby Gap • Brooks Brothers • The Children's Place • The Disney Store • Eileen Fisher • Gap Kids Gymboree • Hannah Andersson Jacadi • Kay Bee Toys • Kids Footlocker Limited Too • Neiman Marcus Nordstrom • Oilily • Stride Rite Shoes Talbot's Kids & Babies

Palisades Park Center

West Nyack, NY
914-348-1000

Directions: Take the George Washington Bridge to the Palisades Interstate Parkway North. Exit 9E to the New York State Thruway. Take 87 South to 287 East, then take Exit 12, West Nyack Palisades Center.

Stores:

Baby Gap • Barnes & Noble • Disney Store • Gap Kids • Gymboree • JC Penny Kids Footlocker • Limited Too • Lord & Taylor • Old Navy • The Children's Place Waldenbooks

Woodbury Commons Mall

Harriman, NY
914-928-4000

Directions: Take the upper level of the George Washington Bridge; make a right onto the Palisades Parkway North. Take the Palisades to Harriman (Exit 16). Immediately after the toll, you will see the mall entrance.

Stores: *All stores here are discount stores and/or outlets.*

Carter's Childrenswear • The Children's Place • JM Originals • Kay Bee Toy Liquidators • Maternity Works Neiman Marcus Last Call • Off 5th Oilily • Oshkosh B'Gosh • Patagonia World of Fun

LONG ISLAND

Roosevelt Field Shopping Center

Glen Cove, NY
516-742-8000

Directions: Take the Long Island Expressway to the Northern State Parkway (Exit 38). Take the Northern State to the Meadowbrook Parkway, and get off at Exit M2, Mall Exit. The mall will be directly in front of you.

Stores:

Bloomingdale's • The Children's Place The Disney Store • FAO Schwarz • Gap Kids • Gymboree • JC Penny • Jordan Marie • Kay Bee Toys • Kids Footlocker Limited Too • Macy's • Noodle Kidoodle Nordstrom • The Right Start • Stern's Stride Rite • United Colors of Benetton

Sunrise Mall

Sunrise Highway, Massapequa, NY

516-795-3225

Directions: Take the Long Island Expressway to Route 110 South. Get off at Sunrise Highway (Exit 27 West). Go down two street lights and make a right. The mall is on Sunrise Highway.

Stores:

The Children's Place • The Disney Store Gap Kids/ Baby Gap • JC Penny • Kay Bee Toys • Kids Footlocker • Limited Too Lobel's Stride Rite • Macy's • Motherhood Maternity • Noodle Kidoodle Old Navy • Stern's

Walt Whitman Mall

Dix Hills, NY

516-271-1741

Directions: Take the Long Island Expressway to Route 110 (Exit 49 North). Take Route 110 north five miles; the mall is on the right-hand side of Route 110.

Stores:

Bloomingdale's • The Children's Place The Disney Store • Gap Kids • Gymboree Lord & Taylor • Macy's • Mimi Maternity Saks Fifth Avenue • Warner Bros. Studio Store

CONNECTICUT
Stamford Town Center

Tresser Boulevard, Stamford, CT

203-324-0935

Directions: Take I 95 North to Exit 8. Make a left at the first light, Atlantic Street. Go to the third traffic light and make a right onto Tresser Boulevard. From Tresser Boulevard, make a left into the mall entrance.

Stores:

Brooks Brothers • The Disney Store Elizabeth Wood • FAO Schwarz Gap Kids • Gymboree • Kay Bee Toys Kids Foot Locker • Limited Too Mimi Maternity • Motherhood Maternity Macy's • Saks Fifth Avenue • Waldenkids

12 · toys, toys, toys

You're about to rediscover the magic of toys, because you're going to be playing with them more than you can imagine. Having a baby is a great excuse to act like a kid again, and New York's toy stores, from the venerable FAO Schwarz to the tiniest neighborhood specialty shop, will help you to remember what it was like when a toy store was the greatest place in the world. Of course, the world of toys has changed since you were a kid, so here are some tips to get you started on picking the right toys, including where to find them.

Jennifer Bergman from West Side Kids (one of our favorite toy stores) believes that play is a child's version of work. Healthy, happy, imaginative play is crucial to a growing child's development. The more creative play-time a child has, the more likely that she or he will become a creative, well rounded adult. Creative thinking is important whether you are a doctor, an accountant, an actor or a painter. Be creative with your child, play with abandon . . . but remember: no toy can replace you, and you can only enhance the toy.

Toys must be safe, durable, and age-appropriate—no buttons, long strings, ribbons, or small parts for children under three years of age. If a toy or toy part can fit through the cardboard center of a toilet paper roll, it's too small.

✳ If you're looking for a specific item, call ahead. Some stores will gift wrap and deliver nearby, so you might be able to shop over the phone.

✳ There are a few Web sites (see the Web Directory) that are excellent for ordering toys. Once you know what you want, check the Web for the best prices.

✳ Pay attention to return policies and store credits. Some stores, like FAO Schwarz and Toys

"R" Us, have an "anything, anytime" return policy, which can be useful if your youngster, like Alexander on his first birthday, receives three Barney dolls.

AGE-SPECIFIC TOYS

Jennifer from West Side Kids suggests these toys for the specific age groups, but remember, more does not equal better. Stick to one or two toys that your child enjoys for each stage:

1st Month

At this age, babies are just beginning to focus on the face, and see high contrast images. So consider black and white toys for a newborn.

- **Stim-Mobile (Wimmer Ferguson)**
- **Pattern-Play Cards (Wimmer Ferguson)**
- **B&W crib bumper books**
- **B&W Board Books**
- **B&W Gymini (Tiny Love)** Hang one item at a time! Don't overwhelm your little one. By hanging single items you learn what their favorites are.
- **Infant Mirror (Wimmer Ferguson)**
- **Tracking Tube (Early Start)**
  Great for the stroller
- **Lullaby Light Show (Tomy) or IRC Lullaby Dream Show (Tomy)**

2nd Month

Baby can now grasp a rattle, and will begin to lift her head and rollover.

Continue with above toys and introduce:
Pat Mat: We recommend a pat mat with bright color objects rather than pastels.
- **Activity Blanket (Discover & Go Playmat, Wimmer Ferguson)**
- **Bumper Books (Whoozit, Lamaze)** Hang as low as you can in the crib so the baby can focus on the graphics.
- **Small Rattles (Ambi, Haba, Sassy, etc.)** Place the rattle in the palm of the baby's hand and watch them grasp it.
- **Foot & Wrist rattles (Manhattan Baby, Eden)**
- **Whoozit (B&W Side) (Manhattan Toy)**

3rd Month

As your baby begins to turn in the direction of voices or sounds, it is a great time to introduce musical toys.

- **Rattles with bells (i.e., Geo Rattles from Imagiix)**
- **Wiggly Giggler Rattle (Hands On Toys)**
- **Pull down musical toys (i.e. Winnie the Pooh from Gund)**
- **Whoozit Musical (Manhattan Toy)**

4th Month

Now the baby is beginning to raise her chest, and is reaching and teething.

- **Crib Activity Gym (Fisher Price Busy Box, Kick & Play Piano)**
- **Soft multi-textured blocks**
- **Clack Rattle (Lamaze)**
- **Smiley Face Mirror (Sassy)**
- **Discovery Links (Lamaze)**
- **Teethers**

123 Discovery Lane (Tiny Love)
  Activity Arch (Tiny Love)
  Happy Sounds Ball (Tomy)
  Videos: Baby Mozart, Baby Bach, Baby
    Beethoven, Baby Einstein,
    So Smart series

5th Month

Your baby can now hold her head steady, roll over, reach for objects, grasp a rattle, raise herself up on her arms, and sit. And put everything in her mouth, too.

You no longer need black and white toys. Your baby should be able to focus on more detail.

In addition to the above toys, introduce more manipulative toys, such as:

  Twin Rattle (Ambi)
  Stroller Fun (Early Years)
  Fisher Price Soft Snap & Lock Beads

6th - 7th Month

Now your child can sit, bear her own weight when held up, and comprehend cause and effect. He may pass object from hand to hand or look for objects dropped onto the floor. To help with separation anxiety, play lots of hide & seek games using cups, puppets, boxes, and your hands. Your baby will begin to understand that if the toy always comes back so will you.

  Stacking Cups (Small World Toys,
    Sassy, Galt, etc)
  Fascination Station (Sassy)
  Activity Spiral (Early Years)
  Bath toys: Squirts, sieve, cups,
    floating toys, bath books

Sand toys: small shovel, sieve, and bucket
Neobaby Pick n Pull (Tomy)
Cloth & Vinyl Books
Baby Shakespeare video

8th - 9th Month

Now your baby can bear weight on her legs. She'll work to get a toy out of reach, look for a dropped object, pull herself up to standing position, play patty-cake, and nest.

  Babysongs video series
  Balls in a Bowl (Early Learning)
  Lift the Flap Books
  Chuckling Charlie

10th - 11th month

You baby's becoming aware of his environment, and is beginning to interact with toys as well as becoming more independent. He may be pulling himself up, cruising, and making a razzing sound.

  Baby's First Blocks (TC Timber)
  Bouncing Billy (Tomy)
  Mozart Magic Cube
  Tommy Toot (Ambi)
  Plastic kazoo

1 Year

Your baby may be walking, responding to your voice, cruising, making razzing sounds, and trying to nest, stack, and sort.

It may be time to introduce:

Simple Peg Puzzles
Pull Toys Battat's Spinning Bus, Troller,
  Ambi Max, World on Wheels (Bozart)
Push Toys: Fisher-Price Corn Popper

Activity Cube (Anatex)
Pounding Bench (either plastic or wood)
    or Pound a Ball (many versions)
First Dolls (Corolle Calin, bath babies,
    Raggedy Ann, etc.)
Stacking Rings (Fisher Price, Sassy,
    Lamaze, Brio, etc.)
Pop up Friends (many versions)
    (Creature pops up when correct
    manipulation is done.)
Umbrella Stroller
Sound Puzzle Box (Battat)
Flashcards

18 months

Your baby is gaining more control of fine motor skills, and is beginning to follow your direction.

Lock Box (Tag Toys)
Pathfinder (Anatex)
Shape Sorter (Gazoobo)
Brio Builder Pounding Board

2 Years

At 2 years of age, your child is beginning to build and create, and is interested in how things work. She's becoming verbal, reciting her ABC's and 123's.

Picture Cube Puzzles (Selecta)
Magic Sound Blocks (Small World Toys)
See Inside Puzzles (Ravensburger)
Tricycle
Figure 8 wooden train set (TC Timber,
    Brio, Thomas)
Tomy Bring-Along CD Player
Object recognition puzzles

Bop Bag
Trucks all sizes
Beginning phonics toys like
    Leapfrog's Phonics Bus
Play pretend toys
Art Supplies
I Spy Preschool Game
Brio Builder level 1

3 Years

Can you believe it? Your child's a pre-schooler! His construction and manipulative skills are increasing, and he's learning to play well with others. He is beginning to understand the concept of counting and reciting the ABC's. His fantasy world is expanding, and he's able to make associations.

Tangrams (Mr. Mighty Mind)
Marble Maze (Quercetti)
Pretend & Play Cash Register
Gearations (Tomy)
Flashlight (Playskool)
Leap Frog Think 'n Go phonics
Bingo Bears
Floor Puzzles (approx. 12-25 pieces)
Games: Barnyard Boogie Woogie, Hi-Ho
    Cherri-o, Footloose, Kids on Stage,
    Colorforms Silly Faces, Maisy's ABC
    Game, Four First Games, Snail's Pace,
    Lotto
Sequencing games: Things I Can Do
    (Educa), Tell-a-Story (Ravensburger),
    Step-by-Step (Educa) Magnetic
    Letters & Numbers
Animal Ball Park (Tomy)

Art Supplies
Lacing Aids: Lacing Cards, beads, shoes
THE STORES
A Bear's Place*
789 Lexington Avenue bet. 61st
and 62nd Streets
826-6465
Return Policy: Store credit only.

This friendly shop features educational toys for children under twelve. There are spelling board games, a Velcro rainbow board, musical instruments, puzzles, and a wonderful puppet theater. All toys sold here are JPMA approved. Gift-wrapping is available. A Bear's Place also has a large selection of upholstered furniture, and they offer customized and handpainted pieces as well, such as cribs, changing tables, and beds.

The Children's General Store
2473 Broadway at 92nd Street
580-2723
Grand Central Station
107 E. 42nd Street Lexington Passage
682-0004
Return Policy: Store credit only.

These shops carry an appealing selection, from puppets to cards, books, and tutus. For older children there are musical instruments, how-to kits, dollhouse furniture by Ambi, and Plan toys. Free gift-wrap.

Classic Toys
218 Sullivan Street bet. Bleecker
and W. 3rd Streets
674-4434
Return Policy: Store credit only.

A unique mix of vintage and new toys, including toy soldiers, miniature cars, figurines, and well-known characters (Star Trek, Disney), as well as a selection of dinosaurs, farm animals, and stuffed animals.

Cozy's Cuts for Kids*
1125 Madison Avenue at 84th Street
744-1716
448 Amsterdam Avenue at 81st Street
579-2600

Besides haircuts, Cozy's also sells inexpensive toys and party favors, such as mini-Play-Doh kits, toy cars, barrettes, beach balls, pencils, stickers, egg slime, and Pokemón key chains, as well as more educational material like books and puzzles. You can also find children's videos, handmade costumes, board games, and artist aprons—Pamela has found many party favors here for Rebecca and Benjamin's birthdays.

Cute Toonz
372 Fifth Avenue at 34th Street
967-6942
Return Policy: Store credit and exchange only within three weeks.

Lots of great Disney, Sesame Street, and other cartoon characters in all shapes and forms. Shop here for T-shirts, knapsacks, cups, stuffed animals, watches, and Hello Kitty accessories. A great place for small gifts and party   favors.

Dinosaur Hill
306 E. 9th Street bet. First
and Second Avenues
473-5850
www.dinosaurhill.com
Return Policy: Liberal.

This specialty toy and clothing store has quality marbles, marionettes, mobiles, T. C. Timber toys, and handcrafted toys. It also carries clothing, including an extraordinary selection of hats, mostly for children ages newborns to six. Free gift-wrap.

The Disney Store
711 Fifth Avenue at 55th Street
702-0702
39 W. 34th Street
279-9890
147 Columbus Avenue at 66th Street
362-2386
300 W. 125th Street at Eighth Avenue
749-8390
www.thedisneystore.com
Return Policy: Refund with receipt.

You and your youngster will have a lot of fun browsing through the colorful displays of every Disney character you've ever heard of—and probably a few you haven't—in the form of stuffed animals, videos, books, figurines, art kits, and clothing. Costumes are especially popular here. Gift boxes are free.

E.A.T. Gifts
1062 Madison Avenue at 80th Street
861-2544

Return Policy: Store credit, or exchange only with receipt an item in original packaging.

This Upper East Side store is full of fantastic things, including all sorts of stuffed animals, toy cars, bath toys, puzzles, puppets, and an excellent selection of children's books. Beware—this is not a spot for bargain-hunters! There are also gift items for older children—from funky jewelry, to activity kits and journals. This store is excellent for party planning, offering paper goods and balloons. There are tons of little toys, ideal for filling party bags, and a great selection of piñatas, in the shapes of ballet slippers, basketballs, even Elvis Presley ($30 each)! Kelly loves their selection of hard plastic bowls and plates featuring Arthur, Classic Pooh, Curious George, Madeline, and many other favorite characters. The famous E.A.T. restaurant is just next door.

The Enchanted Forest*
85 Mercer Street bet. Spring
and Broome Streets
925-6677
www.sohotoys.com
Return Policy: Store credit only.

Walk in, and you and your little one are in a forest complete with trees, bridges, and waterfalls. The woodland decor and classical music create a peaceful ambiance for browsing. Explore the selection of handmade toys from all over the world: magnetic play theaters from the Czech Republic, animal whistles from India, puzzles from Egypt and Greece, and an assortment of wooden toys and rattles. You'll also find blocks, books, plush stuffed animals, and a great selection of puppets. The Enchanted Forest offers jewelry, lovely kaleidoscopes, musical instruments, and other fine crafts for mom and dad. Free gift-wrap.

FAO Schwarz*
767 Fifth Avenue bet. 58th and 59th Streets
644-9400
www.fao.com
Return Policy: Lenient.

FAO Schwarz is a city landmark and major tourist attraction. But that is because it has the best and largest range of toys in the world: from wonderful dolls (see the Barbie Boutique), board games, a jungle of stuffed animals, and an endless selection of arts and crafts. Whether you are looking for classic toys or modern favorites you will find it here. All the hottest fads and rages are generally in stock. This is an exciting place for a child. They will love it, and so will Grandma. Yes, it's expensive, but you can find a large amount of gift items for $50 or less. Gift-wrap is free. During the holiday season, the lines of people waiting to get in wrap around the block!

Gepetto's Toy Box
10 Christopher Street bet. Greenwich Avenue and Gay Street
620-7511
www.nyctoys.com
Return Policy: Store credit only.

Gepetto's carries toys by manufacturers like Ambi, Playmobil, Sigikid, and others. It features a nice selection of musical mirrors, photo albums, and other specialty gifts. Free gift-wrap.

Hom Boms
1500 First Avenue bet. 78th and 79th Streets
717-5300
Return Policy: Refund within 30 days with original packaging and receipt.

Among other things, Hom Boms carries soft, plush toys for infants, wooden pull-along toys for toddlers, and activity kits for older children, and features major brands like Playmobil, Brio, and Madame Alexander. Of course, no toy store is truly complete without an art supply section. You will find everything from basic Crayola crayons to glitter pens and stickers here. Hom Boms offers free gift-wrap and delivery in the area.

Kay-Bee Toys
901 Avenue of the Americas bet. 32nd and 33rd Streets
629-5386
2411 Broadway at 89th Street
595-4389
www.kbkids.com
Return Policy: Refund with receipt within thirty days, otherwise store credit only.

Kay-Bee Toys is a chain, with shops in many malls. It carries the most popular name brands such as Fisher Price and Preschool, as well as arts-and-crafts and water toys. This is the place to find the hot toy of the moment. Prices are usually discounted, the sales are wonderful, and if you need a quick $5 toy for your child who went on the potty for the first time, this is the place.

Kidding Around*

68 Bleecker Street bet. Broadway and
Lafayette
598-0228
60 W. 15th Street bet. Fifth and Sixth Avenues
645-6337
Return Policy: Store credit only.

Kidding Around has a nice infant section with rattles, mobiles and squishy toys, and a larger selection of toys for one- to eight-year-olds. There are unique puppet theaters, musical instruments, Native American and African American dolls, and a nice French doll line. You'll find Brio, Ambi, Battat, and Playmobile here, as well as beach balls, and books. They will also supply you with personalized party bags. Free gift-wrap.

Little Extras*

676 Amsterdam Avenue at 93rd Street
721-6161
Return Policy: Refund if the item is in salable condition.

Pretty, roomy, and inviting, Little Extras is a great source for gifts. They stock black-and-white toys for newborns, bibs with cute sayings, and the educational New Beginnings line. In addition, the store carries some furniture, including stools, tables and chairs, and toy chests, as well as the best quality bathrobes and towels (which can be monogrammed) for children. Free gift-wrap and personalizing.

Mary Arnold Toys

1010 Lexington Avenue bet. 72nd
and 73rd Streets
744- 8510
Return Policy: Refunds with a receipt within thirty days. Otherwise store credit only.

A neighborhood favorite for decades, here you'll find the fine brands from Fisher-Price to Madame Alexander, as well as videos, games, dolls, puppets, and arts and crafts galore. The staff can create party favor bags or a special gift basket. Free gift-wrap and local delivery.

New York Firefighter's Friend

263 Lafayette Street bet. Prince
and Spring Streets
226-3142
www.nyfirestore.com
Return Policy: Store credit or exchange with receipt within 7 days.

Located just a few doors from the Ladder 20 fire station, Firefighter's Friend offers all the things an aspiring little firefighter might need. You can find books, and toys like fire trucks, stuffed fire bears, and fire helmets. This store also offers clothing items such as rain boots, raincoats, and baseball caps—all in firefighter fashion. No gift-wrap here, but they will ship anything via UPS or priority mail. Also, go next door to their police-theme store, New York 911—it is a great place to find gifts for your little law enforcer.

Ovations Baby

791-9300

Return Policy: Credit only.

Ovations Baby specializes in distinct and unique custom baskets and gifts for babies. They will prepare custom-made gift baskets of all kinds; their newborn baskets are particularly impressive, whether you spend $50 or $500. The staff is helpful and the quality of the clothing and merchandise is superb. Gift-wrap is free. Phone orders only.

Penny Whistle Toys*

1283 Madison Avenue bet. 91st
and 92nd Streets
369-3868
448 Columbus Avenue bet. 81st
and 82nd Streets
873-9090
www.pwt-toys.com
Return Policy: Store credit only.

These are terrific toy stores known for their commitment to high quality and their unique toys and games. Penny Whistle carries many top-of-the line brands like Brio, Tiny Love, Playmobile, Koosh, and Sassy. Great games, puzzles, and art and crafts kits are available, too. The friendly, easygoing staff will help you find the perfect age-appropriate gift, and wrapping is free. There is also a location on Route 27 in Bridgehampton.

Promises Fulfilled

1592 Second Avenue bet. 82nd
and 83rd Streets

472-1600

Return Policy: Store credit only.

You'll find a varied selection for babies and lots of choices when you need a birthday present for an older child (from costumes to construction kits). You can also buy personalized and coordinated accessories for your child's room: toy chests, benches, frames, bookends, clocks, coat racks, mirrors, and lamps. The most popular items are the hand-painted rocking chairs, and personalized birthday party favors. Cute baby books and photo albums are a specialty. Free gift-wrap. Their East Hampton location is a favorite of the Weinberg kids!

Toys "R" Us

1514 Broadway at 44th Street
(646) 366-8858
24-32 Union Square East
674-8697 · www.toysrus.com
Return Policy: Refund with a receipt,
otherwise store credit only.

Toys "R" Us discounts every well-known name-brand toy. It carries a lot of Fisher-Price, Safety 1st, Playskool, and Mattel; these are all the latest toys, and the prices and selection on books, videos, and Barbie dolls are usually the best in town.

Warner Bros. Studio Store

1 Times Square at 42nd Street
840-4040
www.wbstore.com
Return Policy: Refund with receipt,

otherwise store credit only.

This big, bright, and colorful store offers entertainment as well as shopping. As you might expect, it's a world of Bugs Bunny, Tweety Bird, Scooby-doo, and other Warner Brothers-related toys, stuffed animals, clothing, and accessories. They also stock Pokemón—which can help if you need a Pikachú in a toy pinch! The mail-order service offers free gift-wrap.

West Side Kids*
498 Amsterdam Avenue at 84th Street
496-7282
Return Policy: Store credit only.

This is a terrific neighborhood store, with excellent service and a varied selection of educational toys, quality books, and "imagination" items for playing pretend, such as miniature brooms, rakes, and kitchen utensils. There is also a selection of puzzles, games, and art supplies, plus a great assortment of small toys for party favors. Check out their array of Halloween and dress-up costumes, too. Free gift-wrap.

Wynken, Blynken, & Nod's
306 E. 55th Street bet. First
and Second Avenues
308-9299
Return Policy: Full refund within 7 days; exchange within 30 days.

This small, sweetly cluttered store is filled with unusual things for your child. Part toy store, part clothing store, part art/antique gallery, and part classroom, Wynken, Blynken, & Nod's has an old-fashioned, circus feel, and is the perfect place to get a gift for your little one. They carry nineteenth-century dolls, bronze ballerinas, vintage carousel horses, stage props, and folk art, in addition to more everyday toys like stuffed animals, hand crafted puzzles, activity kits, wooden toys, and curiosity kits. (There's clothing here, too: laurenceleste, Vitamins, cach cach, Twice Upon a Time, Malina, and Baby Baubles.) The owner, Deborah, teaches music-centered Mommy and Me classes in the space in back.

Zany Brainy
112 E. 86th Street bet. Park
and Lexington Avenues
427-6611
2407 Broadway bet. 87th and 88th Streets
917-441-2066
www.zanybrainy.com
Return Policy: Refund with a receipt, otherwise store credit only.

What a great selection! These big, bright, and colorful toy stores (which used to be Noodle Kidoodle) have fair prices on all the most popular brands, and carry puzzles, games, a large selection of educational toys, and arts-and-crafts supplies. These stores also have computers for toddlers to play with, and a toy train set up in the middle of the store to keep the little ones occupied while you browse.

Zittles
969 Madison Avenue bet. 75th and 76th
Streets, 3rd floor of Zitomer

737-2037
www.zittles.com
Return Policy: Refund with receipt within ten days, otherwise store credit only.

It looks like a pharmacy downstairs, yet upstairs it is a treasure trove of children's commercial, educational, and specialty toys. You'll find dolls, puzzles, books, arts and crafts, videos, games, computer games, "dress up" items, and toys from brands like Battat, Ambi, Brio, Fisher-Price, and Leap Frog. The store will ship and deliver locally. Free gift-wrap. Get on their mailing list or go to their Web site, where they advertise their "playdates." Eight to ten times per year, representatives from companies like Lego, Brio, and Thomas come and let children play with their new toys. A nice way to spend an afternoon.

Costumes

At least once a year (more if you have a child like Benjamin who loves to dress up like a superhero), you will need to pick up a costume for your little one. You can easily find selections at your regular toyshops, clothing stores, and department stores. The following specialty stores, however, are the authorities when it comes to Halloween and costume parties. These are the great stores to check out:

Abracadabra Superstore
19 West 21st Street between Fifth and Sixth Avenues
627-5194
www.abracadabra.superstore.com

This is truly a superstore of all things scary —monsters, skeletons, ghosts, and ghouls. Also, you can find clown supplies, makeup, horror props, masks, and costumes. Children's costumes for sale include characters from Powerpuff Girls, Disney classics, Star Wars, and much more. For infants, they have costumes like bunnies, angels, and Teletubbies. This store is not for the weak of heart. If your child is frightened easily, we suggest leaving your little trick-or-treater at home. Abracadabra has excellent magic shows 2 or 3 times each weekend; call for show times.

M. Gordon Novelty
933 Broadway bet. 21st and 22nd Streets
254-8616

M. Gordon is a warehouse of props and costumes. They carry over a thousand different hats, wigs, and masks portraying celebrities like Einstein, Elvis, and Michael Jackson, as well as monsters and other characters like Spiderman, Superman, Cinderella, and Snow White.

Halloween Adventure
104 Fourth Avenue bet. 11th and 12th Streets
673-4546
www.halloweenadventure.com

Open year round, Halloween Adventures is crammed with beautiful costumes, novelties, and accessories. They have a magic department (with a professional magician to give demonstrations on Saturdays) and a professional make-up department. Children's costumes range from Disney and Star Wars characters, to knights, wizards, angels, fairies, and princesses.

13 · books, videos, audio tapes, cds, catalogs, and magazines

No doubt about it: city babies—and their moms—love city bookstores! Together they can listen to stories, pick out videos and CDs, and, best of all, discover the joys of children's books. This multimedia universe is one of the most exciting aspects of baby culture today. In every case, talented writers, artists and musicians are creating lasting treasures for your children.

This section lists the best children's bookstores in New York and all they hold, from the classic must-haves, like *Goodnight Moon* or *Where the Wild Things Are*, to useful adult titles such as *Practical Parenting Tips*. We have recommended our favorite audio tapes and CDs (essential for those long car rides) and videos, not only to entertain the kids but to provide you with a few moments of peace. We have also listed some of the best parenting magazines, along with a selection of catalogs to assist you with at-home shopping.

Of course, the Web has totally changed and enriched the way we get our parenting information. Don't fail to read through the many great sites listed in the Web Directory at the end of the book.

BEST BOOKSTORES FOR CHILDREN

Bank Street Bookstore*
610 W. 112th Street at Broadway
678-1654
www.citysearch.com/nyc/bankstbooks
Return Policy: Store credit only.

With more than 40,000 titles for children, parents, and educators, Bank Street Bookstore is perhaps the best resource in the city for children's books. The knowledgeable staff can guide you on age-appropriate books.

Best Reading Tip We've Ever Heard

Carry a book with you and read to your child whenever and wherever you can:
* over breakfast in the morning
* on a bus
* in the pediatrician's office

Barnes & Noble
Locations throughout the city.
www.bn.com
Return Policy: Generous.

Barnes & Noble has an enormous selection. Its children's sections are comfortable, with plenty of room to sit and read with your child. Call to find out about story times and author appearances, particularly at Barnes & Noble Junior stores.

Books of Wonder
16 W. 18th Street bet. Fifth and Sixth Avenues
989-3270
www.booksofwonder.com
Return Policy: Store credit only.

This is a very special children's bookstore carrying new, out-of-print, vintage, and rare books, with an entire section devoted to the Wizard of Oz—not to mention a great selection of illustrated books. No television or movie tie-ins here, (meaning no Barney- or Sesame Street-type books.) Call for information on story hours.

Bookberries
983 Lexington Avenue at 71st Street
794-9400
Return Policy: Hardcover returns for credit, or an exchange, paperbacks cannot be returned.

This intimate bookstore has a great selection of books for all ages, with a darling elevated section for kids in the back. The area is carpeted with plenty of space to sit down and read. The selection includes all of the classics, from *Curious George* to *Eloise*, and everything is clearly marked by age group. The staff is very friendly.

Borders Books & Music
550 Second Avenue bet. 32nd and 33rd Streets
685-3938
461 Park Avenue at 57th Street
980-6785
www.borders.com
Return Policy: Refund or exchange with reciept within 30 days.

Borders has a lovely children's department with small tables to sit at as you peruse your and your child's favorite books. Like Barnes & Noble, Borders has everything; a coffee bar, the latest magazines, and a newspaper rack make this store complete. Call ahead for the monthly children's calendar.

Lenox Hill Bookstore

1081 Lexington Avenue between 72nd and 73rd Streets
472-7170
Return Policy: Store credit only.

This brightly-lit store has a small but adequate selection of kids books, tucked in a back corner. It includes everything from board books by Sandra Boynton to *Madeline*. There is a roomy floor and bench to read on and the staff is extremely friendly and helpful.

Logos Bookstore

1575 York Avenue bet. 83rd and 84th Streets
517-7292
Return Policy: Store credit only.

Logos is a very neighborhood-oriented little bookstore, and a popular place to take your kids. There is a wide selection of books for children of all ages, on topics including religion, poetry, science, nature, and history. Logos also offers special events for children, including birthday parties and reading groups. Owner Harris Healy is very knowledgeable and hands-on.

The Strand Bookstore

828 Broadway at 12th Street
473-1452
www.strandbooks.com
Return Policy: Refund within three days with receipt.

This family-owned bookstore is famous for its "eight miles of books," and has been since 1927. There is a huge selection of discounted books, mainly used and out-of-print, but also some publisher's overstock and reviewer's copies—all at fabulous prices. The children's department is mostly in the basement, where kids can lose themselves in the nooks and crannies of the windy spaces with shelves crammed with books. On the third floor you'll also find a nice selection of rare children's books.

CHOOSING A BOOK FOR YOUR CHILD

There are so many benefits to reading with your child: it will familiarize him with speaking patterns, increase his vocabulary, develop his attention span, introduce him to new concepts, and most importantly, help him learn to enjoy reading. Books provide influences that will be key in forming his personality. As a New York parent, you have an abundance of resources available to help you find the newest in children's literature and give you an opportunity to rediscover old classics. Sometimes all of this information can be overwhelming, but there are a few pointers we can give you to make the process of choosing a book for you and your child to share as smooth as possible. We have searched high and low throughout the city, visiting bookstores and libraries, and speaking with the experts. Here is what we've come up with:

Don't be afraid to ask for help from the children's department at your favorite bookstore or from the children's librarian at your local New York Public Library branch. That's what they're there for and they will be happy to help you!

✳ Especially for very small children, pick books that are durable (cloth books and board books are very popular) and with pages that little fingers will be able to turn. Bright, simple illustrations are always great!

✳ For slightly older children, be sure to follow your child's interests. If he likes sports or history, choose books with simple story lines in these areas. Children especially enjoy books about kids their own age in different historical periods. (The American Girl series is a favorite of Rebecca's.)

✳ Books should be challenging and stimulating—they should give children a chance to ask questions, think about possible solutions, use their imagination, and have fun!

✳ Read your child the books that you read as a child. It will be more enjoyable for both of you if you like what you are reading too.

✳ Most importantly, let your child be active in choosing the books she wants to read. She might feel ready to start exploring simple chapter books (like *Winnie the Pooh*, *Pippi Longstocking*, or the *Ramona* series from Beverly Cleary) when she is about five or six years old and first learning how to read. Take turns reading aloud (you'll probably have to do most of the reading at first). Your child will grow into the book and enjoy the challenge.

✳ Many suppliers and carriers of children's books maintain web sites. You can go to these to find new releases, locate places to borrow or purchase a specific book, and even order a book!

✳ Barnes and Noble publishes a great book for choosing reading material for your child: *The Barnes and Noble Guide to Children's Books*. It can be purchased in the Children's Section of any Barnes and Noble store.

Making the Most of Reading with Your Child

When reading aloud with your child, set aside a certain time each day and make it part of his daily routine. Snuggle up together and make it a time that you share. Let him be active in the reading process, encourage him to point out and describe pictures, suggest possible endings and ask questions. Older babies can participate by pointing and helping to turn the pages. Use silly voices for the characters—it will make storytelling more enjoyable for all involved. Introduce your child to the reading process early on, and tell short, simple stories to your newborn. A parent's voice evokes special responses from a child and it is never too early to take advantage of this. Also, don't be afraid to read just one or two words per page and skip the rest. This is how a one or two-year-old reads. Toddlers like to jump around a lot, and the constant stimulation is good for them. Turn those pages quickly!

BEST BOOKS FOR YOUNG CHILDREN

There are so many great books out there for children of all ages! For newborn babies to children ages 5 or 6, there are three main categories to use as guidelines. Baby books (infant-2 years) are simple and repetitive with lots of pictures. These books are bright and colorful, and connected to the baby's surroundings in some way. They should be sturdy and rounded at the corners for safety. The most popular forms of these books are bath books (great in the tub), cloth books (perfect for the crib), board books, and touch and feel books.

Once your child is around two, you can introduce her to preschool books. These books are concept-based and should be helpful in developing a sense of humor. They also begin to teach children about social interaction and the difference between right and wrong. They should be easy, fun, and colorfully illustrated. Preschool books are especially popular in pop-up form.

Finally, picture books should have slightly more complex story lines and illustrations. They often address a key life issue: siblings, sharing, potty training, starting school, and so on. These come in hard cover and paperback and some have plush figures as well. Classic books have been kept in a separate category—they're great for all ages. We've also included some special needs books that explain issues like divorce or adoption to young children.

It is important to remember that reading levels are just recommended ages and that what may be right for one three-year-old may be too advanced, or too simple for another. Your child will let you know when she is ready to move on by showing interest in more difficult concepts and reading material. The age ranges given for the following books are generally appropriate for most children in that age group. Use your judgment and enjoy.

Baby books

Board Books:

***Little Spot* Board Books by Eric Hill**
(*Spot's First Words, Spot at Home, Spot in the Garden, Spot's Toy Box*)

These books tell simple stories that are easy for small children to follow. Spot helps children learn to associate words and images.

Sesame Street Board Books
(*Elmo's Guessing Game, Ernie and Bert Can . . . Can You?, Ernie Follows His Nose, Hide and Seek With Big Bird*)

Sesame Street has been entertaining and educating children for years, and these books help even the youngest children learn useful concepts. *Hide and Seek with Big Bird* was one of Benjamin's favorites.

Neil Ricklen Board Books
(*Daddy and Me, Mommy and Me, Baby's Clothes, Baby's Colors,* etc.)

These books use one word per picture to describe familiar situations. They are adorable and use real baby photographs rather than illustrations.

Sandra Boynton Board Books
(*Snoozers, A to Z, Moo, BAA, La La La!, Doggies*, etc.)

Kids love the rhyming sentences with cute cartoon pictures. Pamela's kids love these books, and come back to them time and time again.

Anne Geddes Board Books
(*Garden Friends, Colors, Dress-ups, Faces*)

There's nothing babies love more than looking at other babies, and photographer Anne Geddes shows them in a whole new light. There are baby mushrooms, baby flowers, and many baby animals.

Helen Oxenbury Board Books
(*Working, Dressing, Friends*)

These great books teach little ones about the basics with simple illustrations and single words.

Thomas and the Freight Train

This is an early introduction to the beloved little train.

Cloth Books:
Thomas the Tank Engine Says Good Night
This cute book is perfect for the crib.

Cloth Books by Eric Hill
(*Animals, Clothes, Home*)

These charming books by the creator of Spot are perfect for little ones.

Bath Books:
Bath Books by Eric Hill
(*Spot Goes Splash, Spot's Friends, Spot's Toys*)

Make a splash with Spot, the adorable puppy!

Bath Books by Beatrix Potter
(*Benjamin Bunny, Jemima Puddle-Duck, Mr. Jeremy Fisher, Mrs. Tiggy-Winkle, Peter Rabbit*)

Looking at these classic characters will make baths more enjoyable for your little one.

Babar's Bath Book

This elephant makes a great friend in the tub.

Sesame Street Bath Books
(*Elmo Wants a Bath, Ernie's Bath Book*)

No one knows bath time like the experts, Ernie and his rubber ducky.

Preschool Books
The Clifford Books by Norman Bridwell
(*Clifford the Big Red Dog, Clifford and the Big Storm, Clifford and the Grouchy Neighbors, Clifford Goes to Hollywood, Clifford the Small Red Puppy, Clifford's Big Book of Stories*)

Everybody loves the Big Red Dog! Follow him and Emily Elizabeth through their adventures in this popular series by Norman Bridwell.

The Arthur Books by Marc Brown
(*Arthur's Really Helpful Word Book, Arthur Goes to School, Arthur's Neighborhood*)

Starring the adorable aardvark Arthur, these books help small children learn about word association and social interaction.

My Very First Mother Goose by Iona Opie

This is a great rhyming book for the very young.

Spot Books by Eric Hill

(*Where's Spot?*, *Spot Goes to a Party*, *Spot Goes to School*, *Spot Goes to the Beach*, *Spot Goes to the Farm*, *Spot Sleeps Over*, *Spot's Birthday Party*, *Spot's First Christmas*, *Spot's First Walk*)

These books are great for every preschooler. Kids can lift flaps to accompany Spot as he makes his way through many of his big firsts.

Peter Rabbit Books by Beatrix Potter

(*Peter Rabbit and Friends: A Stand-Up Story Book*, *Peter Rabbit: A Lift-the-Flap Rebus Book*, *Peter Rabbit's ABC 123*)

These books make learning interactive and fun.

Sesame Street Preschool Books by various authors

(*The Sesame Street Word Book*, *Elmo's Lift-and-Peek Around the Corner Book*, *Tickle Me My Name is Elmo*, *Sesame Street Lift-and-Peek Party!*, *Lift and EEEEK! Monster Tales: There's a Monster in the Closet*, *The Monster at the End of This Book*)

Kids love reading about characters from their favorite show—and everyone loves Elmo!

Everyone Poops by Taro Gomi

This book uses simple illustrations and explanations, showing kids that going to the bathroom is perfectly natural. (You will love this book, too.)

Going to the Potty by Fred Rogers

Mr. Rogers patiently and supportively explains potty training to parents and children.

Classics

Beatrix Potter books

(*The Complete Tales*, *The Tale of Benjamin Bunny*, *The Tale of Peter Rabbit*, *The Tale of Squirrel Nutkin*, *The Tale of Tom Kitten*, *The Tale of Two Bad Mice*)

For generations, children have enjoyed the cute, trouble-making little animals in Beatrix Potter's stories.

Curious George by H.A. Rey

(*The Adventures of Curious George*, *Curious George Gets a Medal*, *Curious George Learns the Alphabet*, *Curious George Rides a Bike*, *Curious George Takes a Job*, *Curious George Flies a Kite*, *Curious George Goes to the Hospital*)

Curious George loves life in the city with the man in a yellow hat, but his curiosity for new things can get him into trouble!

Dr. Seuss Books

(*One Fish, Two Fish, Red Fish, Blue Fish*, etc.)

These are silly, rhyming stories with amusing drawings and creative characters with the power to bring you back to your own childhood as well.

The Giving Tree by Shel Silverstein
(*Giraffe and a Half, The Missing Piece, The Missing Piece Meets the Big O*)

This is the story of the life-long friendship between a little boy and a very generous tree.

Goodnight Moon*
by Margaret Wise Brown

Everyone loves this timeless, charming picture book about a little rabbit who says goodnight to everything, including the moon outside his window.

Harold and the Purple Crayon
by Crockett Johnson
(*Harold's ABC, Harold's Purple Crayon*)

Join Harold as he draws his way through adventures.

The Little Engine That Could* by Watty Piper

This inspiring tale about the brave little engine has been popular for over 70 years for good reason.

Madeline by Ludwig Bemelmans
(*Madeline and the Bad Hat, Madeline and the Gypsies, Madeline in London, Madeline's Rescue, Mad About Madeline*)

Follow Madeline and her friends on their adventures in Paris.

Make Way for Ducklings by Robert McCloskey
(*Blueberries for Sal, One Morning in Maine, Time of Wonder*)

This classic book tells the tale of Mrs. Mallard and her eight ducklings crossing a busy Boston street.

Pat the Bunny, Pat the Cat,
Pat the Puppy by Dorothy Kunhardt

Your child will love touching the soft bunny and Daddy's scratchy face.

The Very Hungry Caterpillar* by Eric Carle
(*The Grouchy Ladybug, The Very Busy Spider, The Very Lonely Firefly*)

This is a beautiful, interactive picture book about a caterpillar, who eats and eats until eventually, turning into a butterfly.

Where the Wild Things Are
by Maurice Sendak
(*Alligators All Around: An Alphabet, Chicken Soup With Rice: A Book of Months*—one of Rebecca's favorites, *One Was Johnny: A Counting Book, Pierre: A Cautionary Tale in Five Chapters and a Prologue, In the Night Kitchen*)

When Max gets sent to his room without dinner, he sails off to the land of the Wild Things, where he can misbehave as much as he wants. But is this as great as it sounds? Also, check out *Chicken Soup with Rice*. This is how Rebecca and Benjamin learned the months of the year.

Other great reading recommendations:
Goodnight, Gorilla by Peggy Rathmann
Brown Bear, Brown Bear, What Do You See? by Bill Martin, Jr. (illustrated by Eric Carle). Also, Polar Bear, Polar Bear, What Do You See?
Jamberry by Bruce Degan

Time for Bed by Mem Fox
(illustrated by Jane Dyer)

Snowy Day by Ezra Jack Keats

Bus Stops by Gomi

Lady with the Alligator Purse
by Nadine Bernard Westcott

*Jesse Bear, Jesse Bear, What You Will
Wear* by Nancy White Carlstrom

Peek-A-Boo by Jan Olmerod

Silly Sally by Audrey Wood

10, 9, 8 by Molly Bang

*Eating the Alphabet: Fruits and
Vegetables from A to Z* by Lois Ehlert

Special Needs Books

Adoption Is for Always
by Linda Walvoord Girard

At Daddy's on Saturdays
by Linda Walvoord Girard

*Dinosaurs Divorce:
A Guide for Changing Families*
by Laurence Krasny Brown

Let's Talk About It: Divorce
by Fred Rogers

*Lifetimes: The Beautiful Way
to Explain Death to Children*
by Bryan Mellonie

Over the Moon: An Adoption Tale
by Karen Katz

*Tell Me Again About the Night
I Was Born* by Jamie Lee Curtis

We Adopted You, Benjamin Koo
by Linda Walvoord Girard

What's Heaven? by Maria Shriver

When a Pet Dies by Fred Rogers

*When Dinosaurs Die: A Guide
to Understanding Death*
by Laurence Krasny Brown

BEST BOOKS FOR PARENTS

As a new mother, you'll want to stock your shelves with books by experts such as Penelope Leach, Dr. Spock, and T. Barry Brazelton. Here are a few more titles. You can pick these books up at any of the major bookstores or order them online. Also, don't forget to take advantage of your local library!

GENERAL

*The Baby Book: Everything You Need
to Know About Your Baby from
Birth to Age 2* by William Sears, M.D., and
Martha Sears, R.N.

*Games Babies Play** by Julie Hagstrom and
Joan Morrill

*Mother's Almanac** by Marguerite Kelly and
Elia S. Parsons

*The Parent's Guide to Baby and Child Medical
Care* by Terril H. Hart, M.D.

*The Pediatrician's Best Baby Planner
for the First Year of Life*

by Daniel W. Dubner, M.D. and
D. Gregory Felch, M.D.

Practical Parenting for the 21st Century
by Julie Ross*
Practical Parenting Tips by Vicki Lansky
*Solve Your Children's Sleep Problems**
by Richard Ferber

Pamela couldn't have survived the last seven years without this book! It's not for everyone, but it's definitely worth a close look.
*25 Things Every New Mother Should Know**
by Martha Sears, R.N. and William Sears, M.D.
*What to Expect the First Year**
by Arlene Eisenberg, Heidi E. Murkoff, and Sandee E. Hathaway

This is referred to as the bible—as it should be. This is the month-by-month guide to your baby's first year.
Your Amazing Newborn
by M. Klaus and J. Kennell
Your Baby's First Three Years by Dr. Paula Kelly

Breastfeeding

Breastfeeding: The Nursing Mother's Problem Solver by Claire Martin, Nancy Funnemark Krebs, ed.

The Breastfeeding Book: Everything You Need to Know About Nursing Your Child From Birth to Weaning by Martha Sears, R.N.

The Complete Book of Breastfeeding by Marvin S. Eiger, M.D. and Sally Wendklos Olds

Successful Breastfeeding
by Nancy Dana and Anne Price

*The Womanly Art of Breastfeeding**
by La Leche League

Toddlers

The Girlfriends' Guide to Toddlers
by Vicki Iovine

The Vicki Iovine books are hilarious! Written for mothers by a mother who has seen it all with her four children.

Kids Book to Welcome a New Baby
by Barbara J. Collman

How to Take Great Trips with Your Kids
by Sanford and Joan Portnoy

The Smart Parents' Guide to Kids T.V.
by Milton Chen, Ph.D.

Special Interests

Twins from Conception to Five Years
by Averil Clegg and Anne Woolett

The Single Mother's Book: A Practical Guide to Managing Your Children, Career, Home, Finances, and Everything Else by Joan Anderson

In Praise of Single Parents
by Shoshana Alexander

New York's 50 Best Places to Take Children
by Allan Ishac

The Manhattan Family Guide to Private

Schools by Victoria Goldman and Catherine Hausman
The Parent's Guide to New York City's Best Public Elementary Schools by Clara Hemphill

VIDEOS

Almost all the superstores and many toy stores carry both children's entertainment and grown-up videos, covering a range of topics concerning new parents—breastfeeding, child development, and baby proofing. Also, don't forget your local library, HMV, Tower Records, Coconuts, Blockbuster Video, and Champagne Video, all of which sell and/or rent children's and parenting videos. Champagne Video is especially reasonable—two movies for $1.50, with a well-stocked children's section. There are four locations in Manhattan—three on the Upper East Side and one on the West Side. For a location near you, call 517-8700. We must add that children under two should not spend much time in front of the television. Experts recommend no more than one hour of TV per day!

Best Videos for Children

During your child's first two or three years, he is going to fall madly in love with Barney, Big Bird, Ernie, Winnie-the-Pooh, or some character that hasn't even been invented yet. You'll be renting or buying any number of videos featuring these lovable creatures, even if, like Kelly, you once swore no child of yours would ever watch a purple dinosaur sing.

Here's a listing of videos based on popular television series (the titles give you an idea of what each is about). All the tapes listed here offer either fun or instruction:

BARNEY
(Best for nine months and up)

Children love sharing adventures with Barney and Baby Bop. Your child will love the sing-a-long songs, even if they drive you crazy.

Barney's Alphabet Zoo
Barney's Birthday*
Let's Pretend with Barney*
Riding in Barney's Car
Barney and Mother Goose*
And more . . .

DISNEY'S SPOT SERIES
(Best for newborns to nine months)

The Spot video series is just as charming as Eric Hill's books.

Spot Goes to the Farm
Spot Goes to School*
Spot Goes to a Party
Where's Spot?*
Sweet Dreams Spot

DISNEY CLASSICS
(Best for age two or three and up)

Everybody loves the Disney classics, even Mom and Dad. The animation is enjoyable for all ages and the tales are timeless.

A Bug's Life
Aladdin
A Goofy Movie
Cinderella
The Fox and the Hound
The Great Mouse Detective

The Lion King
Mulan
Pocahontas
Snow White and the Seven Dwarfs
Toy Story
One-Hundred-and-One Dalmatians
The Aristocats
And more...

DISNEY'S WINNIE-THE-POOH SERIES
(Best for eighteen months and up)

Follow Winnie, Piglet, Tigger, and the others as they make their way from adventure to adventure. These videos are great because, aside from being fun, they teach valuable lessons.

Pooh Party
Pooh Learning
Cowboy Pooh
Sharing and Caring
*Making Friends**
Winnie-the-Pooh and the
   Blustery Day
Winnie-the-Pooh and a
   Day for Eeyore
*Winnie-the-Pooh and Tigger Too**
Winnie-the-Pooh and
   the Honey Tree

RICHARD SCARRY
(Best for toddlers ages 2 to 4)

Join the little worm Lowly and his friends in their animated adventures.

Richard Scarry's Learning Songs
Best Sing-along Mother
   Goose Video Ever!

Best Busy People Video Ever!
Best Counting Video Ever!
Best ABC Video Ever!
Best Silly Stories and Songs Ever!
Best Birthday Party Ever!

SESAME STREET
(Best for twelve months and up)

Sesame Street videos are as educational as the television show. Elmo, Bert, Ernie, Big Bird, and other beloved characters will help teach your little one how to sing, spell, and say their ABCs.

My Sesame Street Home Video
Play-Along
Sesame Street Sing Along
Big Bird Sings
The Best of Bert and Ernie
Do the Alphabet
The Best of Elmo
Sing, Hoot & Howl with the
   Sesame Street Animals
Sesame Street's 25th Birthday
   Celebration

JULIE ANGIER-CLARK'S BABY SERIES
(Best for newborn to age two)

What's better than cultural enrichment that's fun, too? This series was not around when our kids were newborns, but our new mommy friends swear by them as the only videos their newborn will focus on.

Baby Bach
Baby Einstein
Baby Mozart
Baby Shakespeare

MISCELLANEOUS
(Eighteen months and up)
Here are some additional favorites of ours:
Baby Songs
Shari Lewis' "Don't Wake Your Mom!"
Wee Sing Grandpa's Magical Toys

VIDEOS FOR PARENTS

Videos are an easy, convenient way to pick up parenting tips and gain some know-how. They will save you precious time by allowing you to stay at home with your little one. The Lifetime cable channel also offers some interesting parenting programming. Check your local listings.

Baby's Early Growth, Care, and Development

Baby's First Months 'What Do We Do Now?' Developed by twelve pediatricians, this video leads parents from birth through their baby's first few months. New parents are instructed on the daily care of a newborn.

The First Two Years—A Comprehensive Guide To Enhancing Your Child's Physical and Mental Development This award-winning video observes babies involved in everyday activities. The developmental periods are divided by age: one day to three months, three to six months, six to twelve months, and twelve to twenty-four months. Other topics include breastfeeding, early child care, infant nutrition, physical growth, and mobility/motor skills.

Dr. Jane Morton's Guide to Successful Breastfeeding Using a case study and graphics, this video shows the critical steps to comfortable, effective breastfeeding, including how to avoid common problems.

Touchpoints: The Definitive Video Series on Parenting, Volume 1: Pregnancy, Birth, and the First Weeks of Life* This practical guide to child development defines touchpoints as periods preceding rapid growth in learning, which are significant to future development. Points covered include pregnancy, delivery, preparation for birth, and the first weeks of your baby's life to three months.

Your Baby—A Video Guide To Care and Understanding with Penelope Leach A comprehensive and practical guide to newborn baby care and development, this video demonstrates techniques of everyday care in a variety of situations.

What Every Baby Knows—A Guide To Pregnancy An instructive video with sensible information concerning the development of children from birth to three months. This tape also explores a father's emotional involvement during pregnancy, gives a detailed profile of one couple's delivery, and looks at typical issues that arise in the early months after birth.

Exercise/Well-Being

Jane Fonda's Pregnancy, Birth, and Recovery This exercise program demonstrates pregnancy and recovery workouts, baby massage, and infant care, and skills to physically prepare for birth.

Kathy Smith's Pregnancy Workout* Both mothers-to-be and three different childbirth experts instruct mothers on how to maintain their energy and strength. Divided into prenatal and postnatal sections, the ninety-minute tape covers exercise for the new mothers up to six weeks after giving birth. Pamela used this tape to exercise at home, and found it challenging.

Safety Videos

Barney Safety Barney and friends instruct little ones on safety with cars, traffic, and in the home.

Fire Safety for Kids with Beasel the Easel This video, endorsed by educators and fire-fighters, teaches basic fire safety to children ages two and up. Children will enjoy the cast of characters and an original soundtrack.

CPR To Save Your Child or Baby* This award-winning video carefully explains the step-by-step procedures of CPR, including instructions on the Heimlich maneuver and choking rescue. If you haven't had a chance to take a CPR-instruction class, this is the next best thing.

Infant and Toddler Emergency First Aid (Volume 1: Accidents, Volume 2: Illnesses) These videos are endorsed by the American Academy of Pediatrics. The tapes explain emergency medical services including the proper procedures and actions to take when giving CPR or dealing with choking or poisoning.

Mr. Baby Proofer A tape designed to teach parents how to make their home a baby-safe environment, this hands-on guide also describes key safety products.

Choosing Quality Child Care This video answers questions such as how to recognize quality child care, how to make sure a child is safe, and what to ask during an interview.

AUDIO CASETTES AND CDS FOR CHILDREN

Just because you have a baby doesn't mean you have to spend the next few years listening to terrible, sappy music. There's some great music being written for children these days; don't be amazed when you find yourself humming the tunes to yourself (even in the company of other adults). In fact, you can find a lot of the adult music you like re-recorded for children. Much of the music recommended here is in *Baby's Best* by Susan Silver, or the Music for Little People catalog (800-409-2757). Also, don't hesitate to listen to your own music in the car. Pamela's friend Elizabeth only listened to classical music on car rides with her son, and he not only became accustomed to it, but he enjoys it, even now as a seven-year-old!

RAFFI
Baby Beluga
Bananaphone*
Grocery Corner Store and Others
Singable Songs for the Very Young

JOANIE BARTEL
Joanie Bartel's award-winning sound really appeals!
Lullaby Magic*
Bathtime Magic
Dancin' Magic*

Morning Magic
Sillytime Magic

SESAME STREET
The Best of Elmo
Ernie's Side by Side
Family and Friends
Sesame Street Silly Songs
Sing-Along Travels
Sing the Alphabet

OTHER SUGGESTIONS
A Child's Gift of Lullabies
  by Someday Baby
G'Night Wolfgang by Ric Louchard
Hap Palmer's Follow Along Songs*
Hush-A-Bye Dreamsongs
Lullabies of Broadway by Mimi Bessette
Lullaby Berceuse by XYZ
Peter, Paul, and Mommy by Peter,
  Paul, and Mary*
Shakin' It by Parachute Express
Sleep, Baby Sleep by Nicolette Larson*
The Lullaby and Goodnight Sleep Kit
Sugar Beats* (Rebecca and Benjamin
  love all of the Sugar Beats' music.)
The Beatles for Kids

CHILDREN'S CATALOGS

Shopping by catalog can be the world's greatest convenience; there are loads of them, all filled with great things for babies and children, and all of these great things can be delivered right to your doorstep. Most of these catalogs also have Web sites, which make shopping online easier than ever. Here are a few of our favorites offering one-of-a-kind accessories, toys, and practical imported clothing not available in stores.

Biobottoms
730 E. Church Street, Suite 19
Martinsville, VA 24148
(800) 766-1254
www.biobottoms.com
  Cotton and dress-up clothing for infants, toddlers, and older children.

Chinaberry Book Service*
2780 Via Orange Way, Suite B
Spring Valley, CA 91978
(800) 776-2242
www.chinaberry.com
  Chinaberry has wonderful books for children, with the most detailed descriptions we've ever seen!

Constructive Playthings*
13201 Arrington Road
Grandview, MO 64030
(800) 832-0572
www.ustoy.com
  An array of colorful, entertaining toys for young boys and girls, with a section called "First Playthings" that's especially good for newborns to one-year-olds.

The Walt Disney Catalog of Children's Clothing
www.disneystore.com
(800) 328-0612
  All of the merchandise, including characters from your child's favorite Disney characters and movies.

Hanna Andersson*
1010 NW Flanders Street
Portland, OR 97209
(800) 222-0544
www.hannaandersson.com

Hanna Andersson carries moderately priced, superior quality cotton play clothes for young children, including swimwear and hats, plus some matching outfits for parents. And these clothes last forever!

L.L. Bean Inc.
Freeport, ME 04033-0001
(800) 441-5713
www.llbean.com

Casual clothes for rugged kids. L.L. Bean is one of the few companies to offer clothing for larger body types.

Lilly's Kids
Lillian Vernon Corp.
Virginia Beach, VA 23479-0002
(800) 285-5555
www.lillianvernon.com

From Lillian Vernon, a catalog with well priced toys, games, and costumes.

The Natural Baby Catalog
7835 Freedom Avenue
North Canton, OH 44720
www.kidsstuff.com

The Natural Baby Catalog carries natural, ecological, and health-minded products, including cloth diaper covers, bedroom furniture, many beautifully crafted wooden toys, and books.

Ecobaby Organics, Inc.
332 Coogan Way
El Cajon, CA 92020
888-ECOBABY
www.ecobaby.com

This catalog has more than organic baby accessories—they also have non-toxic furniture, and a selection of breast pumps. They augment Natural Baby Catalog very nicely.

One Step Ahead*
75 Albrecht Drive
Lake Bluff, IL 60044
(800) 274-8440
www.onestepahead.com

One Step Ahead is good for baby products, including carriers/strollers, car seats, cribs, bottle holders, and some toys and clothing. Safety, travel, and mealtime helpers are also available.

Oshkosh B'Gosh
1112 Seventh Avenue, P.O. Box 2222
Monroe, WI 53566-8222
(800) MY BGOSH (800-692-4674)
www.oshkoshbgosh.com

Oshkosh is simple, all-American kid's wear, including classic denim overalls and jeans for your toddler or young child, in both boys' and girls' sizes. They have a store on Fifth Avenue.

Parenting and Family Life
P.O. Box 2153, Dept. PA7
Charleston, WV 25328
(800) 468-4227

www.cambridgeeducational.com

Extensive selection of videos on parenting, discipline, and health-and-safety issues.

Patagonia Mail Order

P.O. Box 8900
Bozeman, MT 59715
(800) 336-9090
www.patagonia.com

Patagonia is known for its own brand of rugged everyday clothing and parkas, as well as its cozy fleece jackets.

Perfectly Safe*

7245 Whipple Avenue, NW
North Canton, OH 44720
(800) 837-KIDS (800-837-5437)
www.kidsstuff.com

Safety gates, bathtub spout covers, and other items to child-proof a home.

Play Fair Toys

P.O. Box 18210
Boulder, CO 80308
(800) 824-7255
www.playfairtoys.com

Games, blocks, nesting animals, videos, and many other play items that just may help your little one learn to play fair.

The Right Start Catalog*

Right Start Plaza
5334 Sterling Center Drive
Westlake, CA 91361-4627
(800) LITTLE-1 (800-548-8531)
www.rightstart.com

Nursery accessories, safe plastic toys, diaper bags, car seats, jogging strollers, baby carriers, and more. This was a staple of Pamela's for the first few years of Rebecca's life.

Rubens & Marble Inc.

P.O. Box 14900
Chicago, IL 60614
773-348-6200

Rubens & Marble has basic white, 100 percent cotton clothing and bedding for infants. Excellent prices.

Toys to Grow On

P.O. Box 17
Long Beach, CA 90801
(800) 542-8338
www.ttgo.com

Every kind of toy you can think of, for newborn to pre-teens.

Troll's Learn & Play

100 Corporate Drive
Mahwah, NJ 07430
(800) 247-6106
www.learnandplay.com

Creative toys, costumes, activity books, videos, art supplies, and counting toys, mostly for ages two and up.

MAGAZINES FOR PARENTS

There's always something to do with children in New York. Check these publications for monthly calendars plus services and helpful articles just for New York parents. Many are free at local shops. Here are some of the better ones.

Big Apple Parents' Paper
9 E. 38th Street between Madison
and Fifth Avenues, 4th floor
New York, NY 10003
889-6400
www.parentsknow.com

This monthly publication features topical articles on parenting and kids. It has been around for over ten years and is an invaluable resource for Manhattan parents.

New York Family
141 Halstead Avenue, Suite 3D
Mamaroneck, NY 10543
914-381-7474
www.parenthoodweb.com

Started by two moms, this monthly magazine offers useful event calendars as well as features on everything from children's health to traveling with kids.

The Expectant & New Parents Guide
37 W. 72nd Street
New York, NY 10023
787-3789

Think of this as a mini *What to Expect When You're Expecting*, geared especially toward New York parents. You can pick it up at your pediatrician's office.

Parent Guide
419 Park Avenue South
New York, NY 10022
213-8840
www.parentguidenews.com

This monthly magazine is for New York families with young children offering information on schools, camps, entertainment, and more.

National Magazines

Two of our favorite magazines are *Parents* and *Child*, but all those listed offer practical advice and information on parenting and child development.

American Baby
249 W. 17th Street bet. Seventh
and Eighth Avenues
New York, NY 10011
462-3500
www.healthykids.com

A monthly magazine for expectant parents and parents of one-year-olds and under.

Baby Talk
1325 Avenue of the Americas (on 53rd Street
bet. Sixth and Seventh Avenues)
New York, NY 10019
522-8989

A monthly magazine for expectant parents and parents of two-year-olds and under.

Child*
P.O. Box 3173
Harlan, IA 51593-2364
(800) 777-0222
www.parents.com

A popular, authoritative magazine full of information for parents of newborns through teens.

Parents*
685 Third Avenue
New York, NY 10017
878-8700
www.parentsmagazine.com
A monthly magazine for expectant parents and parents of preteens and under.

Practical Parenting Newsletter
8326A Minnetonka Boulevard
Deephaven, MN 55391
612-475-1505
A bimonthly newsletter for expectant parents and parents of grade school age children and under.

Sesame Street Parents*
P.O. Box 52000
Boulder, CO 80322-2000
Provides information for parents about children age two through six, as well as a specially-sized little magazine for your children to read and color in, featuring favorite Sesame Street characters.

Twins Magazine
5350 South Roslyn Street, Suite 400
Englewood, CO 80111
888-55-TWINS (888-558-9467)
www.twinsmagazine.com
The only bimonthly national magazine for parents of twins.

Working Mother
135 W. 50th Street
New York, NY 10020
445-6100
www.workingwomannetwork.com
A monthly magazine for parents of infants through teens.

the city baby brooklyn guide

14 · brooklyn babies

Since the publication of the first edition of *City Baby*, many of our friends have opted to leave Manhattan for Brooklyn after having children. We thought maybe it's because rents are a bit lower there, and the pace slower. As we investigated further, we discovered that a virtual migration was underway, one that has resulted in a proliferation of stores and services catering specifically to Brooklyn families. From Park Slope to Prospect Park and the streets of Cobble Hill, we saw moms, dads and city babies everywhere.

Clearly, it was time to dedicate an entire chapter to Brooklyn. To provide the most up-to-date and reliable information on the borough, we went straight to the real sources for the lowdown-Brooklyn moms. We asked our Brooklyn friends, Jill in Park Slope and Alexandra in Brooklyn Heights, to scout their respective neighborhoods for what's new, what's hot, and what's tried-and-true. The listings below reflect their personal best bets for superstores, children's clothing and shoe stores, toy stores, bookstores, maternity shops, kid-friendly restaurants, classes for kids, play-grounds, and fun outings your kids will love. With their recommendations in hand, we visited each and every place. Many of them will delight you—even if you don't live in Brooklyn.

SHOPPING
Superstores

Happy Days
533 Fifth Avenue bet. 13th and 14th Streets
718-768-1433
Return Policy: Full refunds within seven days if items are unused, and in original packaging; exchanges within 30 days with receipt.

Happy Days is so huge it might as well be K-Mart, with fluorescent lights, white floors, and racks and racks of stuff. They have all kinds of inexpensive children's clothing, (including school uniforms) and accessories; strollers from brands like Cosco, Graco, Combi, Kolcraft, and Evenflo; car seats, infant carriers, cribs, bedding, baby monitors, and more.

Heights Kids
85 Pineapple Walk bet. Henry Street and Cadman Plaza
718-222-4271
Return Policy: Refund with receipt; without a receipt, store credit or exchange only.

Heights Kids is pleasant and spacious and just on the verge of being a superstore. There is a large selection of toys, clothing, and other products for kids under age 3. There are strollers by Maclaren, Martinelli, and Combi; Kolcraft bassinets and portable playpens; Britax car seats and Evenflo infant carriers; Peg Perego Prima Pappa highchairs; clothing from Catimini and Deux Par Deux; Medela breast pumps; Lamaze educational toys; and beautiful handmade quilts. The staff is knowledgeable and helpful. They even repair strollers (replacing wheels, etc.), and will deliver large items and ship gifts. Alexandra has purchased clothing, infant toys, and safety gates here.

MB Discount Furniture
2311 Avenue U bet. E. 23rd and E. 24th Streets
718-332-1500
Return Policy: Store credit, exchange, or refund.

Hands-down, MB is the best merchandised store in Brooklyn (and nicer than many in Manhattan). It stocks everything from cribs and strollers to bedding, accessories, gift items, clothes, swings, highchairs, playpens, and car seats. Unique model rooms are set up on one side of the store and custom bedding is a specialty here. Agnes, the owner, says they "will make anything you want," even adult bedding. Crib brands include Morigeau-Lepine, Bonavita, C & T, Pali, Tracer, and Ragazzi; strollers include Peg Perego, Baby Trend, Combi, and Inglesina. The store also carries bottles, nipples, diaper bags, and layettes from brands like Absorba, Baby Steps, Mini Clasix, and Carter's. MB Discount Furniture has a price guarantee, and will match the lowest prices found elsewhere.

Go Fish
260 Fifth Avenue bet. Carroll and Garfield
718-622-8237
This consignment shop has everything: cribs, strollers, clothes, toys, shoes, and books. Only items in good condition are accepted, so the selection is always very good.

Kids' Clothing and Shoe Stores

Children's Emporium
293 Court Street bet. DeGraw
and Douglass Streets
718-875-8508
www.achildrens.com
Return Policy: Store credit only.

This neighborhood favorite carries discounted name-brand clothing, in sizes newborn to 14, by Deux Par Deux, Chevignon, Flapdoodle, and Berlingot. They also carry shoes from Elefanten, Brakkies, Dr. Martens, Aster, and Baby Botte.

Fidgets
169 Seventh Avenue bet. Garfield
and 1st Streets
718-788-2002
Return policy: Store credit or exchange.

Fidgets has been a Park Slope favorite for over ten years. They carry clothing from sizes newborn to 14, as well as stroller and crib accessories, bibs, potty chairs, purses, shoes, great baby gifts, and toys like puppets, stuffed animals, and puzzles. Fidgets is customer service oriented, and will mail gifts, take special orders, and provide free gift wrapping.

Good Footing
94 Seventh Avenue at Union Street
718-789-2500
www.goodfooting.com
Return Policy: Full refund or exchange within one week of purchase, with receipt and if shoes are in good condition.

Keds, Aster, Birkenstock, and Brakkies are some of the shoe brands you'll find here for children size 8 and up. It's a pleasant place to shop, with brick walls and wood floors. The owners also own 3rd Street Skate on 3rd Street and Seventh Avenue, where you can buy children's helmets, roller skates, ice skates, and protective gear.

The Green Onion
274 Smith Street bet. Sackett
and DeGraw Streets
718-246-2804
Return Policy: Full refund within 14 days with receipt; after two weeks, store credit only.

This charming, bright store specializes in baby stuff, but carries casual clothing up to size 7. Brands include Zutano, Kushies, Petit Elephant, So Fun, Cotton Kaboodle, and Zyno, and prices are moderate. The Green Onion also carries shoes, and a ton of accessories, including cribs, bedding, and blankets. They also do layettes, and offer a baby registry.

Hoyt & Bond Store
248 Smith Street bet. Douglass
and DeGraw Streets
718-488-8283
Return Policy: Exchange or store credit.

Clothes both classic and trendy are featured at this upscale, minimalist store. Brands include Petit Bateau, laurenceleste, Petit Elephant, Honore, and Hoyt & Bond's own label, which is carried by Barney's and other elegant stores. Shoes from the London label

Start-Rite are offered. Our friends in Brooklyn love this shop; it truly saves a trip to Manhattan for dressy, one-of-a-kind clothing.

Johnnie's Bootery
208 Smith Street bet. Baltic and Butler Streets
718-625-5334
Return Policy: Full refund within two weeks with receipt and original packaging.

Johnnie's has been around for 60 years. It is a no-nonsense establishment packed with boxes of shoes in sizes ranging from infant to adult. Brands include Stride Rite, Minibel, Reebok, and New Balance. The salespeople are experts in measuring feet.

Jumpin' Julia's
240 Seventh Avenue bet. 4th and 5th Streets
718-965-3535
Return Policy: Full refund within seven days; exchange or store credit within fourteen days.

A neighborhood favorite, Jumpin' Julia's carries attractive, mainly European clothing, in sizes newborn to 14. Brands include Berlingot, Sucre d'Orange, and Deux Par Deux; and shoes are by Elefanten. You can also find quilts, bibs, hats, special occasion dresses, finger puppets, mobiles, lamps, and more.

Les Amis
50 Hicks Street bet. Middagh and Cranberry Streets
718-858-3179
Return Policy: Exchange or store credit.

Formerly known as 50 Hicks 'n Kids, this small neighborhood shop carries good quality, moderately priced children's clothing, shoes, gift items, and cute accessories from all over the world. Clothing is by Slaphappy, Molehill, Cotton Kaboodle, Manna, and Skivvydoodles; shoes are from Baby Botte, Rite Step, and other brands. Clothing designed by one of the owners, Fern, bears a house label. Fern will also make costumes and clothing to order. The friendly, community-minded owners maintain a bulletin board for mothers, and occasionally stage special events, such as storytimes and face painting. Call for information.

Lester's
1111 Avenue U bet. E. 12th Street and Coney Island Avenue
718-645-5636
Return Policy: Store credit only. No returns on party clothes or christening items.

This is the original Lester's, where the clothing selection for infants and toddlers is fabulous, as well as discounted, between ten and twenty percent. The store takes up about two city blocks, and you can easily spend an entire day shopping there. For Manhattan parents, it is definitely worth the trip. We found clothing from Catamini, L'Agneau D'Or, Petit Bateau, Mini Basix, Miniman, Jean Bourget, Sophie Dess, and Pappa & Cicca. The layette department is well-stocked, and the sales help wonderfully attentive. Lester's also sells sheets and towels (we spotted Blauen linen), bedding, mobiles, car seats, and diaper bags.

Lisa Polansky
121 Seventh Avenue bet. President
and Carroll Streets
718-622-8071
Return Policy: Store credit or exchange within
one week or purchase.

This little store has no shop sign, even though it has been here for 26 years. Neighborhood parents just seem to know where it is; but you can spot it by the racks of clothing outside. Along with a fantastic selection of shoes from brands like Dr. Martens, Converse, Frye, and Baby Botte, there is a smaller selection of clothing from unusual designers. The stock is constantly changing, new shipments arrive daily, and all the merchandise is discounted. Sizes are newborn and up. One warning: it is a tight fit for a stroller.

Peek A Boo Kids
90 Seventh Avenue bet. Union
and Berkeley Streets
718-638-1060
Return Policy: Exchange or store credit only.

A wonderful new addition to the Park Slope shopping scene, Peek A Boo Kids is the largest children's clothing store in the neighborhood. This is the place to go for upscale European clothes and fancy dresses, in sizes newborn to 6x. Brands include Absorba, Baby Graziella, Deux Par Deux, Aletta, Marinus, and Little Me; and for fancy dresses, Zoe and Sylvia White. The shop specializes in layettes, and you can also find underwear, pajamas, Elefanten shoes, and other baby products, like bouncy seats, jogging strollers, and infant carriers. A television set and VCR in the back of the store keeps the kids entertained while you browse.

Rachel's
4218 Thirteenth Avenue bet. 42nd
and 43rd Streets
718-435-6875
Return Policy: Store credit only.

Located in an Orthodox Jewish enclave in Borough Park, Rachel's has earned well-deserved fame for its large selection (over 200 clothing brands) and low prices. Clothing comes in sizes newborn to 16, and the selection of boys pants alone is staggering. The layette department is well-stocked, with brands like Carter's, Baby Dior, Jordache, Oshkosh B'Gosh, Baby Guess, Jean Bourget, Petit Bateau, and Baby Mini. You will also find an excellent selection of coats, jackets, and snowsuits. Rachel's is worth the trip if you aren't from the neighborhood.

Tuesday's Child
1904 Avenue M bet. E. 19th Street
and Ocean Avenue
718-375-1790

Tuesday's Child carries high-end French, Italian, and American brands such as Pinco Pallino, Armani, Clo Clo, Petit Bateau, Magil, and Sonia Rykiel—many at discounted prices. They also have a nice selection of accessories, and the staff will help put outfits together according to the latest European fashions.

Windsor Shoes

233 Prospect Park West at Windsor Place
718-369-2192
Return Policy: Exchange or store credit only.

Located right down the street from the park, this shoe store features sneakers, slippers, sandals, boots, and Tevas in styles ranging from sporty to funky. Brands include Stride Rite, Minibel, Skechers, and Fila. Watch for great sales.

Youngworld

452 Fulton Street at Hoyt Street
718-852-7890
Return Policy: Full refund with receipt within 30 days.

This sprawling, downtown store is part of a chain in New York, Baltimore, and Philadelphia. Youngworld is beautifully merchandised and well-lit, with all of the clothing laid out by size. Most of the stock is casual, from brands like French Toast, Mickey & Co, Gasoline, and Robert Stock. Prices are some of the lowest we've seen. Downstairs you can find every accessory imaginable, from bottles to cribs. Stroller brands include Kolcraft and Graco.

Toy, Book, and Gift Stores

Barnes & Noble

267 Seventh Avenue at 6th Street
718-832-9066
106 Court Street bet. State
and Schermerhorn Streets
718-246-4996
www.bn.com

These Barnes & Noble stores have great kids' sections with weekly readings, child-friendly atmospheres, and in-house Starbucks. A rainy-day heaven!

Booklink

99 Seventh Avenue bet. President
and Union Streets
718-783-6067

Booklink offers a nice selection of children's books and a slew of Harry Potter accessories.

Brooklyn's Best Books and Toys

92 Seventh Avenue at Union Street
718-636-9266

This is a lovely store, with its murals, stuffed animals hanging from the ceiling, and a young and friendly staff known to don costumes for work. There's a small but choice selection of children's books, clothing, costumes, masks, and tutus, and all kinds of toys. They also have a nice variety of educational products, arts and crafts materials, and puzzles. The shop hosts "circle time" every Wednesday morning, with occasional musical guests. A play space in back is reserved for the kids.

The Clay Pot

162 Seventh Avenue bet. 1st and
Garfield Streets
718-788-6564

This shop has a small, but lovely, selection of children's gifts: personalized baby bowls and cups, finger puppets, picture frames, embroidered pillows and bibs, felt balls, ceramic figures, and sterling silver items like cups and spoons. It may not be the place to bring young children, however, given the many breakables.

Community Bookstore

143 Seventh Avenue bet. Garfield
and Carroll Streets
718-783-3075

You will find a good selection of children's books here, along with a coffee bar, and a lovely garden. Unfortunately, space is so tight that a stroller barely fits in, so it's best to come without it.

Court Street Books

163 Court Street bet. Dean and Pacific Streets
718-875-3677

The back room of this bookstore—painted in a brilliant red—is brimming over with childhood favorites. Your kids will love this bookstore, too.

The Laughing Giraffe
at the Monkey's Wedding

234 Court Street bet. Baltic and Kane Streets
718-852-3635
www.laughinggiraffe.com

This shop's fanciful name leads you to expect the unexpected, and we promise you won't be disappointed by their unique and imaginative selection of toys. You will also find tons of games, trains, puzzles, and crafts materials from companies like T.C. Timber, Ravensburger, Playmobil, Marklin, and Creativity for Kids.

Little Things Toystore

1457 Seventh Avenue bet. Garfield
and Carroll Streets
718-783-4733

Belying its name, this is a big toy store bursting with games, puzzles, dolls, stuffed animals, musical instruments, arts and crafts materials, videos and books—and, to complete the mix, a back wall lined with items for infants. Pamela has received wonderful gifts from her Park Slope friends, wrapped in the shop's distinctive purple paper.

Nancy Nancy

244a Fifth Avenue bet. President
and Carroll Streets
718-789-5262

This sweet store is filled with funky things for kids—and the kitsch-lover in us all. It stocks great party favors, and party planning is a specialty. The goodie bags are especially appealing and you can always find a nice gift.

The Toy Box

93 Pineapple Walk bet. Henry Street and
Cadman Plaza
718-246-5440

The Toy Box is just as impressive and well-kept as its sister store, Heights Kids. Here you can find puzzles, books, computer games, Kettler tricycles, Razor scooters, stickers, party kits and invitations, as well as items from popular brands like Playmobil, Thomas, and Lego. Plus, they sell activity kits that will keep kids busy on rainy afternoons, everything from make-your-own dolls to body glitter and scrapbooks. The owner will recommend age-appropriate toys, and will also deliver large items and gifts, or party balloons. He once loaned Alexandra a Felt Friends easel for her daughter's birthday party. This is a neighborhood gem!

Victoria Station

247 Court Street bet. Kane
and McGraw Streets
718-522-1800
Return Policy: Refund within one week;
store credit after one week.

This charming store stocks all kinds of unusual, old-fashioned toys-tea sets, wind-up animals, plush toys, ceramic dolls, dollhouses, solid wood yo-yos, marbles and push puppets. A case in back holds collectible items with predictable price tags: a vintage Shirley Temple doll goes for $700!

Brooklyn Women's Exchange

55 Pierrepont bet. Henry and Hicks Streets
718-624-3435

Founded in 1852, The Women's Exchange is a veritable treasure trove, with all kinds of handmade clothing, toys, quilts, and children's accessories, plus carefully selected Brooklyn- and New York-theme books (both children's book and guides for parents). About 300 crafts-people from all over the country consign items here-everything from adorable hand-smocked dresses to elaborately carved wooden train sets and rocking horses. Toys are especially inventive, like a felt pelican with-surprise!—fish spilling from its zippered mouth. Prices are reasonable, even for such top-quality goods.

Maternity Clothing

Boing Boing

204 Sixth Avenue at Union Street
718-398-0251
Return Policy: Exchange or store credit within seven days, with receipt.

A dream for new mothers and moms-to-be, Boing Boing has found a distinct niche in Park Slope. Not only does it offer a fashionable selection of toddler and maternity clothing (with lots of nursing wear), but it functions as much as a community center-cum-rest-stop as a store. Two plush armchairs in back are available for nursing moms, and when we visited the store, a woman came in off the street, nursed her baby, and left. Bulletin boards offer information on parenting groups, child-care, and anything else. A front courtyard, which gives moms a place to rest while kids play with the toys, adds to the laid-back, nurturing atmosphere. You can also find a great selection of parenting books, breast pumps, and baby slings and carriers.

FOOD, ACTIVITIES, AND FUN
Restaurants

The Big Pizza Cafe

137 Seventh Avenue bet. Garfield
and Carroll Streets
718-398-9198

During a day of shopping, "Park Slope's

perfect pizzeria" is the place to stop in and grab a slice and a soda. You'll be delighted with its large variety of gourmet pizzas, inexpensive pastas, heroes, and salads.

Connecticut Muffin Co.
171 Seventh Avenue at 1st Street
718-768-2022
115 Montague Street bet. Clinton
and Henry Streets
718-875-3912
206 Prospect Park West at 15th Street
718-965-2067

This popular chain is one of Park Slope's premier meeting places for neighborhood moms, who often come in with their babies for a morning muffin, or for coffee, tea, cakes, and cookies, too.

Dizzy's
511 9th Street at Eighth Avenue
718-499-1966

"A finer diner," Dizzy's caters to kids, although highchairs are not provided. Crayons and crates of toys keep kids happy while they wait for favorites like Mac & Cheese, burgers, hot dogs, mini-omelets and pancakes. The decor is bright and funky, and Prospect Park's only a block away.

Heights Cafe
84 Montague Street at Hicks Street
718-625-5555

Although a bit more upscale than our other Brooklyn Heights listings, this spacious cafe remains kid-friendly. The menu is loaded with pizzas, salads, pastas, and sandwiches—all standard fare but with a gourmet twist.

Lassen & Hennigs
114 Montague Street bet. Henry
and Hicks Streets
718-875-8362

Because Lassen & Hennigs has such an outstanding deli and bakery, lots of moms get lunch here to take to the park. And Alexandra swears it's a great place to "pick up" other new moms. After the birth of her daughter, she met one of her best mommy friends here.

Living Room Cafe
188 Prospect Park West at 14th Street
(In the Pavilion Theatre)
718-369-0824

Located right across from Prospect Park, this whimsical place is a child's dream. There are games to play, and all sorts of fun to be had. Open only on the weekends (Friday evenings, Saturdays and Sundays), it's a nice place to stop on your way to a park outing.

Monty Q's
158 Montague Street bet. Clinton
and Henry Streets
718-246-2000

You can grab a quick gourmet meal at Monty Q's, where pizza, salad, pasta, sandwiches, and other goodies are tantalizingly displayed on the counter. The restaurant is clean and roomy, but be advised: strollers are not always welcome during the crowded lunch hours.

New World Coffee

125 Seventh Avenue at Carroll Street
718-638-9633

You can tell by the basket of toys in plain sight, that this is a popular meeting spot for mothers with children.

Park Slope Brewing Company

356 Sixth Avenue at 5th Street
718-788-1756
40 Van Dyke Street at Dwight Street
718-246-8050
62 Henry Street bet. Cranberry
and Orange Streets
718-522-4801

In each of its locations, this establishment offers a congenial atmosphere, comfort food, and a long, inviting bar. It's a fun spot to take the kids early on Friday and Saturday nights, when they can order from a children's menu that's filled with favorites like PB&J, chicken fingers, grilled cheese, and burgers.

2nd Street Cafe

189 Seventh Avenue at 2nd Street
718-369-6928

The children's menu here is replete with all the favorites, plus veggie and turkey burgers. The regular menu of soups, salads, and sandwiches—there's a coffee bar, too—makes this an appealing place for parents to unwind with the kids. Children are invited to cover the walls with artwork, crayons courtesy of the management.

Starbucks

164 Seventh Avenue bet. Garfield
and First Street
718-369-1213

A nice place to sip a latte while your kids amuse themselves with the toys and books provided.

Sweet Melissa's

276 Court Street bet. Butler
and Douglass Streets
718-855-3410

This is a bakery/cafe is famous for its gorgeous special order birthday cakes.

Teresa's

80 Montague Street bet. Hicks
and Montague Terrace
718-797-3996

Teresa's has no children's menu, but kids and parents alike will find an appealing selection of sandwiches, soups, and salads, along with Eastern European fare like pierogies and kielbasa. And breakfast is served all day long. Wood floors, open spaces, and a small bar all contribute to the warm atmosphere. In the summer, the outdoor cafe is a nice place to feed noisy toddlers who are easily diverted by passers-by.

Two Boots

514 2nd Street bet. Seventh
and Eighth Avenues
718-499-3253

The "boots" of Italy and Louisiana kick in

for great pizza with creative toppings, and a variety of Cajun and pasta specialties. Everybody loves Two Boots and we know why! It's fun, with a sparkling décor enhanced by lively music. Every evening this place is packed with kids, who love getting bits of dough to play with from the pizza man. To arrange a pizza-making birthday bash, call Piper, the general manager, who will help you plan your party.

Kids' Classes, Mommy and Me

ArtsCetera
212 Smith Street bet. Baltic and Butler Streets
718-643-6817

Founded in 1998, ArtsCetera houses its own art, dance, and music classes, as well as those of associate programs. Afternoon Art is a class that nurtures the artist in every child through painting, sculpture, collage, and more; Young Music Makers is for children 3 1/2 to 5. [See also Music for Aardvarks & Other Mammals, and Music Together described on page 251.] A prenatal yoga class is offered on Mondays, and the Smith Street studio is available for birthday parties, rehearsals, mother's groups, and meetings.

Brooklyn Central YMCA
153 Remsen Street, 2nd floor,
bet. Court and Clinton Streets
718-625-3136
www.ymcanyc.org

Youth programs at this popular Y include preschool gymnastics, hockey, basketball, and flag football.

Brooklyn Conservatory of Music
58 Seventh Avenue at Lincoln Place
718-622-3300

Sing, Sounds, Leaps & Bounds is the conservatory's noteworthy program for toddlers.

Brooklyn Heights Synagogue
131 Remsen Street bet. Clinton
and Henry Streets
718-522-2070
www.bhsbrooklyn.org

This vibrant, liberal synagogue offers a Gan Playgroup twice a week for 3- and 4-year-olds. Playtime, arts and crafts and other activities, all highlight Jewish culture. The playgroup meets Tuesdays from 2:45 to 3:45 P.M., and Thursdays from 3:30 to 4:30 P.M. Religious school for kindergartners and up meets daily, and on Fridays there are free Welcoming Shabbats for all age groups. Support groups for new mothers, Mommy and Me classes, and family bagel breakfasts are offered the first Sunday of each month. Call for specifics.

Brooklyn Museum
200 Eastern Parkway at Washington Avenue
718-638-5000
www.brooklynart.org

Located next door to Brooklyn Botanic Garden, the Brooklyn Museum offers children's programs and special events throughout the year. A unique and popular program, Stories & Art, invites storytellers, authors, and illustrators to tell tales inspired by the museum's collections. It meets every Saturday at 4 P.M. Sign-language-interpreted versions of these classes are also offered.

Brooklyn Public Library

Grand Army Plaza
718-230-2100
431 Sixth Avenue bet. 8th and 9th Streets
718-832-1853
www.brooklynpubliclibrary.org
www.bplkidzone.org

The Brooklyn Public Library is, of course, a fantastic resource for everyone in the family. The main branch not only holds an extensive collection of classic children's books, (as well as games and toys), but offers a Reading is Fundamental (RIF) program that encourages kids to build personal book collections—a child may take home a free book after each club meeting. After school, the library staff is always available to help children with homework and computers, or to read aloud to them. Free art classes are also offered, but advance registration is required; and there is a cafe.

Brooklyn Botanic Garden

1000 Washington Avenue
bet. Crown and Montgomery Streets
718-623-7223
www.bbg.org

At the Brooklyn Botanic Garden, your city babies age 3 and up can learn to become amateur farmers and gardeners. Kids plant, harvest, and tend to gardens, and participate in everything from gathering herbs and flowers for scented sachets to filling in ponds and cleaning tools. Time is allocated for creative play in the interactive Discovery Garden. Classes and camps are also offered.

Dance Studio of Park Slope

808 Union Street, 2nd floor, bet. Sixth
and Seventh Avenues
718-789-4419

This popular dance studio offers a variety of great classes for children age 20 months and up. Tots on the Go is a movement class for kids 20 months to 3 years and their parents or caregivers; Rhythm and Motion is a creative movement class for 3 year olds; and classes in tumbling, ballet, jazz, and tap are offered for kids 4 and up.

The Early Ear

511 9th Street bet. Eighth Avenue
and Prospect Park West
212-877-7125 (general number)

Babies as young as four months are introduced to music in a highly regarded program. Forty-minute classes are limited to ten children, with two teachers, one to accompany and the other to demonstrate. Sing-a-long, games, play activities and mini-musical instruments are incorporated.

Eastern Athletic Club

17 Eastern Parkway at Grand Army Plaza
718-789-4600
43 Clark Street bet. Henry and Hicks Streets
718-625-0500

Children ages 6 months to 12 years come

here for lessons in swimming, gymnastics, tennis, ballet, soccer, in-line skating, basketball, hip-hop dance, creative movement, squash, and even fencing. According to Jill, the swimming classes are excellent, though registration is tricky: it is by lottery only. Classes are open both to members and non-members.

Beth Elohim's Early Childhood Center

Eighth Avenue at Garfield Place
718-499-6208

The center offers a great class, "Tots on the Move," as well as a variety of other options for children ages 6 months to 3 years. Children and moms or caregivers enjoy art, cooking, and swimming together. There is also a nursery and a drop-in center.

Grace Church School

254 Hicks Street bet. Joralemon
and Remsen Streets
718-624-4030

"Together-time" for 15 to 23-month-olds and their moms or caregivers offers tots a taste of preschool. Be sure to enroll early; classes are held during the school year, and you may need to apply months in advance.

Just Wee Two

Congregation Mount Sinai
250 Cadman Plaza West bet. Clinton
and Clark Streets
(800) 404-2204

"Just Wee Two" is a program that lets children 14 months to 3 years and their moms

enjoy music, arts and crafts, story time, and playtime in a classroom environment. Separation classes are also available for toddlers age 2 ½ to 3 ½, and up.

Kid Fit

25 Dean Street bet. Court and Smith Streets
718-852-7670

Jose was children's gymnastic program manager at Eastern Athletic Club before he opened this terrific space on the ground floor of a brownstone. Along with a well-trained staff, he offers excellent gymnastics classes, baby tumbling, and Daddy and Me classes on Saturdays, as well as rock climbing, karate, and dance. Alexandra's daughter Charlotte thoroughly enjoyed coming to this clean, colorful space, where the waiting area is equipped with a ball pit and slide. Kid Fit also hosts sensational birthday parties and holiday camps.

Music for Aardvarks & Other Mammals

125 Henry Street bet. Clark and Pierrepont
Streets (at Zion Lutheran Church)
212 Smith Street bet. Baltic and
Butler Streets (ArtsCetera)
61 Park Place bet. Fifth and Sixth Avenues
(at Father Dempsey Center)
718-643-6817
www.musicforaardvarks.com

David Weinstone uses his original songs to introduce kids to music-making. Kids up to 4 years old sing, move, and play instruments with parents or caregivers. The songs reflect universal childhood themes and celebrate growing up in an urban environment. David brings a non-traditional voice to children's music, with influences of rock, blues, ballads, folk, and pop. His tapes and compact discs come with the program.

Music Together

125 Henry Street bet. Clark and
Pierrepont Streets (at Zion Lutheran Church)
212 Smith Street bet. Baltic and Butler
Streets (at ArtsCetera)
718-643-6817
www.musictogether.com

Music Together is a forty-five minute class in which mommies and children sing, dance, chant, and play with various instruments. At the start of the program, parents receive a cassette tape, a compact disc, and a charming illustrated song book. They are encouraged to play the tape at home, and moms report that children come to love the songs. Music Together has ten to twelve children per class. There are also classes for babies and toddlers, and classes that are not divided by age—infants and toddlers are mixed together. This class is also taught in Park Slope at the Brooklyn Society of Ethical Culture located at Prospect Park West and Second Street.

Power Play

432 Third Avenue, bet. Seventh
and Eighth Streets
718-369-9880

A wide range of gymnastics is offered for younger children ages 9 months and up. Age-appropriate equipment is provided in bright, colorful environment that houses a sandbox, a tree house, a big play house and a play stage. This is a great place for parties.

Prospect Park YMCA

357 Ninth Street bet. Fifth and Sixth Avenues
718-768-7100
www.ymcanyc.org

This popular Y offers swimming, karate, and gymnastics for little ones, as well as arts and crafts, song and dance, soccer, basketball, and volleyball. Many are offered as after-school child care programs. Holiday Camps are also offered.

Spoke the Hub Dancing Company

748 Union Street bet. Fifth and Sixth Avenues
718-857-5158
295 Douglass Street bet. Third
and Fourth Avenues
718-643-5708
www.spokethehub.org

In these friendly neighborhood studios—one in a brownstone, the other in a loft warehouse—the emphasis is more on exploration and creativity than technique. Four different classes are offered : Sing, Dance, and Make Believe is for kids ages 2 to 4 years and their parents or caregivers; Creative Dance is for kids ages 3 to 6; Modern Dance is for 6 to 8 year olds; and Afro-Caribbean Dance class is for 5 to 7 year olds. Spoke the Hub also produces events and performances showcasing community members and children, along with professional dancers.

Terrace Dance Studio
273 Prospect Park West at 17th Street
718-768-5505
www.terracedance.com

Known as "the best little dance school in Brooklyn," Terrace offers classes in ballet, jazz, tap, gymnastics, and hip-hop for children ages 3 and up. Many children stay in these classes for years, some even until they go off to college.

Playgrounds

Carroll Park
Carroll Street at Court Street

Located in the heart of charming Carroll Gardens, this playground is large, leafy, and filled with benches. Kids love the huge jungle gyms and sprinklers.

Park Slope Playground
Berkeley Place bet. Fifth and Sixth Avenues

This is a pleasant playground, with several jungle gyms, sprinklers, and benches—and screaming kids, of course. Another plus: there is a bathroom with an attendant.

Pierrepont Playground
Brooklyn Heights Promenade

A beautiful playground at the water's edge, Pierrepont offers spectacular views of the Brooklyn Bridge, the Statue of Liberty, and lower Manhattan. It's a great place to sit and rest—even without the kids. Wrought-iron gates, lush trees, old-fashioned lampposts, and the sprawling jungle gyms make this a favorite hangout for Heights' kids. In the summer, volunteers give free arts and crafts instruction.

P.S. 321 Playground
Seventh Avenue bet. 1st and 2nd Streets

Small and somewhat barren, this playground is open only on weekdays after school. The two jungle gyms will entertain preschoolers after a day of shopping and eating with mom on Seventh Avenue. It is most popular in the evenings.

Third Street Playground
Prospect Park West at 3rd Street

This is the nicest—and largest—playground in Park Slope, with jungle gyms, tire swings, swing sets, sprinklers, and a sandbox. The space is lined with trees. It is *the* Park Slope hangout.

Tot Lot
Garfield Place and Prospect Park West

To get to this simple climbing structure for babies and toddlers, use the Garfield Street entrance.

Outings

The Brooklyn Aquarium at Coney Island
Surf Avenue and Coney Island Boardwalk
at W. 8th Street
718-265-3400

Visitors from all over the world come to this famed aquarium to see the sea lions and other water creatures. Even the youngest children are amazed and delighted by the "underwater" views.

Brooklyn Botanic Garden
1000 Washington Avenue bet. Crown and Montgomery Streets

718-623-7200
www.bbg.org

Founded in 1910, the Brooklyn Botanic Garden is visited by more than 750,000 people each year. More than 12,000 kinds of plants from around the globe are displayed on 52 acres and in the acclaimed Steinhardt Conservatory. There's always something new to see, and kids love the educational Discovery Garden.

Brooklyn Children's Museum
145 Brooklyn Avenue at St. Mark's Avenue
718-735-4400
www.brooklynkids.org

The Brooklyn Children's Museum was the world's first museum of its kind. With its interactive exhibitions, based on a collection of more than 20,000 plants, animals, and cultural artifacts, it is a stimulating place to spend a day with the little ones. The museum is closed on Mondays and Tuesdays.

Prospect Park
718-965-8951
www.prospectpark.org

With its 526 verdant acres, Prospect Park offers urbanites a peaceful retreat from the city's stresses. There is a 60-acre lake on the east, a 90-acre meadow on the west, and Brooklyn's last natural forest in between. The Park's many popular attractions include the Picnic House overlooking the Long Meadow, the Carousel, the Lefferts Homestead Historic House Children's Museum, the Kate Wollman Center and Rink, the Boathouse located on the Lullwater, and five playgrounds. Prospect Park hosts hundreds of events annually, including concerts, sporting events, performing arts, festivals, and tours.

Prospect Park Children's Wildlife Center
450 Flatbush Avenue bet. Empire Boulevard and Grand Army Plaza
718-399-7321
www.wcs.org

This children's zoo, arguably New York City's best zoo, is rarely crowded and one we highly recommend. Among the many highlights is the Discovery Trail, a fascinating walk along a path through grassy fields where your curious toddler can come face-to-face with prairie dogs and watch wallabies and many other animals cavort in a replication of their natural habitat. While on the trail, an enormous tortoise once crossed Alexandra's and Charlotte's path. Zookeepers circulate and offer information about the animals. Kids can also try on "turtle shells," "hatch" from oversized "eggs," and measure how far they can jump compared to a mouse or kangaroo. At the always popular petting zoo, children can feed goats, sheep, and a cow with pellets sold in candy dispensers for 50 cents a handful. Other exhibits include sea lions and indoor displays of various animals from around the world. Jill's kids love it here.

The Puppetworks, Inc.
338 Sixth Avenue at 4th Street
718-965-3391
www.puppetworks.org

Using hand-carved wooden marionettes, Puppetworks performs classic and traditional fairy and folk tales. These shows, popular with Brooklyn kids for more than twenty years, are presented on Saturday and Sunday afternoons. They do birthday parties, too.

The NY Transit Museum
Boerum Place and Schermerhorn Street
718-243-3060

"Drive" a bus, or board an antique train at this fun museum, housed in a de-commissioned subway station.

web site directory

The Internet has revolutionized our lives as parents. What follows is a list of Web sites, organized by topic, which we found particularly useful. But sites open up and close down with frequency, so use this list as a point of reference, but update it with your own discoveries. For city parents who enjoy surfing the Web, some of these listings may be familiar.

GENERAL

www.newyork.urbanbaby.com
A comprehensive guide for city families throughout the five boroughs.

www.newyork.citysearch.com
What's happening in the greatest city in the world, including kids activities within designated areas.

www.ci.nyc.ny.us
The official New York City Web site for general information, event listings, and much more.

www.metmuseum.org
The Metropolitan Museum of Art's official Web site.

web.gc.cuny.edu/library/Research/newc.htm
City University of New York—listings range from museums and restaurants, to cultural and theater events.

www.nyckidsarts.org
Arts and arts education programming in New York City. Click on Kids Culture Catalog, for lists of over 230 arts and cultural organizations that offer programs for children. Also an events calendar, and listings of after-school classes.

BROOKLYN

www.brooklyn.about.com
Top Brooklyn sights, a FAQ sheet, and more.

www.bplkidzone.org
The Brooklyn Public Library site offers fun online games and links.

www.brooklynonline.com
All things Brooklyn.

www.hellobrooklyn.com
Pediatricians, classes, preschools, shopping, and much more, all for the Brooklyn family.

www.about.brooklyn.com
Brooklyn FAQS and links.

PARENTING

www.babycenter.com
A wealth of information on everything baby-related, i.e. maintaining fitness during pregnancy.

www.abcparenting.com
Comprehensive parenting site.

www.parentsoup.com
Connect with other parents through the many chat rooms on this extensive site.

www.familywonder.com
A site for family entertainment, with activities, news, parenting tips-and a huge selection of toys.

www.parentsoup.com/library
A library of parenting articles from this site.

MEDICAL, NUTRITION AND FITNESS

www.acog.org
The American College of Obstetrics and Gynecology. Current information, doctors listings.

www.my.webmd.com
Articles on pregnancy, childbirth preparation, normal deliveries, alternative medicine and nutrition.

www.ivillage.com
Fantastic site for pregnant women and new moms. A month-by-month chart on what to expect throughout your pregnancy.

www.parentsoup.com
Great features, including "Ask the OB-GYN."

www.cfmidwifery.org
The Citizens for Midwifery, promoting Midwifery Model of Care. State-by-state information, contacts, and a helpful news directory.

www.mana.org
The Midwive's Alliance of North America.

www.midwiferytoday.com
Midwifery, birthing, books, products, feature articles, and a weekly newsletter.

www.moonlily.com/obc
The Online Birth Center offers loads of information on midwifery, pregnancy, birth, breastfeeding and nannies.

www.bradleybirth.com
The Bradley Method of Natural Childbirth's Web site includes a national directory of instructors, and a suggested diet for pregnant women.

www.lamaze-childbirth.com
Locates a Lamaze educator in your area, and describes this style of birth preparation.

www.childbirth.org
Everything you need to know about birthing—from complications and Cesareans to VBAC and postpartum stress.

www.thebabycorner.com
A complete resource for childbirth, breastfeeding, and parenting information.

www.birthcenters.org
From the National Association of Childbearing Centers, everything you need to know about birth centers.

www.birthpsychology.com
Articles on the psychological and emotional effects of pregnancy.

www.travelingtikes.com
For moms who want to exercise with their kids. Backpacks, baby joggers, and other resources for kids on the go.

www.nutrio.com
A comprehensive nutrition and fitness resource.

www.expectingfitness.com
Exercise guidelines and suggested regimes for pregnant women.

www.fitnessfind.com/pregnancy.html
Information on staying fit during pregnancy—nutrition, stretches, guidelines and workout information.

www.yogadirectory.com
Listings and links to everything yoga: classes, private instructors, events and more.

www.maternityshoppe.com
Tips on fitness, skin care, and massage for pregnant women.

CHILD CARE: PEDIATRICIANS, NANNIES

www.kidsgrowth.com
Pediatric advice by topic, from abdominal pains to vision disorders. Very current information.

www.childbirth.org
Information about doulas.

www.dona.com
Doulas of North America. Locate a doula in your area.

www.webnannies.com
A good place to find and discuss issues pertaining to childcare.

www.liveandlearn.com
Good pointers on what to look for in a caregiver.

www.careguide.net
Search by state for child care centers, nannies, and preschools.

www.ci.nyc.ny.us
The New York City Department of Health Bureau of Day Care's Web site offers tips on choosing a licensed day care program.

www.metlife.com
Offers advice on choosing child care.

JUST FOR MOMS

www.athomemothers.com
The official Web site of the magazine *At Home Mother*.

www.clubmom.com
"If you're a mom, you're a member."

www.girlfriendsguide.com
By far, the hippest Web page for moms and moms-to-be.

www.mothering.com
The Web site for *Mothering Magazine*.

www.hipmama.com/talk/cgi-bin/talk.cgi
Chat with other moms on topics ranging from health, adoption, single parenting and more.

www.momsonline.oxygen.com
Chat with other moms and get some hot parenting tips.

www.parentsplace.com
Join in chats on breastfeeding, miscarriage, parenting gifted children, or in general chats for expecting mothers or parents.

AND ONE FOR DADDIES

www.fathersworld.com
A web ring with links to all kinds of sites for fathers, including resources for single dads, at-home dads and fathering in general.

PARTY PLANNING

www.birthdayexpress.com
A complete resource for all things birthday-related.

www.birthdaypartyideas.com
Get tons of ideas for elaborate, original, and just plain fun birthday parties for your kids.

www.amazingmoms.com
All kinds of advice for planning an unforgettable birthday party for your little one.

www.greatentertaining.com

This site offers party supplies, party themes, recipes, and all kinds of other advice on throwing a great birthday party for your kid.

BIRTH ANNOUNCEMENTS, PORTRAITS AND OTHER NOVELTIES

www.bluemountain.com

From this electronic greeting card service you can an e-mail birth annoucement around the globe for free.

www.AnnounceNet.net

Create a personalized birth announcement Web page, with your baby's photographs and graphics selected from the site's library.

www.hallmark.com

Find e-cards here announcing your baby's birth.

www.ecards.com

Another fun e-card site, with cards announcing pregnancy or your baby's arrival.

www.sears-portrait.com

This site from Sears Portrait Studio has games, parenting advice, greeting cards, tips for getting better portraits of your kids, and much more.

www.familyheirlooms.com

A service that transforms baby's first shoes into bronzed heirlooms.

www.e-stork.com

Another place where you can create a personal Web page announcing your baby's birth and include photos, birth stats, and more.

ONLINE SHOPPING
Maternity Clothing

www.babystyle.com

Shop by basics and by style.

www.gap.com

Click on the Gap's online only maternity line: basics and a splash of fun.

www.imaternity.com

The Maternity Everything Store. Stylish and comfortable clothing and accessories, with free shipping.

www.maternitymall.com

Links to Motherhood Maternity, Motherhood Nursing Wear, A Pea in the Pod, and others.

www.onnamaternity.com

On'na Maternity specializes in career fashions with basics and twin-sets in nice colors.

www.pumpkinmaternity.com

For hip moms. Bootcut jeans, three-quarter shirts, and great underwear and accessories.

www.annacris.com

Contemporary collection of career, casual, and special occasion maternity wear is great.

www.maternityzone.com

A great site for moms-to-be, with the Belly Basics Pregnancy Survival Kit, diaper bags, lingerie, nursing clothes, and tons of fashionable maternity wear.

www.mothers-in-motion.com

Exercise clothing for moms-to-be.

www.maternityclothes.com

Your source for Maternity Vintage Levis, and other hip maternity fashions.

Baby Necessities

www.babyage.com
A broad range of baby products at great prices.

www.babystyle.com
Great nursery items.

www.babyuniverse.com
Baby Universe has a wealth of information on subjects from bathing to shopping for your child.

www.buybuybaby.com
Accessories, cribs and cradles, strollers, car seats and more.

www.rightstart.com
Strollers, car seats, nursery accessories, and home safety items.

www.thebabylane.com
Slings, baby blankets, and other items.

www.babygear.com
An amazing source for all thing baby-related from a large listing of products by category.

www.ebrick.com
Everything for your baby, including diapers, strollers, cribs, and clothes.

www.baby-express-stores.com
Baby furniture and much more.

www.interiordec.about.com/homegarden/interiordec/msubchilddecor.htm
Articles on decorating your child's room—including creative ideas, trends, and safety tips.

Baby Clothing

www.babystuff.com
Popular brands at great prices.

www.frenchkids.com
French Kids Online carries the best French and European brands for children's apparel.

www.kidsdirectory.com
A great resource listing stores in forty different U.S. cities.

www.kidstyle-nyc.com
An online boutique of funky gifts and clothing for hip, urban kids.

www.thebabyoutlet.com
Great baby wear and free shipping for your purchases.

www.designeroutlet.com
Shop for designer overstocks.

www.rainbee.com
Over 10,000 children's products from over 250 designers and manufacturers.

www.webclothes.com
Beautiful infant and children's clothing.

www.hannahanderson.com
Beautiful clothes made from soft fabrics in fun and elegant patterns.

www.cwd.kids
Cute clothing and costumes for boys and girls.

www.babyuniverse.com
A nice source for layettes and clothing.

Toys

www.rightstart.com
A wonderful array of fun and educational children's toys.

www.amazon.com
Good selection of toys.

www.smarterkids.com
Awesome site that helps children learn, discover, and grow.

www.zanybrainy.com
Tons of toy and book listings, split by age and category.

www.nuttyputty.com
A great online toy store. Shop by age, toy category, or brand.

www.smarttoys.com
Games, puzzles, plush toys, beanie babies, and everything else.

www.shopping.yahoo.com/toys
Yahoo! has an extensive selection of toys, classified by age and category.

www.boardgames.com
All your favorite board games for rainy afternoons.

www.playthings.com
The latest toy news, bestsellers and coming attractions.

Books and Bookstores

www.bn.com

www.citysearch.com/nyc/bankstbooks
Bank Street Bookstore lists new books, featured authors and events.

www.booksofwonder.com
Information about New York's largest children's bookstore.

www.nypl.org/branch/kids
The New York Public Library's "On-Lion" site for kids. Recommended reading, events in the city, magazine links and other New York kids links.

www.bplkidzone.org
The Brooklyn Public Library's kid site is amazing—tons of links, programs, book lists and games.

www.alanbrown.com
Book reviews for and by kids.

www.bookhive.org
Search for any kind of book on this site.

www.cataloglink.com
Hundreds of catalogs are at your fingertips here.

www.storknet.org/bkstore/index.html
A wonderful source for parenting books.

www.amazon.com

www.borders.com

www.childrensbooks.about.com
Great information and articles on choosing children's books; books with strong female characters, books for reluctant readers, and recent award winners.

INDEX

city baby yellow pages

AQUARIUMS

The Brooklyn Aquarium at Coney Island, Surf Avenue and Coney Island Boardwalk at W. 8th Street, (718) 265-3400

AU PAIR AGENCIES

Au Pair America, 102 Greenwich Avenue, Greenwich, CT 06830, (800) 9AU-PAIR (1-800-928-7247)

Au Pair USA/Interexchange, 161 Sixth Avenue, 13th Floor, (800) AUPAIRS (800-287-2477)

Au Pair Childcrest, 6965 Union Park Center, Suite 100, Salt Lake City, UT 84047, (800) 574-8889

BABY NURSES/DOULAS

All Metro Health Care, 50 Broadway, Lynbrook, NY 11563, 516-887-1200

Avalon Registry, 162 W. 56th Street, Suite 507, 245-0250

Beyond Birth (Doulas), 1992 Commerce Street, Suite 40, Yorktown Heights, NY 10598, 914-245-2229, (888) 907-BABY

Bohne's Baby Nursing, 16 E. 79th Street, Suite G-4, 879-7920

Doula Care, Ruth Callahan, 70 W. 93rd Street, 749-6613

Foley Nursing Agency, 790 Madison Avenue, Suite 501, 794-9666

Fox Agency, 30 E. 60th Street, 753-2686

In a Family Way,124 W. 79th Street, Suite 9-B, 877-8112

Mother Nurture Doula Service, P.O. Box 284, Glen Oaks, NY 11004, (718) 631-BABY (718-631-2229)

BABY PRODUCTS, see SUPERSTORES

BABY PROOFING

All Star Baby Safety, Inc., (877) 668-7677

Babyproofers Plus, (800) 880-2191

BABY-SITTING SERVICES

Avalon, 245-0250

Barnard College Baby-Sitting Service, 854-2035

Baby-Sitting Guild, 682-0227

Beth Israel School of Nursing, 614-6110

Instant Sitter, My Child's Best Friend Nanny Services, 206-9910

Pinch Sitters, 260-6005

BALLET, see CHILDREN'S CLASSES, DANCE

BALLOONS

Balloonacy, 608-5335/(800) 320-GIFT

Balloon-A-Grams of New York, 212 W. 17th St. bet. Seventh and Eighth Avenues, 989-9338

Basically Balloons, (800) 472-5970

Inflatably Yours, 318 W. 77th Street bet. West End and

Riverside Drive, 580-2776

BATHROOMS
East Side
Barney's, Madison Avenue at 61st Street, 826-8900
Bergdorf Goodman, Fifth Avenue at 57th Street, 753-7300
Bloomingdale's, Third Avenue at 59th Street, 705-2000
Bendel's, Fifth Avenue at 55th Street, 247-1100
Lord & Taylor, Fifth Avenue at 39th Street, 391-3344
Saks Fifth Avenue, Fifth Avenue at 50th Street, 753-4000
FAO Schwarz, 767 Fifth Avenue at 59th Street, 644-9400
The New York Palace Hotel, 455 Madison Avenue at 50th Street, 888-0131
The Hotel Pierre, 2 E. 61st Street bet. Madison and Fifth Avenues, 838-8000
The Regency Hotel, 540 Park Avenue at 60th Street, 759-4100
Tiffany & Company, 727 Fifth Avenue at 57th Street, 755-8000
The Waldorf Astoria, 301 Park Avenue at 50th Street, 355-3000

West Side
The Empire Hotel, 44 W. 63rd Street bet. Broadway and Columbus Avenue, 265-7400
Macy's, Herald Square, 151 W. 34th Street bet. Broadway and Seventh Avenue, 695-4400
The Mayflower Hotel, 15 Central Park West at 61st Street, 265-0060
Manhattan Mall, 100 W. 32nd St. at Sixth Avenue, 465-0500
New York Hilton, 1335 Sixth Avenue at 53rd Street, 586-7000

Downtown
ABC Carpet & Home, 888 Broadway at 19th Street, 473-3000
Bed, Bath & Beyond, 620 Avenue of the Americas at 19th Street, 255-3550
Millenium Hilton, 55 Church Street bet. Fulton and Dey Streets, 693-2311
SoHo Grand Hotel, 310 W. Broadway bet. Grand and Canal Streets, 965-3000
South Street Seaport (The Fulton Market), 11 Fulton Street, 732-7678
Tribeca Grand Hotel, 2 Avenue of the Americas bet. White and Walker Streets, 519-6600
World Financial Center, The Winter Garden, West Street bet. the World Trade Center and the Hudson River, 945-0505

BIRTH ANNOUNCEMENTS
Berkeley Stationers, Inc., 19 W. 44th Street bet. Fifth and Sixth Avenues, 719-5181
Blacker & Kooby, 1204 Madison Avenue at 88th Street, 369-8308
FranMade, 250 W. 89th Street bet. Broadway and West End Avenue, 799-9428
Hudson Street Papers, 357 Bleecker Street between 10th and Charles Streets, 229-1065
Hyde Park Stationers, 1070 Madison Avenue at 80th Street, 861-5710
Jamie Ostrow, 876 Madison Avenue at 71st Street, 734-8890
Kate's Paperie, 561 Broadway at Prince Street, 941-9816; 8 W. 13th Street at Fifth Avenue, 633-0570; 1282 Third Avenue at 74th Street, 396-3670
Laura Beth's Baby Collection, 300 E. 75th Street, Suite 24E, 717-2559
Lincoln Stationers, 1889 Broadway at 63rd Street, 459-3500
Little Extras, 676 Amsterdam Avenue at 93rd Street, 721-6161
Paper Emporium, 835A Second Avenue at 44th Street, 697-6573
Papyrus Cards & Stationery, 1270 Third Avenue at 73rd Street, 717-1060; 852 Lexington Avenue bet. 64th and 65th Streets, 717-0002; 130 World Trade Center Mall, 432-0500; 107 E. 42nd Street at Lexington Avenue (Grand Central Station), 490-9894; 2157 Broadway bet. 75th and 76th Streets, 501-0102
Rebecca Moss, Ltd., 510 Madison Avenue at 53rd Street, 832-7671
Mrs. John L. Strong, Barneys, 660 Madison Avenue at

61st Street, 2nd Floor, 833-2059

Tiffany & Co., 727 Fifth Avenue at 57th Street, 755-8000

Venture Stationers, 1156 Madison Avenue at 85th Street, 288-7235

BIRTHDAY CAKES, CUPCAKES, AND COOKIES

Cakes 'N Shapes, LTD., 403 W. 39th Street bet. Ninth and Tenth Avenues, 629-5512

Carvel, 1631 First Avenue at 85th Street, 879-6210; 1091 Second Avenue bet. 57th and 58th Streets, 308-4744; Home Delivery, 422-7835

CBK Cookies of New York, 226 E. 83rd Street bet. Second and Third Avenues, 794-3383

Cupcake Cafe, 522 Ninth Avenue at 39th Street, 465-1530

Dean & Deluca, 560 Broadway at Prince Street, 226-6800

Grace's Market Place, 1237 Third Avenue at 71st Street, 737-0600

Haagen-Dazs, 187 Columbus Avenue bet. 68th and 69th Streets, 787-0265; 1221 Third Avenue bet. 70th and 71st Streets, 288-7088; 300 W. 23rd Street at Eighth Avenue, 929-2255; 33 Barrow Street bet. Seventh Avenue and Bleecker, 727-2152

Lafayette Bakery, 26 Greenwich Avenue between Tenth Avenue and Charles Street, 242-7580

Magnolia Bakery, 401 Bleecker Street at 11th Street, 462-2572

My Most Favorite Dessert Company, 120 W. 45th Street bet. Sixth Avenue and Broadway, 997-5032/997-5130

Soutine, 104 W. 70th Street bet. Columbus and Amsterdam Avenues, 496-1450

Sylvia Weinstock Cakes, 273 Church Street bet. White and Franklin Streets, 925-6698

Veniero Pasticceria, 342 E. 11th Street bet. First and Second Avenues, 674-7264

William Greenberg Desserts, 1100 Madison Avenue bet. 82nd and 83rd Streets, 861-1340; 1383 Third Avenue bet. 78th and 79th Streets, 988-8548

BIRTHDAY PARTIES

Central Park Carousel, 396-1010, ext. 14

Chelsea Piers Gymnastics, Pier 62, 23rd Street at Twelfth Avenue, 336-6500

Child's Play, Central Presbyterian Church, 593 Park Avenue at 64th Street, 838-1504

Circus Gymnastics, 2121 Broadway at 74th Street, 799-3755

Eli's Vinegar Factory, 431 E. 91st Street at York Avenue, 987-0885, ext. 4

Gymtime, 1520 York Avenue at 80th Street, 861-7732

Jodi's Gym, 244 E. 84th Street bet. Second and Third Avenues, 772-7633

Linda Kaye's Birthday Bakers Party Makers, 195 E. 76th Street bet. Third and Lexington Avenues, 288-7112

Party Poopers, 104 Reade Street at Broadway, 587-9030

Playspace, 2473 Broadway at 92nd Street, 769-2300

Seventy-Fourth Street Magic, 510 E. 74th Street bet. York Avenue and the East River, 737-2989

BIRTHDAY PARTY ENTERTAINERS

Bobby DooWah, 914-366-8291/772-7633 (Jodi's Gym).

Cynthia's Musical Parties, 717-6141

Hollywood Pop Gallery, 777-2238

Arnie Kolodner, 265-1430

Madeline the Magician, 475-7785

Marcia the Musical Moose, 567-0682 or 914-358-8163

Magical Musical Marion, 917-922-9880

Only Perfect Parties, 869-6988

Party Poopers, 587-9030

Send in the Clowns, (718) 353-8446

Silly Billy, 645-1299

Ronni Soled, Parties Perfect, 744-3194

Tilly the Clown, 721-1867

BIRTHING CENTERS

The Birthing Center (affiliated with St. Luke's-Roosevelt Hospital Center), 1000 Tenth Avenue bet. 58th and 59th Streets, 523-BABY

Elizabeth Seton Childbearing Center (affiliated with St. Vincent's Hospital), 222 W. 14th Street bet. Seventh and Eighth Avenues, 367-8500

A
B
C
D
E
F
G
H
I
J
K
L
M
N
O
P
Q
R
S
T
U
V
W
X
Y
Z

BOOKSTORES

Bank Street Bookstore, 610 W. 112th Street at Broadway, 678-1654

Barnes & Noble, locations throughout the city, 807-0099 (main store)

Books of Wonder, 16 W. 18th Street bet. Fifth and Sixth Avenues, 989-3270

Bookberries, 983 Lexington Avenue at 71st Street, 794-9400

Borders Books & Music, 550 Second Avenue bet. 32nd and 33rd Streets, 685-3938; 461 Park Avenue at 57th Street, 980-6785

Lenox Hill Bookstore, 1081 Lexington Avenue between 72nd and 73rd Streets, 472-7170

Logos Bookstore, 1575 York Avenue bet. 83rd and 84th Streets, 517-7292

The Strand Bookstore, 828 Broadway at 12th Street, 473-1452

BREASTFEEDING CONSULTANTS AND RESOURCES

Beth Israel Medical Center, Lactation Program, 420-2939

Màire Clements, R.N., I.B.C.L.C., 595-4797

La Leche League, 794-4687

Jan Wenk, IBCLC, 917-313-1085

BREAST PUMP RENTALS

Upper East Side

Calagor Pharmacy, 1226 Lexington Avenue at 83rd Street, 369-6000

Clayton & Edwards Pharmacy, 1327 York Avenue at 71st Street, 737-6240

Falk Drug, 259 E. 72nd Street at Second Avenue, 744-8080

Goldberger's Pharmacy, 1200 First Avenue at 65th Street, 734-6998

Kings Lexington Pharmacy, 1091 Lexington Avenue bet. 76th and 77th Streets, 794-7100

Timmerman Pharmacy, 799 Lexington Avenue bet. 61st and 62nd Streets, 838-6450

Upper West Side

Apthorp Pharmacy, 2211 Broadway at 78th Street, 877-3480

Chateau Drug, 181 Amsterdam Avenue bet. 68th and 69th Streets, 877-6390

Regine Kids, 2688 Broadway bet. 102nd and 103rd Streets, 864-8705

Suba Pharmacy, 2721 Broadway at 104th Street, 866-6700

Sandra Jamrog, Home delivery, 866-8257, jjjamrog@aol.com

Midtown

NYU Medical Center, 560 First Avenue at 32nd Street, 263-BABY

Elizabeth Seton Childbearing Center, 222 W. 14th Street bet. Seventh and Eighth Avenues, 367-8500

St. Luke's Roosevelt Hospital Center, 1000 Tenth Avenue at 58th Street, 523-4000

Westerly Pharmacy, 911 Eighth Avenue at 54th Street, 247-1124

Downtown

Barren Hospital Medical Center, 49 Delancey Street bet. Eldridge and Forsyth Streets, 226-6164

C.O. Bigelow Apothecaries, 414 Sixth Avenue bet. 8th and 9th Streets, 533-2700

Elm Drugs, 298 First Avenue bet. 17th and 18th Streets, 777-0740

Kings Pharmacy, 5 Hudson at Reade Street, 791-3100

Little Folks, 123 E. 23rd Street bet. Park and Lexington Avenues, 982-9669

Miriam Goodman, Home Delivery, 219-1080

CAKES, see BIRTHDAY CAKES

CAMPS

A.C.T Summer Camp Program, The Cathedral of St. John the Divine, 1047 Amsterdam Avenue bet. 110th and 111th Streets, 316-7530

Ballet Academy East, 1651 Third Avenue, 3rd floor, bet. 92nd and 93rd Streets, 410-9140

Bank Street Summer Camp, 610 W. 112th Street bet. Broadway and Riverside Drive, 875-4420

Chelsea Piers Summer Sports Camp, W. 23rd Street at the Hudson River, Pier 62, 336-6666

Columbia Grammar Summer Camp, 26 W. 94th Street bet. Columbus Avenue and Central Park West, 749-6200, ext. 225

Columbus Gym Summer Camp, 606 Columbus Avenue bet. 89th and 90th Streets, 721-0090

Corlears Summer Camp, 324 W. 15th Street bet. Eighth and Ninth Avenues, 741-2800

Dalton Day Camp, 53 E. 91st Street bet. Park and Madison Avenues, 423-5431

Discovery Programs, 251 W. 100th Street at West End Avenue, 749-8717

Hi Art!, 362-8190

Jodi's Gym, 244 E. 84th Street bet. Second and Third Avenues, 772-7633

Language Workshop for Children, Summer Day Camps, 888 Lexington Avenue at 66th Street, 396-1369

Little Red School House, 272 Sixth Avenue at Bleecker Street, 477-5316, ext. 239

The Lucy Moses School for Music and Dance, 129 W. 67th Street bet. Broadway and Amsterdam Avenue, 501-3360

Marymount Summer Day, 1026 Fifth Avenue bet. 83rd and 84th Streets, 744-4486

Montessori International Day Camp, 347 E. 55th Street bet. First and Second Avenues, 223-4630

New Town Day Camp at Sol Goldman Y, 344 E. 14th Street bet. First and Second Avenues, 780-0800, ext. 241

92nd Street Y, 1395 Lexington Avenue at 92nd Street, 415-5536

The Poppyseed Pre-Nursery, 424 West End Avenue at 81st Street, 877-7614

Renanim Pre-School and Summer Camp, 336 E. 61st Street bet. First and Second Avenues, 750-2266; 133-35 E. 29th Street bet. Lexington and Third Avenues, 685-3330

Rhinelander Children's Center, 350 E. 88th Street bet. First and Second Avenues, 876-0500

Rodeph Sholom Camp and School, 70 W. 83rd Street bet. Central Park West and Columbus Avenue, 362-8800

Summer Breeze Day Camp, 1520 York Avenue at 80th Street, 734-0922

Summer Days Camps, 510 E. 74th Street bet. York Avenue and the East River, 737-2989

Trinity Day Camp, 101 W. 91st Street bet. Amsterdam and Columbus Avenues, 932-6983

West Side YMCA Kinder Camp, 5 W. 63rd Street at Central Park West, 875-4112

CATALOGS

Biobottoms, 730 E. Church Street, Suite 19, Martinsville, VA 24148, (800) 766-1254

Chinaberry Book Service, 2780 Via Orange Way, Suite B Spring Valley, CA 91978, (800) 776-2242

Constructive Playthings, 13201 Arrington Road, Grandview, MO 64030, (800) 832-0572

The Walt Disney Catalog of Children's Clothing, (800) 328-0612

Hanna Andersson, 1010 NW Flanders Street, Portland, OR 97209, (800) 222-0544

L.L. Bean Inc., Freeport, ME 04033-0001, (800) 441-5713

Lilly's Kids, Lillian Vernon Corp., Virginia Beach, VA 23479-0002, (800) 285-5555

The Natural Baby Catalog, 7835 Freedom Avenue, North Canton, OH 44720

One Step Ahead, 75 Albrecht Drive, Lake Bluff, IL 60044, (800) 274-8440

Oshkosh B'Gosh, 1112 Seventh Avenue, P.O. Box 2222 Monroe, WI 53566-8222, (800) MY BGOSH (800-692-4674)

Parenting and Family Life, P.O. Box 2153, Dept. PA7, Charleston, WV 25328, (800) 468-4227

Patagonia Mail Order, P.O. Box 8900, Bozeman, MT 59715, (800) 336-9090

Perfectly Safe, 7245 Whipple Avenue, NW, North Canton, OH 44720, (800) 837-KIDS (800-837-5437)

Play Fair Toys, P.O. Box 18210, Boulder, CO 80308, (800) 824-7255

The Right Start Catalog, Right Start Plaza, 5334 Sterling Center Drive, Westlake, CA 91361-4627, (800) LIT-TLE-1 (800-548-8531)

Rubens & Marble Inc., P.O. Box 14900, Chicago, IL 60614, 773) 348-6200

Toys to Grow On, P.O. Box 17, Long Beach, CA 90801, (800) 542-8338

Troll's Learn & Play, 100 Corporate Drive, Mahwah, NJ 07430, (800) 247-6106

CHILD CPR & SAFETY INSTRUCTION
Baby-Life, 201-836-1616
Save-A-Tot, 317 E. 34th Street, 725-7477
Tot-Saver, 5 E. 98th Street, 241-8195

CHILD PROOFING, see BABY PROOFING

CHILDBIRTH EDUCATORS
BODY BY BABY, Jane Kornbluh, 677-6165
Choiceful Birth and Parenting, Ellen Krug, CSW, C.C.E., (718) 768-0494
Ellen Chuse, C.C.E., (718) 789-1981
Mary Lynn Fiske, C.C.E., AAHCC, (718) 855-1650
Judith Halek, 309 W. 109th Street bet. Broadway and Riverside Drive, 222-4349
The International Cesarean Awareness Network (ICAN)/NY Chapter, 662-2554 (Dierdre McLary), (718) 275-3389 (Vanessa Anton-Paultre)
Martine Jean-Baptiste, C.N.M., C.C.E., 769-4578
Risa Lynn Klein, 1490 Second Avenue bet. 77th and 78th Streets, 249-4203
Gayatri Martin, R.N., Choices for Childbirth, 725-1078
Diana Simkin, Upper East Side locations, 348-0208
Nancy Vega, 206 W. 104th Street bet. Broadway and Amsterdam Avenues, 316-6337
Wellcare Center, 161 Madison Avenue bet. 32nd and 33rd Streets; 349 Henry Street (at Long Island College Hospital in Brooklyn), 696-9256

CHILDREN'S CLASSES
Art
Art-N-Orbit, Reebok Sports Club East, 160 Columbus Avenue at 67th Street; Reebok Sports Clubs West, 330 E. 61st Street bet. First and Second Avenues; Jewish Community Center of the Upper West Side; 15 W. 65th Street, 8th floor, bet. Columbus Avenue and Central Park West; The Children's Museum of Manhattan, 212 W. 83rd Street bet. Broadway and Amsterdam Avenue, 420-0474

Create a Day, 57 E. 75th Street bet. Park and Madison Avenues, 452-2560

Funworks for Kids, 201 E. 83rd Street at Third Avenue, 759-1937/(917)432-1820

Gymtime/Rhythm and Glues, 1520 York Avenue at 80th Street, 861-7732

Hi Art!, 362-8190

Computer
Futurekids, 1628 First Avenue bet. 84th and 85th Streets, 717-0110

The Techno Team Lab, Reebok Sports Club, 160 Columbus Avenue at 67th Street, 501-1425

Dance
American Youth Dance Theater, 434 E. 75th Street, #1C, bet. First and York Avenues, 717-5419

Ballet Academy East, 1651 Third Avenue, 3rd floor, bet. 92nd and 93rd Streets, 410-9140

Greenwich House Music School, 46 Barrow Street bet. Bleecker and Bedford Streets, 242-4770

In Grandma's Attic, Studio Maestro, 48 W. 68th Street bet. Columbus Avenue and Central Park West; The Basement Space, 102 W. 75th Street at Columbus Avenue; Peggy Levine, 212 W. 92nd Street bet. Broadway and Amsterdam Avenue; Playspace, 2473 Broadway at W. 92nd Street; The Ward Studio, 145 W. 28th Street, #8F, bet. Sixth and Seventh Avenues; Civic Center Synagogue, 49 White Street bet. Church Street and Broadway, 726-2362

Kinderdance(r), Various locations, 579-5270

Manhattan Ballet School, 149 E. 72nd Street bet. Lexington and Third Avenues, 535-6556

The Lucy Moses School for Music and Dance, 129 W. 67th Street bet. Broadway and Amsterdam Avenue, 362-8060

Perichild Program, 132 Fourth Avenue, 2nd floor, bet. 13th and 12th Streets, 505-0886

Gymnastics

Asphalt Green, 555 E. 90th Street bet. York and East End Avenues, 369-8890 for catalog

Chelsea Piers, Pier 62, 23rd Street at Twelfth Avenue, 336-6500

Circus Gym, 2121 Broadway, 2nd floor, at 74th Street, 799-3755

Columbus Gym, 606 Columbus Avenue bet. 89th and 90th Streets, 721-0090

Gymtime Gymnastics, 1520 York Avenue at 80th Street, 861-7732

Jodi's Gym, 244 E. 84th Street bet. Second and Third Avenues, 772-7633

Life Sport Gymnastics, West Park Presbyterian Church, 165 W. 86th Street at Amsterdam Avenue, 769-3131

Sokol New York, 420 E. 71st Street bet. First and York Avenues, 861-8206

Sutton Gymnastics, 20 Cooper Square (Third Avenue at 5th Street), 533-9390

Tumble Town Gymnastics, 118 E. 28th Street, Room 708, bet. Park and Lexington Avenues, 889-7342

Wendy Hillard Foundation, Rhythmic Gymnastics NY, 792 Columbus Avenue, Suite 17T, at 100th Street, 721-3256

Ice Skating

Chelsea Piers, Pier 62, 23rd Street at Twelfth Avenue 336-6500

Rockefeller Plaza Rink, Fifth Avenue bet. 49th and 50th Streets, 332-7654

Skating Club of New York, W. 23rd Street at Chelsea Piers, 627-1976

Wollman Rink, 59th Street at Sixth Avenue, north of park entrance, 396-1010, ext. 15

In-Line Skating

Joel Rappelfeld's Kids on Wheels, 744-4444

NY Central Park Skate Patrol Skate School, Blades West Skate Shop, 120 W. 72nd Street bet. Broadway and Columbus Avenue, 439-1234

NY Skateout, 486-1919

The Roller Rinks at Chelsea Piers, 23rd Street at the Hudson River, 336-6200

Music

Bloomingdale School of Music, 323 W. 108th Street bet. Broadway and Riverside Drive, 663-6021

Campbell Music Studio, 305 West End Avenue at 74th Street; 436 E. 69th Street bet. York and First Avenues, 496-0105

Church Street School for Music and Art, 74 Warren Street bet. W. Broadway and Greenwich Street, 571-7290

Diller-Quaile School Of Music, 24 E. 95th Street bet. Madison and Fifth Avenues, 369-1484, www.diller-quaile.org

Family Music Center, Asphalt Green, 555 E. 90th Street at York Avenue; 275 W. 96th Street at Broadway, 864-2476

Greenwich House Music School, 46 Barrow Street bet. Bleecker and Bedford Streets, 242-4770

Mary Ann Hall's Music for Children, 2 E. 90th Street bet. Fifth and Madison Avenues, (800) 633-0078

Mozart for Children, 129 W. 67th Street bet. Broadway and Amsterdam Avenue; 15 Gramercy Park on 20th Street off Park Avenue; 120 E. 87th Street bet. Lexington and Park Avenues, 942-2743

Music, Fun & Learning, 339 E. 84th Street bet. First and Second Avenues; 263 W. 86th Street at West End Avenue, 717-1853

The Lucy Moses School for Music and Dance, 129 W. 67th Street bet. Broadway and Amsterdam Avenue, 362-8060

Third Street Music School Settlement, 235 E. 11th Street bet. Second and Third Avenues, 777-3240

Turtle Bay Music School, 244 E. 52nd Street bet. Second and Third Avenues, 753-8811

A B C D E F G H I J K L M N O P Q R S T U V W X Y Z

Pottery

Greenwich House Pottery, 16 Jones Street bet. Bleecker and W. Fourth Streets, 242-4106

Swimming

Asphalt Green, 555 E. 90th Street bet. York and East End Avenues, 369-8890

New York Health and Racquet Club, 24 E. 13th Street bet. Fifth Avenue and University Place, 924-4600; 1433 York Avenue at 76th Street, 737-6666

Take Me to the Water, 10 locations, 828-1756

YWCA, 610 Lexington Avenue at 53rd Street, 655-4500

Yoga

B.K.S. Iyengar Yoga Association, 27 W. 24th Street, Suite 800, bet. Broadway and Sixth Avenue, 691-9642

Goodson Parker Wellness Center, 30 E. 76th Street, 4th floor, at Madison Avenue, 717-5273

Next Generation Yoga, 200 W. 72nd Street, Suite 58, bet. Broadway and West End Avenue, 595-9306

CLOTHING STORES

Clothing, Baby and Children's

Au Chat Botté, 1192 Madison Avenue bet. 87th and 88th Streets, 722-6474

Baby Gap, 341 Columbus Avenue at 76th Street; 875-9196; 1535 Third Avenue at 87th Street, 423-0033; 680 Fifth Avenue at 54th Street, 977-7023

Bambini, 1367 Third Avenue at 78th Street, 717-6742

Barney's, 660 Madison Avenue at 61st Street, 826-8900

Bloomingdale's, 1000 Third Avenue bet. 59th and 60th Streets, 705-2000

Bombalulus, 101 W. 10th Street bet. Sixth and Greenwich Avenues, 463-0897; 244 W. 72nd Street bet. Broadway and West End Avenues, 501-8248

Bonpoint, 1269 Madison Avenue at 91st Street, 722-7720; 811 Madison Avenue at 68th Street, 879-0900

Bu & The Duck, 106 Franklin Street bet. Church Street and W. Broadway, 431-9226

Bunnies, 100 Delancey Street bet. Ludlow and Essex Streets, 529-7567

CALYPSO Bébé, 284 Mulberry Street bet. Houston and Prince, 965-8910

CALYPSO Enfant, 280 Mulberry bet. Houston and Prince, 925-6544

Catimini, 1284 Madison Avenue at 91st Street, 987-0688

Century 21 Department Store, 22 Cortlandt Street, bet. Broadway and Church Street, 227-9092

The Children's Place, 36 Union Square East bet. 16th and 17th Streets, 529-2201; 22 W. 34th Street bet. Fifth and Sixth Avenues; 904-1190; The Manhattan Mall, 901 Avenue of the Americas, Level C-2, 268-7696; 1460 Broadway at 41st Street, 398-4416; 2039 Broadway at 70th Street, 441-2374, 2187 Broadway at 77th Street, 441-9807; 173 E. 86th Street bet. Lexington and Third Avenues, 831-5100, 400 World Trade Center, Concourse Level, 432-6100

Chock's, 74 Orchard Street bet. Grand and Broome Streets, 473-1929

Cremebebe, 68 Second Avenue bet. 3rd and 4th Streets, 979-6848

Daffy's, 111 Fifth Avenue at 18th Street, 529-4477; 335 Madison Avenue at 44th Street, 557-4422; 125 E. 57th Street at Lexington Avenue, 376-4477; 1311 Broadway at 34th Street, 736-4477

Gap, Baby, See Baby Gap.

Greenstones, 442 Columbus Avenue bet. 81st and 82nd Streets, 580-4322; Greenstones, Too, 1184 Madison Avenue bet. 86th and 87th Streets, 427-1665

Gymboree, 1120 Madison Avenue bet. 83rd and 84th Streets, 717-6702; 1049 Third Avenue at 62nd Street, 688-4044; 1332 Third Avenue at 76th Street, 517-5548; 2015 Broadway bet. 68th and 69th Streets, 595-7662; 2271 Broadway bet. 81st and 82nd Streets, 595-9071

Ibiza Kidz, 46 University Place bet. 9th and 10th Streets, 533-4614

Jacadi, 1281 Madison Avenue at 91st Street, 369-1616; 787 Madison Avenue at 67th Street, 535-3200

Julian & Sara, 103 Mercer Street bet. Spring and Prince Streets, 226-1989

Kids Generation USA, 875 Sixth Avenue at 31st Street, 947-1667

Kids 'R' Us, 1311 Broadway at 34th Street, 3rd floor, 643-0714

Koh's Kids, 311 Greenwich Street bet. Chambers and Reade Streets, 791-6915

La Layette . . . Et Plus Ltd., 170 E. 61st Street bet. Third and Lexington Avenues, 688-7072

La Petite Etoile, 746 Madison Avenue bet. 64th and 65th Streets, 744-0975

Lester's, 1522 Second Avenue at 80th Street, 734-9292

Little Folks, 123 E. 23rd Street bet. Park and Lexington Avenues, 982-9669

Little O, 1 Bleecker Street at Bowery Street, 673-0858

Lord & Taylor, 424 Fifth Avenue bet. 38th and 39th Streets, 391-3344

Macy's, Herald Square, 151 W. 34th Street bet. Broadway and Seventh Avenue, 695-4400

Madison Avenue Maternity & Baby, 1043 Madison Avenue bet. 79th and 80th Streets, 988-8686

Magic Windows, 1186 Madison Avenue bet. 86th and 87th Streets, 289-0028

New York Exchange for Woman's Work, 149 E. 60th Street bet. Lexington and Third Avenues, 753-2330

Oilily, 870 Madison Avenue bet. 70th and 71st Streets, 628-0100

Old Navy Clothing Co., 610 Sixth Avenue at 18th Street 645-0663; 150 W. 34th Street at Seventh Avenue, 594-0049; 503/511 Broadway bet. Broome and Spring Streets, 226-0838; 300 W. 125th Street bet. Eighth and Frederick Douglass Avenues, 531-1544

Peanut Butter & Jane, 617 Hudson Street bet. Jane and W. 12th Streets, 620-7952

Prince & Princess, 33 E. 68th Street bet. Madison and Park Avenues, 879-8989

Regine Kids, 2688 Broadway bet. 102nd and 103rd Streets, 864-8705

Robin's Nest, 1168 Lexington Avenue bet. 80th and 81st Streets, 737-2004

Saks Fifth Avenue, 611 Fifth Avenue bet. 48th and 49th Streets, 753-4000

Small Change, 964 Lexington Avenue bet. 70th and 71st Streets, 772-6455

Space Kiddets, 46 E. 21st Street bet. Park Avenue South and Broadway, 420-9878

Spring Flowers, 1050 Third Avenue at 62nd Street, 758-2669; 905 Madison Avenue at 72nd Street, 717-8182

Talbot's Kids & Babies, 1523 Second Avenue at 79th Street, 570-1630

Tigers, Tutu's & Toes, 128 Second Avenue bet. St. Mark's and 7th Street, 228-7990

Tutti Bambini, 1490 First Avenue bet. 77th and 78th Streets, 472-4238

Village Kidz, 3 Charles Street bet. Greenwich and Seventh Avenues, 807-8542

Z'Baby Company, 100 W. 72nd Street at Columbus Avenue, 579-BABY; 996 Lexington Avenue at 72nd Street, 472-BABY

Z'Baby Warehouse!, 445 W. 50th Street bet. Ninth and Tenth Avenues, 245-BABY

Zitomer, 969 Madison Avenue bet. 75th and 76th Streets 737-2037

Clothing, Maternity

A Pea in the Pod, 625 Madison Avenue bet. 58th and 59th Streets, 826-6468

A Second Chance, 1109 Lexington Avenue bet. 77th and 78th Streets, 2nd floor, 744-6041

Barney's New York Maternity Department, 660 Madison Avenue at 61st Street, 6th floor, 826-8900

Belly Basics, (800) 4-9-MONTHS

Eileen Fisher, 521 Madison Avenue bet. 53rd and 54th Streets, 759-9888; 1039 Madison Avenue bet. 79th and 80th Streets, 879-7799; 341 Columbus Avenue at 76th Street, 362-3000; 103 Fifth Avenue bet. 17th and 18th Streets, 924-4777; 314 E. Ninth Street bet. First and Second Avenues, (Outlet Store) 529-5715; 395 W. Broadway bet. Spring and Broome Streets, 431-4567

Liz Lange Maternity, 958 Madison Avenue bet. 75th and 76th Streets, 879-2191

Madison Avenue Maternity and Baby, 1043 Madison Avenue bet. 79th and 80th Streets, 2nd floor, 988-8686

Maternity Works Outlet, 16 W. 57th Street bet. Fifth and
Sixth Avenues, 399-9840

Mimi Maternity, 1021 Third Avenue bet. 60th and 61st
Streets, 832-2667; 1125 Madison Avenue at 84th
Street, 737-3784; 2005 Broadway bet. 68th and
69th Streets, 721-1999; 2 World Financial Center,
225 Liberty Street, 2nd floor, 945-6424

Mom's Night Out, 147 E. 72nd Street, Apt. 2F, bet.
Lexington and Third Avenues, 744-6667

Motherhood Maternity, The Manhattan Mall, 32nd Street
bet. Sixth and Seventh Avenues, 564-8170; 1449
Third Avenue bet. 82nd and 83rd Streets, 734-5984;
641 Avenue of the Americas at 20th Street, 741-3488

Pumpkin Maternity, 407 Broome Street at Lafayette,
334-1809

Veronique Delachaux, 1321 Madison Avenue at 93rd
Street, 831-7800

The Dan Howard Maternity Outlet, Route 4 West in
Paramus, New Jersey, (other locations throughout
Long Island and New Jersey) 201-843-4980

Clothing , Resale Shops

Children's Resale, 303 E. 81st Street bet. First and
Second Avenues, 734-8897

Good-Byes Children's Resale Shop, 230 E. 78th Street
bet. Second and Third Avenues, 794-2301

First & Second Cousin New and Resale Children's Shop,
142 Seventh Avenue South bet. 10th and Charles
Streets, 929-8048

Jane's Exchange, 207 Avenue A bet. 12th and 13th
Streets, 674-6268

Second Act, 1046 Madison Avenue at 79th Street, 2nd
floor, 988-2440

Clothing, Trunk Shows & Private Boutiques

Bodyscapes, Inc., 20 W. 22nd Street, Room 502,
243-2414

Judy's Fancies, 689-8663

Little Follies, P.O. Box 111, Englewood, NJ 07631, (800)
242-7881/(212) 585-1940

Monica Noel , 23 Benedict Place, Greenwich, CT 06830,

203-661-0505

Papo d'Anjo, 396-9668 (voice mail), Praça Luis de
Camões n.36 3° Esq., 1200-243 Lisbon Portugal,
011 351 21 324-1790

COFFEE BARS

DT:UT, 1626 Second Avenue bet. 84th and 85th Streets,
327-1327

New World Coffee, 1246 Lexington Avenue at 84th Street,
772-1422; 2151 Broadway at 75th Street, 496-0300;
723 Third Avenue at 45th Street, 599-4142

Starbucks, 2252 Broadway at 84th Street, 721-4157;
120 E. 87th Street at Lexington Avenue, 426-2580;
51 Astor Place, 677-6447; For other locations, call
613-1280

CONCERTS, PLAYS, & PUPPET SHOWS

The Little Orchestra Society, The Lolli Pops Concert
Series, 971-9500

New York Theater Ballet, Florence Gould Hall, 355-6160

The Paper Bag Players, 362-043

The Puppet Company 741-1646

Puppetworks (718) 965-6058,

TADA!, 627-1732

Tribeca Performing Arts Center, 346-8510

The Swedish Cottage Marionette Theater, Central Park at
W. 81st Street, 988-9093

COSTUMES

Abracadabra Superstore, 19 West 21st Street between
Fifth and Sixth Avenues, 627-5194

M. Gordon Novelty, 933 Broadway bet. 21st and 22nd
Streets, 254-8616

Halloween Adventure, 104 Fourth Avenue bet. 11th and
12th Streets, 673-4546

DAYCARE CENTER INFORMATION

Child Care Inc., 275 Seventh Avenue, 929-4999

The Daycare Council of New York, 10 E. 34th Street, 213-2423

The Department of Health, 442-9666 (Childcare Info Line)

DIAPER SERVICES

Diapers Direct, (800) 515-3427

Nature Baby Diaper Service, 48 Harold Street, Tenafly, NJ 07670, (800) 344-3427

Special Deliveries Diaper Service, 47 Purdy Avenue, Port Chester, NY 10573, (800) 582-7638 or 914-937-9184

Tidy Diapers, 50 Commerce Street, Norwalk, CT 06850, (800) 732-2443

DOLL HOSPITALS

Antique Doll Hospital of New York, 787 Lexington Avenue, 838-7527

Iris Brown Antique Dolls, 253 E. 57th Street, 593-2882

Forty Fifty Sixty, 110 W. 25th Street, 463-0980

DOULAS, see BABY NURSES/DOULAS

EMERGENCY NUMBERS

Police, Ambulance, Fire Department, 911

Poison Control, 340-4494/764-7667

FITNESS/HEALTH CLUBS

Bally Total Fitness, Bfit Baby Club, Various locations in all boroughs, (877) 888-3228; (800) FITNESS to find the club nearest you.

David Barton, 30 E. 85th Street bet. Madison and Fifth Avenues, 517-7577; 552 Sixth Avenue at 15th Street, 727-0004

BODY BY BABY, Jane Kornbluh, 677-6165

Equinox, 250 E. 54th Street at Second Avenue, 277-5400; 140 E. 63rd Street at Lexington Avenue, 750-4900; 344 Amsterdam Avenue bet. 76th and 77th Streets, 721-4200; 2465 Broadway bet. 91st and 92nd Streets, 799-1818; 205 E. 85th Street bet. Second and Third Avenues, 439-8500; 897 Broadway at 19th Street, 780-9300

Maternal Fitness, 108 E. 16th Street, 4th floor, between Park Avenue and Irving Place, 353-1947

Med Fitness, 12 E. 86th Street bet. Fifth and Madison Avenues, 327-4197

New York Health & Racquet Club, Various locations throughout the boroughs, (800) HRC-BEST

New York Sports Clubs, Various locations throughout the boroughs, (800) 796-NYSC

92nd Street Y, 1395 Lexington Avenue at 92nd Street, 415-5729

Peggy Levine, 212 W. 92nd Street bet. Broadway and Amsterdam Avenue, 362-5176

Plus One Fitness Clinic, 301 Park Avenue at 49th Street 355-3000, ext. 4970; One World Financial Center, 200 Liberty Street, 945-2525

Reebok Sports Club/NY, 160 Columbus Avenue at 67th Street, 362-6800; 330 E. 61st Street bet. First and Second Avenues, 355-5100; 45 Rockefeller Plaza bet. 50th and 51st Streets, and Fifth and Sixth Avenues, 218-8600

Diana Simkin, 348-0208

The Sports Club/LA, 330 E. 61st Street; 45 Rockefeller Plaza, 3rd floor, 355-5100

Strollercize, Inc., (800)Y-STROLL

Vanderbilt YMCA, 224 E. 47th Street bet. Second and Third Avenues, 756-9600

YWCA, 610 Lexington Avenue at 53rd Street, 735-9750

FURNITURE, see SUPER STORES

HAIR SALONS

Astor Place Hair Designers, 2 Astor Place bet. 8th Street and Broadway, 475-9854

Cozy's Cuts for Kids, 1125 Madison Avenue at 84th Street, 744-1716; 448 Amsterdam Avenue at 81st Street, 579-2600

Fun Cuts, 1567 York Avenue at 83rd Street, 288-0602

Kids Cuts, 201 E. 31st Street bet. Second and Third Avenues, 684-5252

Michael's Children Hair Cutting Salon, 1263 Madison Avenue bet. 90th and 91st Streets, 289-9612

Paul Molé Haircutters, 1031 Lexington Avenue at 74th Street, 988-9176

SuperCuts, 440 Third Avenue at 32nd Street, 447-0070; 1149 Second Avenue at 60th Street, 688-8883; 2481 Broadway at 92nd, 501-8200; 69 University Place at 10th Street, 228-2545; 378 Sixth Avenue at Waverly, 477-7900; for other locations call (800) SUPERCUT/(800-787-3728)

The Tortoise and the Hare, 1470 York Avenue at 78th Street, 472-3399

HOSPITALS

Beth Israel Hospital, 16th Street at First Avenue, 420-2000 (General), 420-2999 (Classes), 420-3895 (Patient Care)

Columbia Presbyterian Hospital/Babies Hospital/Sloane Hospital for Women, 3959 Broadway at 166th Street, 305-2500 (General), 305-2040 (Parent Ed.)

Lenox Hill Hospital, 100 E. 77th Street bet. Lexington and Park Avenues, 434-2000 (General), 434-2273 (Parent Ed.), 434-3152 (Babies' Club)

The Mount Sinai Medical Center, 1176 Fifth Avenue at 98th Street, 241-6500 (General), 241-7491 (Women's and Children's Office), 241-6578 (Breastfeeding Warm Line)

NY Presbyterian Hospital, at the NY Weill Cornell Center, 525 E. 68th Street bet. York Avenue the East River, 746-5454 (General), 746-3215 (Parenthood Prep.)

New York University Medical Center, 560 First Avenue at 32nd Street, 263-7300 (General), 263-7201 (Classes)

Roosevelt Hospital, 1000 Tenth Avenue at 59th Street 523-4000 (General), 523-6222 (Classes)

St. Luke's Hospital, 1111 Amsterdam Avenue at 114th Street, 523-4000 (General), 523-6222 (Parent/Family Ed.)

St. Vincent's Hospital and Medical Center, 170 W. 12th Street at Seventh Avenue, 604-7000 (General), 604-7946 (Maternity Ed.)

HOTLINES, WARMLINES, & OTHER SPECIAL HELP

Adoption

Adoptive Parents Support Group, 475-0222

Adoptive Parents Committee, 304-8479

At-Home Moms

American Mothers at Home, (800) 223-9260

Mothers Network, 875 Avenue of the Americas, Suite 2001, 239-0510

The National Association of Mothers Centers, Levittown, NY, 516-520-2929

Hotline Help

Child Abuse and Maltreatment Reporting Center, (800) 342-3720

Emergency Children's Service, 341-0900 (general), 966-8000 (nights, weekends, holidays)

National AIDS Hotline, (800) 342-AIDS

New York Foundling Hospital Crisis, Intervention Nursery 472-8555

Poison Hotline, 340-4494/764-7667

National SIDS Resource Center, (800) 221-SIDS (800-221-7437)

Single Parents

Parents Without Partners, (800) 637-7974

Single Mothers By Choice, 988-0993

Single Parent Resource Center, 947-0021

Single Parents Support Group, 780-0800 ext. 239

Twins or More

M.O.S.T. (Mothers Of Super Twins), 631-859-1110

National Organization of Mothers of Twins Clubs, Inc., 877-540-2200

Special Needs Groups

Cystic Fibrosis Foundation, 986-8783

Educational Alliance, 780-0800

League for the Hard of Hearing, 917-305-7700

The Lighthouse/New York Association for the Blind, 821-9200

National Down Syndrome Society, 460-9330

Pregnancy and Infant Loss Center, 612-473-9372 Bereavement Group)

Resources for Children with Special Needs, 677-4650

Spina Bifida Information and Referral, (800) 621-3141

United Cerebral Palsy of New York City, 677-7400,

Williams Syndrome Hotline, 248-541-3630

YIA Early Intervention Program, 418-0335

INDOOR PLAYSPACES

Playspace, 2473 Broadway at 92nd Street, 769-2300

Rain or Shine, 202 E. 29th Street bet. Second and Third Avenues, 4th floor, 532-4420

INTERIOR DESIGN & DECORATION

Charm and Whimsy, Esther Sadowsky, Allied A.S.I.D, 114 E. 32nd Street, 683-7609

Funtastic Interiors, Inc., Kimberley Fiterman, A.S.I.D., 60 W. 12th Street, 633-0660

Gracious Home, 1217/1220 Third Avenue at 70th Street, 517-6300, 1992 Broadway at 67th Street, 231-7800

Janovic Plaza, 1150 Third Avenue at 67th Street, 772-1400; 159 W. 72nd Street, 595-2500; 771 Ninth Avenue at 52nd Street, 245-3241; 215 Seventh Avenue at 22nd Street, 645-5454; 292 Third Avenue at 22nd Street, 777-3030; 161 Sixth Avenue at Spring Street, 627-1100; 2475 Broadway at 92nd Street, 769-1440; 125 Fourth Avenue at 12th Street, 477-6930; 1155 Third Avenue at 87th Street, 289-6300

Kids Digs, Carol Maryan Architects, 212 W. 79th Street, suite 1C , 787-7800

Laura Ashley Home, 398 Columbus Avenue at 79th Street, 496-5110

Laura Beth's Baby Collection, 300 E. 75th Street, Suite 24E, 717-2559

Monica Noel, 23 Benedict Place, Greenwich, CT 06830, 203-661-0505

Nursery Lines Ltd., 1034 Lexington Avenue at 74th Street, 396-4445

Plain Jane, 525 Amsterdam Avenue at 85th Street, 595-6916

SmartStart, Susan Weinberg, 334 W. 86th Street, Suite 6C, 580-7365

LACTATION CONSULTANTS, see BREASTFEEDING

LAMAZE, see CHILDBIRTH EDUCATORS

LAYETTE, see CLOTHING STORES

LIBRARIES

Upper East Side

96th Street, 112 E. 96th Street bet. Park and Lexington Avenues, 289-0908

67th Street, 328 E. 67th Street bet. First and Second Avenues, 734-1717

Webster, 1465 York Avenue bet. 77th and 78th Streets, 288-5049

Yorkville, 222 E. 79th Street bet. Second and Third Avenues, 744-5824

Upper West Side

Bloomingdale, 150 W. 100th Street at Amsterdam Avenue, 222-8030

Columbus, 742 Tenth Avenue bet. 50th and 51st Streets, 586-5098

Riverside, 127 Amsterdam Avenue at 65th Street, 870-1810

St. Agnes, 444 Amsterdam Avenue at 81st Street, 877-4380

Midtown

Donnell Library Center, 20 W. 53rd Street bet. Fifth and Sixth Avenues, 621-0636

A B C D E F G H I J K L M N O P Q R S T U V W X Y Z

Downtown

Epiphany, 228 E. 23rd Street bet. Second and Third Avenues, 679-2645

Hudson Park, 66 Leroy Street at Seventh Avenue, 43-6876

Jefferson Market, 425 Sixth Avenue at 10th Street, 243-4334

Kips Bay, 446 Third Avenue at 31st Street, 683-2520

Lower East Side

New Amsterdam, 9 Murray Street bet. Broadway and Church Streets, 732-8186

Tompkins Square, 33 E. 10th Street bet. Avenues A and B, 228-4747

MAGAZINES, NATIONAL

American Baby, 249 W. 17th Street bet. Seventh and Eighth Avenues, 462-3500

Baby Talk, 1325 Avenue of the Americas (on 53rd Street bet. Sixth and Seventh Avenues), 522-8989

Child, P.O. Box 3173, Harlan, IA 51593-2364, (800) 777-0222

Parents, 685 Third Avenue, 878-8700

Practical Parenting Newsletter, 8326A Minnetonka Boulevard, Deephaven, MN 55391, 612-475-1505

Sesame Street Parents, P.O. Box 52000, Boulder, CO 80322-2000

Twins Magazine, 5350 South Roslyn Street, suite 400, Englewood, CO 80111, 888-55-TWINS (888-558-9467)

Working Mother, 135 W. 50th Street, 445-6100

MAGAZINES, NEW YORK

Big Apple Parents' Paper, 9 E. 38th Street between Madison and Fifth Avenues, 4th floor, 889-6400

New York Family, 141 Halstead Avenue, Suite 3D Mamaroneck, NY 10543, 914-381-7474

The Expectant & New Parents Guide, 37 W. 72nd Street New York, NY 10023, 787-3789

Parent Guide, 419 Park Avenue South, New York, NY 10022, 213-8840

MAGICIANS, see BIRTHDAY PARTY ENTERTAINERS

MALLS

Northern New Jersey, Fashion Center, Route 17 and Ridgewood Avenue, Paramus, NJ, 201-444-9050

Paramus Park Mall, Route 17 North, Paramus, NJ, 201-261-8000

Garden State Plaza, Route 17 South, Paramus, NJ, 201-843-2404

The Mall at Short Hills, Short Hills, NJ, 973-376-7350

Riverside Square Mall, Route 4 West, Hackensack, NJ, 201-489-2212

Westchester/Rockland

Palisades Park Center, West Nyack, NY, 914-348-1000

The Westchester, Bloomingdale Road, White Plains, NY, 914-683-8600

Woodbury Commons Mall, Harriman, NY, 914-928-4000

Long Island

Roosevelt Field Shopping Center, Glen Cove, NY, 516-742-8000

Sunrise Mall, Sunrise Highway, Massapequa, NY, 516-795-3225

Walt Whitman Mall, Dix Hills, NY, 516-271-1741

Connecticut

Stamford Town Center, Tresser Boulevard, Stamford, CT, 203-324-0935

MASSAGE

Carapan, 5 W. 16th Street bet. Fifth and Sixth Avenues, 633-6220

Lisa Curry, Traditional Thai Massage, 360-2319

Laura Favin, 324 W. 89th Street bet. West End Avenue and Riverside Drive, 501-0606

Sandra Jamrog, 866-8257

The Medical Massage Group, 108 E. 66th Street, Suite 1A, 328 E. 75th Street, Suite 3, 472-4772

The Quiet Touch, Locations throughout NYC, 246-0008

Skin and Body Contour, 1100 Madison Avenue at 83rd Street, 737-9604

Elaine Stillerman, 108 E. 16th Street, Suite 401, bet. Union Square East and Irving Place, 533-3188

The Stressless Step, 115 E. 57th Street, 5th floor, bet. Lexington and Park Avenues, 826-6222

MATERNITY CLOTHING, see CLOTHING, MATERNITY

MIDWIVES

Beth Israel Midwifery Group, Beth Israel Medical Center Phillips Ambulatory Care Center, 10 Union Square East bet. 14th and 15th Streets, 844-8569

CBS Midwifery, Inc., Barbara Sellars, (affiliated with St. Luke's Roosevelt), 103 Fifth Avenue at 17th Street, 366-4699

Elizabeth Seton Childbearing Center, (affiliated with St. Vincent's Hospital), 222 W. 14th Street bet. Seventh and Eighth Avenues, 367-8500, www.birthingcenters.org

Midwifery Services, Inc., (affiliated with St. Luke's-Roosevelt), 135 W. 70th Street bet. Broadway and Columbus Avenue, 877-5556

SOHO Women's Medical Center, (affiliated with St. Vincent's), 135 Spring Street, 2nd floor, bet. Greene and Wooster Streets, 274-0900

MOMMY AND ME CLASSES

Applause! Kids, 181 E. 73rd Street, #19A (mailing address), 472-0703

Asphalt Green Inc., The A.G.U.A. Center, 1750 York Avenue at 91st Street, 369-8890

Baby Fingers, 164 W. 79th Street, Suite 1D, bet. Columbus and Amsterdam Avenues; 317 E. 89th Street, lower level, bet. First and Second Avenues, 874-5978

Baby Om, Sandra Cameron Dance Center, 20 Cooper Square (Fourth Avenue and E. 5th Street); Peggy Levine Fitness, 212 W. 92nd Street at Broadway, 615-6935

Bloomingdale School of Music, 323 W. 108th Street bet. Broadway and Riverside Drive, 663-6021

C.A.T.S. (Children's Athletic Training School), 593 Park Avenue bet. 63rd and 64th Streets; The Jewish Center, 131 W. 86th Street, 5th floor, bet. Amsterdam and Columbus Avenues; Turtle Bay Music School, 235 E. 49th Street bet. Second and Third Avenues, 751-4876

Chelsea Piers, Pier 62, 23rd Street at Twelfth Avenue, 336-6500

Child's Play, Central Presbyterian Church, 593 Park Avenue at 64th Street, 838-1504; Rutgers Presbyterian Church, 236 W. 73rd Street at Broadway, 877-8227

Children's Tumbling, Suellen Epstein, 9-15 Murray Street at City Hall, 233-3418

Church Street School for Music and Art, 74 Warren Street at W. Broadway, 571-7290

Circus Gymnastics, 2121 Broadway at 74th Street, 799-3755

Columbus Gym, 606 Columbus Avenue bet. 89th and 90th Streets, 721-0090

Create a Day, 57 E. 75th Street at Park Avenue, 452-2560

Diller-Quaile School Of Music, 24 E. 95th Street bet. Madison and Fifth Avenues, 369-1484

Discovery Programs, 251 W. 100th Street at West End Drive, 749-8717

The Early Ear, 48 W. 68th Street bet. Central Park West and Columbus Avenue; 353 E. 78th Street bet. First and Second Avenues; 110 W. 96th Street bet. Amsterdam and Columbus Avenues, 877-7125

Educational Alliance Parenting and Family Center at The Sol Goldman YMHA, 344 E. 14th Street bet. First and Second Avenues, 780-0800 ext. 239

Free to Be Under Three, 253-2040

Funworks for Kids, 201 E. 83rd Street at Third Avenue, 759-1937/(917)432-1820

Gymboree, 401 E. 84th Street at First Avenue; 50 Lexington Avenue at 24th Street; 30 W. 68th Street bet. Central Park West and Columbus Avenue; 210 W. 91st Street bet. Broadway and Amsterdam

Avenue; 64 W. 3rd Street bet. LaGuardia and Thompson Streets, 877-496-5327

Gymtime/Rhythm and Glues, 1520 York Avenue at 80th Street, 861-7732

Hands On! A Musical Experience, Inc., 1365 First Avenue bet. 73rd and 74th Streets, 628-1945; 529 Columbus Avenue bet. 85th and 86th Streets, 496-9929

JAMS, Ansche Chesed Synagogue, W. 100th Street bet. Broadway and West End Avenues; Stephen Wise Free Synagogue, 30 W. 68th Street bet. Central Park West and Columbus Avenue, 595-0563

Jodi's Gym, 244 E. 84th Street bet. Second and Third Avenues, 772-7633

Judy Stevens Playgroup, 77 Franklin Street at Church Street, 941-0542

Kids Co-Motion, West Park Presbyterian Church, 165 W. 86th Street at Amsterdam Avenue; Rebecca Kelly Dance Studio, 579 Broadway bet. Prince and Houston Streets; The Soundings, 280 Rector Place; The Maternal Fitness Studio, 108 E. 16th Street bet. Park Avenue and Irving Place, 431-8489

Kindermusik®, The Greenwich Village Center/The Children's Aid Society, 219 Sullivan Street at W. 3rd Street, 864-2476

The Language Workshop for Children, 888 Lexington Avenue at 66th Street, 396-0830

Life Sport Gymnastics, West Park Presbyterian Church, 165 W. 86th Street at Amsterdam Avenue, 769-3131

The Lucy Moses School for Music and Dance, 129 W. 67th Street bet. Broadway and Amsterdam Avenue, 362-8060

Mary Ann Hall's Music for Children, The Church of Heavenly Rest, 2 E. 90th Street bet. Madison and Fifth Avenues, 203-454-7484/(800) 633-0078

Mary Copeland's Dancing Adventures, Peggy Levine, 212 W. 92nd Street bet. Broadway and Amsterdam Avenue, 362-5176, (718) 601-9639

Mommy and Me, The Greenwich Village Center/The Children's Aid Society, 219 Sullivan Street at W. 3rd Street, 254-3074

Musical Kids, 122 E. 88th Street at Lexington Avenue, 996-5898

Music Together, 48 E. 80th Street bet. Park and Madison Avenues; 1240 First Avenue at 67th Street; 54th Street at Lexington Avenue; 1651 Third Avenue, 3rd floor, bet. 92nd and 93rd Streets, 244-3046 (for all East Side locations); 48 W. 68th Street bet. Columbus Avenue and Central Park West; 102 W. 75th Street at Columbus Avenue; 148 W. 83rd Street bet. Amsterdam and Columbus Avenues; 251 W. 100th Street at West End Avenue, 219-0591 (for all West Side locations), 345 W. 14th Street bet. Eighth and Ninth Avenues, 539-8459; 49 White Street bet. Church Street and Broadway; 594 Broadway, 7th floor, bet. Houston and Prince Streets; 280 Rector Place in Battery Park City; 44 E. 32nd Street bet. Madison and Park Avenues, 358-3801 (for all Lower Manhattan locations), 529 W. 42nd Street bet. Tenth and Eleventh Avenues; 221 W. 57th Street bet. Broadway and Seventh Avenue, 244-5772

Rhinelander Children's Center, 350 E. 88th Street bet. First and Second Avenues, 876-0500

Seventy-Fourth Street Magic, 510 E. 74th Street bet. York Avenue and The East River, 737-2989

Sokol New York Gym, 420 E. 71st Street bet. First and York Avenues, 861-8206

The Sunshine Kids' Club: A Preschool of Music, 230 E. 83rd Street bet. Second and Third Avenues, 439-9876

Sutton Gym, 20 Cooper Square at 5th Street, 533-9390

Take Me to the Water, 828-1756

Tumble Town Gymnastics, 118 E. 28th Street, Room 708, bet. Park and Lexington Avenues, 889-7342

Turtle Bay Music School, 244 E. 52nd Street bet. Second and Third Avenues, 753-8811

YWHA 92nd Street, 1395 Lexington Avenue at 92nd Street, 415-5600

MUSEUMS

The American Museum of Natural History, 79th Street at Central Park West, 769-5100

The Children's Museum of Manhattan, 212 W. 83rd Street bet. Broadway and Amsterdam Avenue, 721-1234

The Children's Museum of the Arts, 72 Spring Street at Broadway, 274-0986

Metropolitan Museum of Art, Fifth Avenue at 82nd Street, 535-7710

Scandinavia House, 58 Park Avenue bet. 37th and 38th Streets, 879-9779

N

NANNY ADVERTISEMENTS/ NEWSPAPERS

Irish Echo, 309 Fifth Avenue, 686-1266

Irish Voice, 432 Park Avenue South, Suite 1503, 684-3366

The New York Times, 229 W. 43rd Street, 354-3900

The Polish Daily News, Nowy Dziennik, 333 W. 38th Street, 594-2266, ext. 31

NANNY AGENCIES

A Choice Nanny, 130 W. 57th Street, 246-KIDS (246-5437)

Best Domestic Services Agency, 2 W. 45th Street, Suite 1000, 685-0351

The Fox Agency, 30 E. 60th Street, 753-2686

Frances Stuart Agency, 1220 Lexington Avenue, 439-9222

Domestically Yours, 535 Fifth Avenue, 986-1900

The London Agency, 767 Lexington Avenue, 755-5064

My Child's Best Friend Nanny Services, 44 E. 32nd Street, 11th floor, 206-9910, www.nynannyservice.com

Nannies Plus, 520 Speedwell Avenue, Suite 114, Morris Plains, NJ, (800) 752-0078, www.nanniesplus.com

NY Nanny Center, 31 Bayles Avenue, South Port Washington, NY 11050, 516-767-5136

Pavillion Agency, 15 E. 40th, Suite 400, 889-6609

Professional Nannies Institute, 501 Fifth Avenue, 692-9510

Robin Kellner Agency, 2 W. 45th Street, 997-4151

Town and Country, 250 W. 57th Street, 245-8400

NANNY SURVEILLANCE, BACK-GROUND CHECKS, & TRAINING

Baby Safe, 444 E. 86th Street, 396-1995

Care Check, 1056 Fifth Avenue, 360-6640

Caring People, Inc., (718) 591-0557

Kid-View, Inc., 299 East Shore Road, Suite 206 Great Neck, NY, (516) 498-9300

Mind Your Business, P.O. Box 1390, Maplewood, NJ 07040, (888) 869-2462

Nanny Vision, 677-2776

NannyWise, Amy Hatkoff, 534-5623

NEW MOTHER CLASSES— HOSPITALS

Beth Israel Hospital, 16th Street at First Avenue, 420-2000 (General), 420-2999 (Classes)

Columbia Presbyterian Hospital, Babies Hospital/Sloane Hospital for Women, Broadway at 166th Street, 305-2500 (General), 305-2040 (Parent Education Program)

The Mount Sinai Medical Center, One Gustave L. Levy Place, Fifth Avenue at 98th Street, 241-6500 (General), 241-7491 (Women & Children's Office), 241-6578 (Breastfeeding Warm Line)

New York Hospital/Cornell Medical Center, 525 E. 68th Street, 746-5454 (General), 746-3215 (Preparation for Parenthood Office)

New York University Medical Center, 560 First Avenue at 32nd Street, 263-7200 (General), 263-7201 (Classes)

Roosevelt Hospital, 1000 Tenth Avenue at 59th Street, 523-4000 (General), 523-6222 (Parent/Family Education)

St. Luke's Hospital, 1111 Amsterdam Avenue at 114th Street, 523-4000 (General), 523-6222 (Parent/Family Education),

St. Vincent's Hospital and Medical Center, 153 W. 11th Street, 604-7000 (General), 604-7946 (Maternity Education)

NUTRITIONISTS

Erica Ilton, R.D., C.D.N., 529-0654

Joanne Diamond, R.D., Women's Health Beth Israel, 844-8620

Danielle M. Schupp, R.D., Reebok Sports Club/NY, 501-1401, ext. 3744

Bonnie Taub-Dix, M.A., R.D., C.D.N., New York City and Long Island, 737-8536; 516-295-0377

Elisa Zied, M.S., R.D., C.D.N., 575 Lexington Avenue, Suite 400, bet. 51st and 52nd Streets, 527-7557

PARENTING CLASSES & GROUPS

BabyWise, Amy Hatkoff, 534-5623

The Early Childhood Development Center, 163 E. 97th Street, 360-7803

Educational Alliance Parenting and Family Center at the Sol Goldman, YM-YWHA, 344 E. 14th Street bet. First and Second Avenues, 780-0800, ext. 239

Elizabeth Bing Center for Parents, 164 W. 79th Street, 362-5304

Fatherhood Forum, 724-2652

The Fourth Trimester, Dr. Donna Steinberg, 182 E. 79th Street, 348-6308

The Jewish Community Center of the Upper West Side, 15 W. 65th Street, 8th floor, bet. Columbus Avenue and Central Park West, 580-0299

Phyllis LaBella, CSW, BCD, Adoption Specialist, Domestic and International, 987-0077

Mother-Baby Discussion and Play Groups, Parent-Infant Program of Columbia University, 560-2444

Mom and Tot Get Together in NYC, Jean Ellen Connelly, 614-0163, Bernadette Depaz, 982-3504

Mothers & More, www.mothersandmorenyc.com

MUNCHmoms, Upper West Side at The Reebok Sports Club, 160 Columbus Avenue at 67th Street; Upper East Side at The Sports Club/LA, 330 E. 61st Street bet. First and Second Avenues; Tribeca at Bubby's Restaurant, 120 Hudson Street at North Moore Street, 717-9922

"New Parents' Get Together," 92nd Street, 1395 Lexington Ave., 996-1100

New Mommies Network, Lori Robinson, 769-3846

New Mother's Luncheons, East and West side locations,

Ronni Soled, 744-3194

The Parent Child Center, 247 E. 82nd Street, 879-6900

The Parent's League, 115 E. 82nd Street, 737-7385

Parenting Horizons, Julie Ross, Central Presbyterian Church, 593 Park Avenue at 64th Street, 765-2377

The Parenting Program, Temple Shaaray Tefila, 250 E. 79th Street at Second Avenue, 535-8008, ext. 248

Ann Profitt, M.A., Battery Park City, 938-0139

Rhinelander Children's Center, 350 E. 88th Street bet. First and Second Avenues, 876-0500

Nancy Samalin, R.N., M.S., 787-8883

Kiki Schaffer, CSW, Mother/Infant Counseling, 529-9247

Lisa Schuman, CSW, CASAC, 590 West End Avenue, Suite 1A, 874-1318

Elizabeth Silk, M.S.S.W., C.S.W., B.C.D., 235 W. 71st Street, 2-Unit 1, 873-6435

The SoHo Parenting Center, 568 Broadway, Suite 205, 334-3744

PARKS AND RECREATION

New York Parks Department, 360-8111

Recreation Office, 408-0243

PARTY ENTERTAINERS, see BIRTHDAY PARTY ENTERTAINERS

PARTY FAVORS

Cozy's Cuts for Kids, 1125 Madison Avenue at 84th Street, 744-1716; 448 Amsterdam Avenue at 81st Street, 579-2600

E.A.T. Gifts, 1062 Madison Avenue at 80th Street, 861-2544

Paper House, 1020 Third Avenue bet. 60th and 61st Streets, 223-3774; 180 E. 86th Street bet. Lexington and Third Avenues, 410-7950; 269 Amsterdam Avenue bet. 72nd and 73rd Streets, 724-8085; 678 Broadway bet. 3rd and Bond Streets, 388-0082

Party Poopers, 587-9030

PHARMACIES, see BREAST PUMP RENTALS

PHOTOGRAPHERS

A Child's Portrait, Nancy Ribeck, 476 Broome Street, Suite 6A, bet. Wooster and Greene Streets, 534-3433

Jami Beere Photography, 646-505-5836

Barry Burns, 311 W. 43rd Street bet. Eighth and Ninth Avenues, 713-0100

Kate Burton Photography, 316 E. 84th Street , 717-9958

Creative Photoworks , 629-9028

Nina Drapacz, 500 E. 85th Street at York Avenue, 772-7814

Fromex, 182 E. 86th Street bet. Third and Lexington Avenues, 369-4821

Jennifer Lee, 40 W. 72nd Street, Suite 53, bet. Central Park West and Columbus Avenue, 799-1501

Karen Michele, 721 Fifth Avenue at 56th Street, 355-7576

Manger-Weil Photography, 1556 York Avenue at 82nd Street, 717-6203

Sarah Merians Photography & Company, 104 Fifth Avenue, 4th floor, at 16th Street, 633-0502

Nancy Pindrus Photography, 21 W. 68th Street bet. Central Park West and Columbus Avenue, 799-8167

Gail Sherman, 88 Central Park West at 69th Street, 877-7210

PLANETARIUMS

Hayden Planetarium, 81st and Central Park West, 769-5100

PLAYS, see CONCERTS, PLAYS, & PUPPET SHOWS

PRIVATE TRAINERS

Jane Kornbluh, 677-6165

Ana Learner, 355-3109

PUPPET SHOWS, see CONCERTS, PLAYS, & PUPPET SHOWS

RESALE SHOPS, see CLOTHING, RESALE SHOPS

RESTAURANTS
Upper East Side

Barking Dog Luncheonette, 1453 York Avenue at 77th Street, 861-3600; 1678 Third Avenue at 94th Street, 831-1800

California Pizza Kitchen, 201 E. 60th Street bet. Second and Third Avenues, 755-7773

China Fun, 1239 Second Avenue at 65th Street, 752-0810; 1653 Broadway at 51st Street, 333-2622; 246 Columbus Avenue at 71st Street, 580-1516

Hi-Life Bar and Grill, 1340 First Avenue at 72nd Street, 249-3600; 477 Amsterdam Avenue at 83rd Street, 787-7199

Il Vagabondo, 351 E. 62nd Street bet. First and Second Avenues, 832-9221

Peppermint Park, 1225 First Avenue at 66th Street, 288-5054

Serendipity, 225 E. 60th Street bet. Second and Third Avenues, 838-3531

Tony's Di Napoli, 1606 Second Avenue at 83rd Street, 861-8686

Upper West Side

Avenue Bistro, 520 Columbus Avenue at 85th Street, 579-3194

The Boulevard Cafe, 2398 Broadway at 88th Street, 874-7400

Gabriela's, 685 Amsterdam Avenue at 93rd Street, 961-0574;315 Amsterdam Avenue at 75th Street, 875-8532

Josephina, 1900 Broadway bet. 63rd and 64th Streets, 799-1000

Louie's Westside Cafe, 441 Amsterdam Avenue at 81st Street, 877-1900

Popover Cafe, 551 Amsterdam Avenue at 87th Street, 595-8555

Midtown East and West

Broadway Diner, 590 Lexington Avenue at 52nd Street, 486-8838; 1726 Broadway at 55th Street, 765-0909

Ellen's Stardust Diner, 1650 Broadway at 51st Street, 307-7575

Hamburger Harry's, 145 W. 45th Street bet. Broadway and Sixth Avenue, 840-0566

Metropolitan Cafe, 959 First Avenue bet. 52nd and 53rd Streets, 759-5600

Chelsea/Flatiron

America, 9 E. 18th Street bet. Fifth Avenue and Broadway, 505-2110

Chat 'n Chew, 10 E. 16th Street bet. University Place and Fifth Avenue, 243-1616

West Village

Arturo's Pizzeria, 106 W. Houston Street at Thompson Street, 677-3820

Cowgirl Hall of Fame, 519 Hudson Street at 10th Street, 633-1133

East Village

Miracle Grill, 112 First Avenue bet. 6th and 7th Streets, 254-2353; 415 Bleecker Street between Bank Street and W. 11th Street, 924-1900

Two Boots, 37 Avenue A bet. 2nd and 3rd Streets, 505-2276; Two Boots to Go-Go, 74 Bleecker at Broadway, 777-1033; Two Boots to Go West, 201 W. 11th Street at Seventh Avenue, 633-9096; Two Boots Pizzeria, 42 Avenue A at 3rd Street, 254-1919

Veselka, 144 Second Avenue at 9th Street, 228-9682

Central Village/NoHo

Noho Star, 330 Lafayette Street at Bleecker Street, 925-0070

Tribeca

Bubby's, 120 Hudson Street at North Moore Street, 219-0666

The Odeon, 145 W. Broadway bet. Duane and Thomas Streets, 233-0507

SoHo

Tennessee Mountain, 143 Spring Street at Wooster, 431-3993

The Chains

Carmine's, 2450 Broadway at 91st Street, 362-2200; 200 W. 44th Street bet. Broadway and Eighth Avenue, 221-3800

Dallas BBQ, 1265 Third Avenue at 73rd Street, 772-9393; 27 W. 72nd Street bet. Columbus Avenue and Central Park West, 873-2004; 132 Second Avenue at 8th Street, 777-5574; 132 W. 43rd Street between Sixth Avenue and Broadway, 221-9000; 21 University Place at 8th Street, 674-4450

EJ's Luncheonette, 1271 Third Avenue at 73rd Street, 472-0600: 447 Amsterdam Avenue bet. 81st and 82nd Streets, 873-3444: 432 Sixth Avenue bet. 9th and 10th Streets, 473-5555

Jackson Hole Burgers, 1611 Second Avenue bet. 83rd and 84th Street, 737-8788; 232 E. 64th Street bet. Second and Third Avenues, 371-7187; 517 Columbus Avenue at 85th Street, 362-5177; 521 Third Avenue bet. 34th and 35th Streets, 679-3264; 1270 Madison Avenue and 91st Street, 427-2820

John's Pizzeria, 260 W. 44th Street bet. Broadway and Eighth Avenue, 391-7560; 408 E. 64th Street bet. First and York Avenues, 935-2895; 48 W. 65th Street bet. Central Park West and Broadway, 721-7001; 278 Bleecker Street bet. Sixth and Seventh Avenues, 243-1680

La Cocina, 217 W. 85th Street bet. Broadway and Amsterdam Avenue, 874-0770; 2608 Broadway bet. 98th and 99th Streets, 865-7333; 762 Eighth Avenue bet. 46th and 47th Streets, 730-1860

Ollie's Noodle Shop & Grille, 200 W. 44th Street at Seventh Avenue, 921-5988; 1991 Broadway bet. 67th and 68th Streets, 595-8181; 2315 Broadway at 84th Street, 362-3712; 2957 Broadway at 116th Street, 932-3300

Theme Restaurants

Hard Rock Cafe, 221 W. 57th Street bet. Broadway and Seventh Avenue, 489-6565

Harley Davidson Cafe, 1370 Sixth Avenue at 56th Street, 245-6000

Jekyll & Hyde, 91 Seventh Avenue South bet. W. 4th and
Barrow Streets, 989-7701

Mickey Mantle's, 52 Central Park South bet. Fifth and
Sixth Avenues, 688-7777

Planet Hollywood, 140 W. 57th Street bet. Sixth and
Seventh Avenues, 333-7827

SHOES

East Side Kids Inc., 1298 Madison Avenue at 92nd Street
360-5000

Great Feet, 1241 Lexington Avenue at 84th Street,
249-0551

Harry's Shoes, 2299 Broadway at 83rd Street, 874-2035

Ibiza Kidz, 42 University Place at 9th Street, 505-9907

Lester's, 1522 Second Avenue at 80th Street, 734-9292

Little Eric, 1131 Third Avenue at 76th Street, 288-8987;
1118 Madison Avenue at 83rd Street, 717-1513

Shoofly, 465 Amsterdam Avenue at 82nd Street, 580-
4390; 42 Hudson Street at Duane Street, 406-3270

TipTop Kids, 149 W. 72nd Street, 874-1004

SUMMER ACTIVITIES, see CAMPS

SUPERSTORES—
BABY PRODUCTS, FURNITURE

In New York

Albee's, 715 Amsterdam Avenue at 95th Street, 662-8902

Baby Depot, 707 Sixth Avenue at 23rd Street, 229-1300

Ben's for Kids, 1380 Third Avenue bet. 78th and 79th
Streets, 794-2330

Little Stars, 669 Lexington Avenue bet. 55th and 56th
Streets, 829-1155

Planet Kids, 247 E. 86th Street bet. Second and Third
Avenues, 426-2040

Regine Kids, 2688 Broadway bet. 102nd and 103rd
Streets, 864-8705

Schneider's, 20 Avenue A at E. 2nd Street, 228-3540

Toys "R" Us, 2430 Union Square East bet. 15th and 16th
Streets, 674-8697; 1514 Broadway at 44th Street,
(646) 366-8858

Outside of New York

The Baby and Toy Superstore, 11 Forest Street,
Stamford, CT, 203-327-1333

Buy Buy Baby, 1019 Central Park Avenue, Scarsdale, NY,
(914) 725-9220; 350 Route 110, Huntington
Station, New York, (631) 425-0404; 240 Route 17
North, Paramus, New Jersey (201) 599-1900

Darling's, 169 South Central Avenue, Hartsdale, NY,
(914) 993-0800; 5 Perlman Drive, Pascack Plaza,
Spring Valley, NY, (914) 352-5600

SPECIALTY STORES

ABC Carpet & Home, 888 Broadway at 19th Street, 473-
3000

Bellini, 1305 Second Avenue bet. 68th and 69th Streets,
517-9233

Chelsea's Kids Quarter, 33 W. 17th Street bet. Fifth and
Sixth Avenues, 627-5524

Cradle & All, 1384 Lexington Avenue bet. 91st and 92nd
Streets, 996-9990

Just for Tykes, 83 Mercer Street bet. Spring and Broome
Streets, 274-9121

Kids Down the Block, 490 Amsterdam Avenue bet. 83rd
and 84th Streets, 496-1546

Kid's Supply Co., 1325 Madison Avenue bet. 93rd and
94th Streets, 426-1200

Little Folk Art, 159 Duane Street bet. Hudson Street and
W. Broadway, 267-1500

Pamela Scurry's Wicker Garden, 1327 Madison Avenue
bet. 93rd and 94th Streets, 410-7001

TOY STORES

A Bear's Place, 789 Lexington Avenue bet. 61st and
62nd Streets, 826-6465

The Children's General Store, 2473 Broadway at 92nd
Street, 580-2723; Grand Central Station, 107 E.
42nd Street Lexington Passage, 682-0004

Classic Toys, 218 Sullivan Street bet. Bleecker and W. 3rd
Streets, 674-4434

Cozy's Cuts for Kids, 1125 Madison Avenue at 84th Street, 744-1716; 448 Amsterdam Avenue at 81st Street, 579-2600

Cute Toonz, 372 Fifth Avenue at 34th Street, 967-6942

Dinosaur Hill, 306 E. 9th Street bet. First and Second Avenues, 473-5850

The Disney Store, 711 Fifth Avenue at 55th Street, 702-0702; 39 W. 34th Street, 279-9890; 147 Columbus Avenue at 66th Street, 362-2386; 300 W. 125th Street at Eighth Avenue, 749-8390

E.A.T. Gifts, 1062 Madison Avenue at 80th Street, 861-2544

The Enchanted Forest, 85 Mercer Street bet. Spring and Broome Streets, 925-6677

FAO Schwarz, 767 Fifth Avenue bet. 58th and 59th Streets, 644-9400

Gepetto's Toy Box, 10 Christopher Street bet. Greenwich Avenue and Gay Street, 620-7511

Hom Boms, 1500 First Avenue bet. 78th and 79th Streets, 717-5300

Kay-Bee Toys, 901 Avenue of the Americas bet. 32nd and 33rd Streets, 629-5386; 2411 Broadway at 89th Street, 595-4389

Kidding Around, 68 Bleecker Street bet. Broadway and Lafayette, 598-0228, 60 W. 15th Street bet. Fifth and Sixth Avenues, 645-6337

Little Extras, 676 Amsterdam Avenue at 93rd Street, 721-6161

Mary Arnold Toys, 1010 Lexington Avenue bet. 72nd and 73rd Streets, 744- 8510

New York Firefighter's Friend, 263 Lafayette Street bet. Prince and Spring Streets, 226-3142

Ovations Baby, 791-9300

Penny Whistle Toys, 1283 Madison Avenue bet. 91st and 92nd Streets, 369-3868; 448 Columbus Avenue bet. 81st and 82nd Streets, 873-9090

Promises Fulfilled, 1592 Second Avenue bet. 82nd and 83rd Streets, 472-1600

Toys 'R' Us, 1293 Broadway at 34th Street, 594-8697; 24-32 Union Square East, 674-8697

Warner Bros. Studio Store, 1 Times Square at 42nd Street, 840-4040

West Side Kids, 498 Amsterdam Avenue at 84th Street, 496-7282

Wynken, Blynken, & Nod's, 306 E. 55th Street bet. First and Second Avenues, 308-9299

Zany Brainy, 112 E. 86th Street bet. Park and Lexington Avenues, 427-6611; 2407 Broadway bet. 87th and 88th Streets, 917-441-2066

Zittles, 969 Madison Avenue bet. 75th and 76th Streets, 3rd floor of Zitomer, 737-2037

VIDEO RENTALS

Blockbuster, 1270 First Avenue at 68th Street, 327-2040; 197 Amsterdam Avenue at 69th Street, 787-0300; 250 E. Houston Street bet. Avenues A and B, 420-8186

Champagne Video, 1416 Third Avenue, 517-8700; 213 W. 79th Street, 873-4600; 1194 First Avenue, 517-5050; 1577 First Avenue, 772-2058

Tower Records, 383 Lafayette at 4th St., 505-1166; 1961 Broadway at 66th St., 799-2500

THE Y ASSOCIATIONS

Vanderbilt YMCA, 224 E. 47th Street bet. Second and Third Avenues, 756-9600

YMCA, 5 W. 63rd Street bet. Central Park West and Broadway, 875-4112

YWCA of the City of New York, 610 Lexington Avenue at 53rd Street, 755-4500

McBurney YMCA Chelsea Center, 122 W. 17th Street bet. Sixth and Seventh Avenues, 741-8725

YOGA CLASSES, ADULT

Mary Ryan Barnes, Yoga for Pregnancy, 175 W. 93rd Street at Amsterdam Avenue, 222-8597

Beth Donnelly, 718-604-0104

Integral Yoga Center, 227 W. 13th Street bet. Seventh and Eighth Avenues, 929-0586

Iyengar Yoga Institute of New York, 27 W. 24th Street, Suite 800, bet. Broadway and Sixth Avenue, 691-9642

Jivamukti Yoga Center, 404 Lafayette Street, 3rd floor, bet. Astor and 4th Streets, 353-0214; 853 Lexington Avenue, 2nd floor, bet. 64th ad 65th Streets, 396-4200

Peggy Levine, 212 W. 92nd Street bet. Broadway and Amsterdam Avenue, 749-1378

Gayatri Martin, R.N., Choices for Childbirth, 220 E. 26th St., 725-1078

Mikelle Terson, 37 W. 76th Street bet. Central Park West and Columbus Avenue, 362-4288

Yoga Zone, 138 Fifth Avenue bet. 18th and 19th Streets 647-9642, 160 E. 56th Street, 12th floor, bet. Third and Lexington Avenues, 935-9642

ZOOS

The Bronx Zoo, 185 Street at Southern Boulevard, (718) 220-5100

Central Park Wildlife Conservation Center, Fifth Avenue at 64th Street, 861-6030

city baby brooklyn yellow pages

CLASSES—CHILDREN'S, MOMMY & ME

ArtsCetera, 212 Smith Street bet. Baltic and Butler Streets, (718) 643-6817

Brooklyn Arts Exchange, 421 Fifth Avenue at 8th Street, (718) 832-0018

Brooklyn Botanic Garden, 1000 Washington Avenue bet. Crown and Montgomery Streets, (718) 623-7223

Brooklyn Central YMCA, 153 Remsen Street, 2nd floor, bet. Court and Clinton Streets, (718) 625-3136

Brooklyn Conservatory of Music, 58 Seventh Avenue at Lincoln Plaza, (718) 622-3300

Brooklyn Heights Synagogue, 131 Remsen Street bet. Clinton and Henry Streets, (718) 522-2070

Brooklyn Museum, 200 Eastern Parkway at Washington Avenue, (718) 638-5000

Brooklyn Public Library, Grand Army Plaza, (718) 230-2100; 431 Sixth Avenue bet. 8th and 9th Streets, (718) 832-1853

Dance Studio of Park Slope, 808 Union Street, 2nd floor, bet. Sixth and Seventh Avenues, (718) 789-4419

The Early Ear, 511 9th Street bet. Eighth Avenue and Prospect Park West, (212) 877-7125 (general number)

Eastern Athletic Club, 17 Eastern Parkway at Grand Army Plaza, (718) 789-4600; 43 Clark Street bet. Henry and Hicks Streets, (718) 625-0500

Beth Elohim's Early Childhood Center, Eighth Avenue at Garfield Place, (718) 499-6208

Grace Church School, 254 Hicks Street bet. Joralemon and Remsen Streets, (718) 624-4030

Just Wee Two, Congregation Mount Sinai, 250 Cadman Plaza West bet. Clinton and Clark Streets, (800) 404-2204

Kid Fit, 25 Dean Street bet. Court and Smith Streets, (718) 852-7670

Music for Aardvarks & Other Mammals, 125 Henry Street bet. Clark and Pierrepont Streets (at Zion

Lutheran Church); 212 Smith Street bet. Baltic and Butler Streets (ArtsCetera); 61 Park Place bet. Fifth and Sixth Avenues (at Father Dempsey Center), (718) 643-6817

Music Together, 125 Henry Street bet. Clark and Pierrepont Streets (at Zion Lutheran Church); 212 Smith Street bet. Baltic and Butler Streets (at ArtsCetera), (718) 643-6817

The Painted Pot, 333 Smith Street bet. Carroll and President Streets, (718) 222-0334

Power Play, 432 Third Avenue bet. 7th and 8th Streets, (718) 369-9880

Prospect Park YMCA, 357 Ninth Street bet. Fifth and Sixth Avenues, (718) 768-7100

Spoke the Hub Dancing Company, 748 Union Street bet. Fifth and Sixth Avenues, (718) 857-5158; 295 Douglass Street bet. Third and Fourth Avenues, (718) 643-5708

Terrace Dance Studio, 273 Prospect Park West at 17th Street, (718) 768-5505

CHILDREN'S CLOTHING & SHOES

Children's Emporium, 293 Court Street bet. DeGraw and Douglass Streets, (718) 875-8508

Fidgets, 169 Seventh Avenue bet. Garfield and 1st Streets, (718) 788-2002

Good Footing, 94 Seventh Avenue at Union Street, (718) 789-2500

The Green Onion, 274 Smith Street bet. Sackett and DeGraw Streets, (718) 246-2804

Hoyt & Bond Store, 248 Smith Street bet. Douglass and DeGraw Streets, (718) 488-8283

Johnnie's Bootery, 208 Smith Street bet. Baltic and Butler Streets, (718) 625-5334

Jumpin' Julia's, 240 Seventh Avenue bet. 4th and 5th Streets, (718) 965-3535

Les Amis, 50 Hicks Street bet. Middagh and Cranberry Streets, (718) 858-3179

Lester's, 1111 Avenue U bet. E. 12th Street and Coney Island Avenue, (718) 645-5636

Lisa Polansky, 121 Seventh Avenue bet. President and Carroll Streets, (718) 622-8071

Peek A Boo Kids, 90 Seventh Avenue bet. Union and Berkeley Streets, (718) 638-1060

Rachel's, 4218 Thirteenth Avenue bet. 42nd and 43rd Streets, (718) 435-6875

Tuesday's Child, 1904 Avenue M bet. E. 19th Street and Ocean Avenue, (718) 375-1790

Windsor Shoes, 233 Prospect Park West at Windsor Place, (718) 369-2192

Youngworld, 452 Fulton Street at Hoyt Street, (718) 852-7890

MATERNITY CLOTHING

Boing Boing, 204 Sixth Avenue at Union Street, (718) 398-0251

OUTINGS

The Brooklyn Aquarium at Coney Island, Surf Avenue and Coney Island Boardwalk at W. 8th Street, (718) 265-3400

Brooklyn Botanic Garden, 1000 Washington Avenue bet. Crown and Montgomery Streets, (718) 623-7200

Brooklyn Children's Museum, 145 Brooklyn Avenue at St. Mark's Avenue, (718) 735-4400

The NY Transit Museum, Boerum Place and Schermerhorn Street, (718) 243-3060

Prospect Park, (718) 965-8951

Prospect Park Children's Wildlife Center, 450 Flatbush Avenue bet. Empire Boulevard and Grand Army Plaza, (718) 399-7321

The Puppetworks, Inc., 338 Sixth Avenue at 4th Street, (718) 965-3391

RESTAURANTS

The Big Pizza Cafe, 137 Seventh Avenue bet. Garfield and Carroll Streets, (718) 398-9198

Connecticut Muffin Co., 171 Seventh Avenue at 1st Street, (718) 768-2022; 115 Montague Street bet. Clinton and Henry Streets, (718) 875-3912, 206 Prospect Park West at 15th Street, (718) 965-2067

Dizzy's, 511 9th Street at Eighth Avenue, (718) 499-1966

Heights Cafe, 84 Montague Street at Hicks Street, (718) 625-5555

Lassen & Hennigs, 114 Montague Street bet. Henry and Hicks Streets, (718) 875-8362

Living Room Cafe, 188 Prospect Park West at 14th Street, (718) 369-0824

Monty Q's, 158 Montague Street bet. Clinton and Henry Streets, (718) 246-2000

New World Coffee, 125 Seventh Avenue at Carroll Street (718) 638-9633

Park Slope Brewing Company, 356 Sixth Avenue at 5th Street, (718) 788-1756; 40 Van Dyke Street at Dwight Street, (718) 246-8050; 62 Henry Street bet. Cranberry and Orange Streets, (718) 522-4801

Peter's Ice Cream, 185 Atlantic Avenue bet. Clinton and Court Streets, (718) 852-3835

2nd Street Cafe, 189 Seventh Avenue at 2nd Street, (718) 369-6928

Starbucks, 164 Seventh Avenue bet. Garfield and 1st Streets, (718) 369-1213

Sweet Melissa's, 276 Court Street bet. Butler and Douglass Streets, (718) 855-3410

Teresa's, 80 Montague Street bet. Hicks and Montague Terrace, (718) 797-3996

Two Boots, 514 2nd Street bet. Seventh and Eighth Avenues, (718) 499-3253

SUPERSTORES

Go Fish, 260 Fifth Avenue bet. Carroll and Garfield Streets, (718) 622-8237

Happy Days, 533 Fifth Avenue bet. 13th and 14th Streets, (718) 768-1433

Heights Kids, 85 Pineapple Walk bet. Henry Street and Cadman Plaza, (718) 222-4271

MB Discount Furniture, 2311 Avenue U bet. E. 23rd and E. 24th Streets, (718) 332-1500

TOY, BOOK, & GIFT STORES

Barnes and Noble, 267 Seventh Avenue at 6th Street, (718) 832-9066; 106 Court Street bet. State and Schermerhorn Streets, (718) 246-4996

Booklink, 99 Seventh Avenue bet. President and Union Streets, (718) 783-6067

00Brooklyn Women's Exchange, 55 Pierrepont bet. Henry and Hicks Streets, (718) 624-3435

The Clay Pot, 162 Seventh Avenue bet. 1st and Garfield Streets, (718) 788-6564

Community Bookstore, 143 Seventh Avenue bet. Garfield and Carroll Streets, (718) 783-3075

Court Street Books, 163 Court Street bet. Dean and Pacific Streets, (718) 875-3677

The Laughing Giraffe at the Monkey's Wedding, 234 Court Street bet. Baltic and Kane Streets, (718) 852-3635

Little Things Toystore, 1457 Seventh Avenue bet. Garfield and Carroll Streets, (718) 783-4733

Nancy Nancy, 244a Fifth Avenue bet. President and Carroll Streets, (718) 789-5262

The Toy Box, 93 Pineapple Walk bet. Henry Street and Cadman Plaza, (718) 246-5440

Victoria Station, 247 Court Street bet. Kane and McGraw Streets, (718) 522-1800

A
B
C
D
E
F
G
H
I
J
K
L
M
N
O
P
Q
R
S
T
U
V
W
X
Y
Z

about the authors

Kelly Ashton holds a B.A. from Yale University and an M.B.A. from Harvard University. She is the mother of seven-year-old Alexander and three-year-old Angela and writes and speaks on child-related topics.

Pamela Weinberg graduated from Brandeis University and is the mother of Rebecca, seven, and Benjamin, four. She runs the West Side New Mother's Luncheon series and frequently speaks on parenting issues.

Visit Kelly and Pam on the Web at www.CityBabyNY.com